12/04

025364

2.95
(FB) 9.95
Pol Sc.

HAVES

WITHOUT

HAVE-NOTS

HAVES

Mortimer J. Adler

WITHOUT

Essays for the 21st Century
on Democracy and Socialism

HAVE-NOTS

Macmillan Publishing Company
New York

COLLIER MACMILLAN CANADA
Toronto

MAXWELL MACMILLAN INTERNATIONAL
New York   Oxford   Singapore   Sydney

Macmillan Publishing Company
866 Third Avenue, New York, NY 10022

Collier Macmillan Canada, Inc.
1200 Eglinton Avenue East, Suite 200
Don Mills, Ontario M3C 3N1

Library of Congress Cataloging-in-Publication Data
Adler, Mortimer Jerome,———
    Haves without have-nots : essays for the 21st century on
democracy and socialism / Mortimer J. Adler.
      p. cm.
    Includes index.
    ISBN 0-02-500561-8
    1. Socialism. 2. Communism. 3. Capitalism. 4. Democracy.
I. Title.
    HX73.A34   1991
    320.5'31—dc20   90-46727   CIP

Macmillan books are available at special discounts for bulk purchases
for sales promotions, premiums, fund-raising, or educational use. For
details, contact:

Special Sales Director
Macmillan Publishing Company
866 Third Avenue
New York, NY 10022

10 9 8 7 6 5 4 3 2 1

Designed by Jack Meserole

PRINTED IN THE UNITED STATES OF AMERICA

Permissions and Acknowledgments appear on page 338.

To Mikhail Gorbachev whose *perestroika* opened the window to this vision of the future in the United States, Eastern Europe, and the Soviet Union

Contents

Preface
Explaining the Unity of This Book   ix

ONE
The End of the Conflict Between Capitalism and
Communism (*with Endnotes and Appendixes*)   1

TWO
A Disputation on the Future of Democracy
(*with Endnotes*)   105

THREE
Robert Bork: The Lessons to Be Learned
(*with Endnotes*)   187

FOUR
Lincoln's Declaration (*with Endnotes*)   218

FIVE
Human Nature, Nurture, and Culture   229

SIX
The New World of the Twenty-first Century: USDR
(*with Endnotes and Appendixes*)   249

Index   327

Preface

Explaining the Unity of This Book

When with sufficient historical perspective the story of the twentieth century is told, I venture to predict that three things will be among the most noteworthy features of the last hundred years. First, it would be impossible, I think, to say anything of prime significance about the twentieth century without highlighting its technological advances. Among the many marvels that these advances engendered is the emergence of what Marshall McLuhan called "the global village." The travel time for going from one place to another anywhere on earth has become little more than a day. The communication time is almost instantaneous. The globe has shrunk to a size much smaller than that of small communities in earlier centuries. These facts underlie the prediction and the promise of this book's closing essay about the new world of the twenty-first century.

The second feature is the rise of constitutional democracy. In the nineteenth century constitutional democracy, in its modern conception, was hardly more than a dream in the minds of a few political thinkers who were regarded as visionary reformers. By the middle of the twentieth century, that dream began to be realized by constitutional amendments and legislative enactments in a relatively small number of countries, mainly in the countries of Western Europe, the

British Commonwealth, and the United States. At the end of the century's ninth decade, the movement toward the ideal of democracy spread with the speed of infection to many countries that had been long deprived of the benefits of political liberty and majority rule.

Finally, one of the most remarkable facts about this century is that totalitarian communism came into existence and (with a few exceptions) ceased to exist within the same hundred years. In the nineteenth century, the misery of the working classes in the early stages of the Industrial Revolution and under the oppressive economic system that Karl Marx called "bourgeois capitalism" inspired the first proposal of socialist reforms. In the second decade of this century, the establishment of totalitarian communism by the dictatorship of the proletariat, replacing private-property capitalism with the ownership of all capital by the state, was the first step taken toward the realization of the socialist ideal. But in the successive decades of this century, totalitarian communism proved to be the wrong method and the ineffective means for achieving the ideal that all varieties of socialism aim at.

The last two features of the twentieth century—its movement toward the democratic ideal in the political sphere and toward the socialist ideal in the economic sphere—explain the title and subtitle of this book, as well as the subject of its opening chapter: the end of the conflict between capitalism and communism. What needs a word of further explanation is that the book's title, when understood in political and economic terms, relates the ideas of democracy and socialism as inseparably as Siamese twins are related.

In relatively advanced democratic societies, all persons (with a few justifiable exceptions) are enfranchised citizens. All are political *haves*, possessing political liberty and the other rights and privileges accorded citizens. The *have-nots* are limited to those below the age of consent, those confined in hospitals for the mentally incompetent, those incarcerated in prisons as felonious criminals, and all those who have ever been convicted. A politically democratic society is a society of *haves without have-nots.*

The socialist ideal lags behind in the degree to which it has been realized anywhere. Socialism is the economic correlate of democracy in precisely the same terms. The socialist ideal is realized in varying degrees in societies in which all or most are haves and there are few or no have-nots—persons grossly deprived of what any human being needs to lead a decent human life. Thus a socialist society, like a democratic society, is also one of haves without have-nots, one in which all (again with a few exceptions) enjoy the right to a decent livelihood.

Communism is antithetical to democracy, but socialism is indispensable to it, for political haves who are not also economic haves cannot discharge their duties as citizens. At the end of the ninth decade of this century, the same countries that began to move toward political democracy also renounced the economic errors of communism and adopted in its place other means to socialism.

Much earlier in the century, the democratic societies whose economic arrangements were those of private-property capitalism corrected the errors of bourgeois capitalism by socializing their economies through a variety of welfare measures. In the United States, we have no qualms about calling all or most of the Western democracies "welfare states," but the widely prevalent mistake of identifying socialism with communism blinds a vast majority of our citizens to the fact that any welfare state is, to some degree, a socialized form of private-property capitalism. That mistake can be corrected only by understanding socialism as an ideal and communism as a wrong and ineffective means toward achieving it. The right means is socialized private property capitalism.

In between Chapters One and Six, Chapters Two, Three, and Four support, in different ways, the argument set forth in Chapter One.

Chapter Two is the report of a disputation about the

future of democracy that occurred in 1977 at the Aspen Institute. Bill Moyers was in the chair. I was one of the disputants; the other two were Lord Quinton, then a fellow of Trinity College, Oxford, and until recently chairman of the British Library; and Maurice Cranston, professor of Political Philosophy at the University of London. I defended the affirmative position on the following three theses: (1) that political democracy *should* prevail everywhere because it is the only perfectly just form of government; (2) that political democracy *can* survive where it now exists and can spread to other countries where it does not now exist; and (3) that political democracy *will* prevail everywhere and will survive and prosper. My two opponents were more qualified and querulous about the first two theses, and expressed grave doubts and reservations about the prediction I defended in the third.

The lessons to be learned in Chapter Three are not limited to the reasons why the nomination of Robert Bork to the Supreme Court of the United States should not have been confirmed by the Senate. The essay is mainly concerned with the basic issue in jurisprudence—that between the legal positivists or realists and those who assert that principles of justice provide us with criteria for judging governments, constitutions, laws, and majorities. This issue has a direct bearing on the development of democracy and socialism in the United States.

Chapter Four was a lecture I delivered in Springfield, Illinois, on an occasion devoted to celebrating Abraham Lincoln's birthday. Lincoln's dedication to the principles of natural law and natural right, expressed in the second paragraph of the Declaration of Independence, justifies the conclusion that he would have been a staunch proponent of the Thirteenth, Fourteenth, Fifteenth, Nineteenth, and Twenty-fourth amendments (the last in 1964), amendments that at long last rectified the injustice in the Constitution of the United States and transformed it into a truly democratic charter. The chapter goes further in suggesting that were Lincoln alive in the middle of the twentieth century, he would have been a socialist reformer as well. He would have argued that life and liberty were not the only natural rights indispensable to the pursuit of happiness, but that among man's unalienable rights is the right to a decent livelihood.

Chapter Five gives support to the predictions about the twenty-first century set forth in Chapter Six. It points out that in the twentieth century, mathematics and the natural sciences, as well as the technology they generate, are transcultural. History, the social sciences, philosophy, and religion are not, at least not yet. Is their becoming so necessary for the political and economic unification of the nations of this earth? Are there obstacles to be overcome that are not intransigent? These questions are answered in Chapter Six.

Of the six chapters that comprise this book, all derive their substance from seminars that I have conducted or lectures that I have delivered at the Aspen Institute. Two of them (One and Two) have been previously published in the *Great Ideas Today*, of which I am the editor. Two of them (Three and Five) have been previously published by the *Aspen Institute Quarterly*. Two of them (Four and Six) have not been previously published.

I am grateful to Encyclopaedia Britannica, Inc., for permission to republish Chapter One and Two and to The Aspen Institute, Inc., for permission to republish Chapters Three and Five.

I am also indebted to my colleagues James O'Toole and John Van Doren for their help in writing the essay on the end of the conflict between capitalism and communism; and to Sidney Hyman, editor of the *Aspen Institute Quarterly*, for his help in writing the essay on Robert Bork. I am grateful to my associates at the Institute for Philosophical Research who have assisted me in the preparation of this book, especially to Marlys Allen, who presided over the preparation of the manuscript.

MORTIMER J. ADLER
Aspen, Colorado,
September 1, 1990

ONE

The End of the Conflict Between Capitalism and Communism

THE QUESTIONS TO BE ANSWERED

In its August 1, 1988, issue, *The New Yorker* magazine published an article by William Pfaff about the Gorbachev reforms in the Soviet Union. The title of the article was "The Question Not Asked." The summer of 1988 was still fairly early in the upheaval occurring in the Soviet Union. Much has happened since then that was only prefigured in the first announcements of *glasnost* and *perestroika*. But the question that Pfaff said had not been asked in 1988 has still not been asked—or answered.

To make that question clear, I must quote some passages from the article. "The true problem" before Mikhail Gorbachev, Pfaff writes, "is not 'reform' of the system and of the economy. He must discover a new basis of legitimacy for Soviet society and for its government. . . . The question not asked, which *has* to be asked, is: What will become of the Soviet Union and the Soviet system if it abandons its intellectual and moral foundations as untrue?" Pfaff continues as follows:

. . . This is a revolution disguised as radical reform that is meant to save the system. That it cannot remain mere reform, however, follows from the fact that the intellectual foundation of the system is contradicted and jeopardized by the nature of the reforms that are required. Gorbachev refers to Lenin to justify his program, yet the program undoes Leninism.

Writing three years ago, Pfaff pointed out that Gorbachev at that point had somewhat obscurely described the purpose of his economic reform as "to assure, during the next two or three years, a transition from an overly centralized command system of management to a democratic system based mainly on economic methods and on optimal combinations of centralism and self-management." Pfaff follows that quotation from Gorbachev with another: "This presupposes a sharp expansion of the autonomy of enterprises and associations, their transition to the principle of profitability and self-financing, and the investment of work collectives with all the powers necessary for this."

Pfaff's comment on this is as follows:

> Gorbachev is determined to renew his system but is constrained to do so in terms of a doctrine that, although it purports to be the most advanced and scientific description of reality that exists, actually does not account for how the modern industrial economy and industrial society work.

And toward the end of his article, Pfaff tells us that

> ... If one takes the language of Gorbachev and his fellow-reformers to mean what it means in the West—"pluralism," "democracy"—they could be said to be attempting, by indirection, to re-start that evolution. But neither in Leninism nor in czarism is there the liberal or constitutional political precedent that the Soviet Union needs—one to which people might refer in attempting to find a new course.

Finally, Pfaff concludes with this statement:

> To break with that system [i.e., Marxism-Leninism] would leave Gorbachev and the reformers without a place to stand, a fulcrum from which to move society, a justification for their own power. They rule Russia by virtue of the Party, Leninism, Marxism. Yet the Party, Leninism, and Marxism are the problem.

I agree with Pfaff that Gorbachev and his fellow reformers cannot succeed if they explicitly renounce Party, Leninism, and Marxism. For more than seventy years now the people of the Soviet Union have been inculcated with commitment to and respect for the doctrines of Karl Marx and Vladimir Lenin and for the Party. This borders on religious reverence and fidelity. They have nothing prior in their history except the autocracy of the Romanovs, and to this they wish never to return. The question not asked, the question that must be asked, is therefore: To what doctrines and institutions can Gorbachev and his fellow reformers appeal for the legitimacy of their proposals?

If they fail to find the answer, their successors—and it is almost certain that they will have successors in this century or the next—must succeed in finding it, for the people of the Soviet Union must be given the intellectual and moral foundations that can legitimatize the *reform* of the system of totalitarian communism, or what may have to be described as its *replacement* by other political institutions and other economic arrangements. If reforming the system cannot produce the desired results, then replacing it must be resorted to. But how can that be done without a complete rejection of Party, Marxism, and Leninism?

The actions taken by Gorbachev at the end of 1989 and in the first months of 1990 appear to have moved *perestroika* in the right direction, both politically and economically, without his having to justify the steps he has taken by appealing to the canonical texts of Marx and Lenin. Though he may have bypassed the question raised by Pfaff, there is another question to be answered.

Marx and Friedrich Engels, like others in the nineteenth century, were socialists before they adopted that form of socialism they called communism. When the Eastern satellites of the Soviet Union—Poland, East Germany, Czechoslovakia, Hungary, and Romania—threw off their Soviet yokes, they proclaimed the tendency of their own internal reforms to be in the direction of socialist democracies. Marx and Engels, in *The Communist Manifesto*, declared progress toward democracy through the enfranchisement of the working class to be an indispensable step toward the realization of their socialist aims; and Lenin, in *The State and Revolution*, made democratic institutions inseparable from the ultimate realization of the socialist ideal.

In other words, Marx and Lenin were not wrong in all respects; nor were they entirely right. The Marxist-Leninist doctrine is not wholly true and sound; but neither is it wholly false and unsound. The millions upon millions of people who have lived under communism in this century have not been totally deluded, deceived, and misguided. Hence the other question to be answered by us as well as by Gorbachev is: What principles in Marxist-Leninist doctrine should be retained and what others should be rejected? The choice is not between the extremes of all or none, but rather in the middle ground of partial retention and partial rejection.

Should not the question to be asked and answered be rephrased as follows: In what limited repect should the Party be retained and continue to function in the Soviet Union; and what principles or propositions in Marxist-Leninist doctrine should be retained while others are rejected? To repeat, the doctrine of Marx and Lenin is not entirely sound, but neither is it entirely unsound.

There are elements in the doctrines of Marx and Lenin that have prevented (and always would have prevented) the Soviet Union from establishing the kind of economic equality that has always been stated as the communist ideal; that make it impossible to achieve political liberty and individual freedom for the people, to increase the supply of consumer goods to a point that raises the standard of living to an acceptable level, and to promote an economy with a plurality of competing private economic agencies or associations; in short, with government regulation of an economy that was for the most part privately managed and operated.

On the other hand, there are also elements in the doctrines

of Marx and Lenin, no less fundamental than the ones which have to be rejected, which can and should be retained to provide the intellectual and moral foundations that would legitimate the radical reforms that would amount in effect to the substitution of democratic socialism for totalitarian communism.

THE PLAN FOR THE ASPEN SEMINAR

I have described my state of mind as a result of reading the Pfaff article and thinking about it in the fall of 1988. This led me to offer to conduct a seminar at the Aspen Institute in the summer of 1989 entitled "Capitalism, Communism, and Their Future." The proposed seminar was oversubscribed; double the largest number that can be accommodated around the seminar table enlisted for it. I was asked to conduct the seminar twice in August 1989, with approximately twenty-five persons in each of the week-long meetings. This happened before the first streaks of dawn glimmered in the darkness of the Cold War.

In planning for the seminar, I produced a volume of readings which, in order to avoid undue length, provided the shortest possible excerpts from the fewest texts that would cover all the salient points we had to consider in order to reach agreement or disagreement about the solution to the Pfaff problem, as I had finally come to formulate it for myself. I should report at once that in both sections of the seminars we reached agreement and shared understanding, by no means completely, but to an extent that is not often achieved in Aspen seminars.

Appendix 1 of this chapter contains the table of contents of the volume of readings prepared for the seminar. In that table of contents, readers will find not only the headings for the six sessions of the seminar but also the names of the authors and the titles of the works assigned for each session. In the light of what happened in the course of the six days of discussion, I would now revise some of the language used in the headings for the sessions. For example, I would head Session III with the words "The Self-Destruction of Totalitarian Communism and Its Capitalization"; and I would change the heading of Session VI to "Conclusion: Coexistence or Convergence, Reform or Replacement."

I did one other thing in preparation for the seminar. In assembling the volume of readings, I found that such basic words as "capitalism," "socialism," and "communism" were used equivocally by the authors included in the volume in a variety of senses and often by the same author in quite different senses. Unless these ambiguities were corrected and some uniformity of verbal usage were adopted by the seminar participants, our discussions would be unclear and would not get very far. I therefore prepared a "Dictionary and Thesaurus of Basic Terms," which appears as Appendix 2.

To that dictionary and thesaurus I would add only two points. The first is that the word "capitalism," when not modified by adjectives as in "private-property capitalism" or "state capitalism," designates a capital-intensive economy without specifying how the productive capital employed is owned and operated. The qualifying adjectives added to the word "capitalism" indicate just that—how the capital is owned and operated.

The second point I would add is that the common future of what is now private-property capitalism or state capitalism (which is identical with Marxist or totalitarian communism) can be described by two phrases. The first of these names the future development of the economy of the United States; the second, the future development of the economy of the Soviet Union. The first phrase is "socialized private-property capitalism." The second is "privately capitalized socialism."

When the full significance of these two names for future developments in the United States and the Soviet Union is grasped, it can be seen how these future developments converge toward a common future that will include not only the

United States and the Soviet Union, but all the capital-intensive industrial economies of the world.

Following this section will be a series of sections in which I will try, as briefly as possible, to summarize the basic insights that developed in the course of the six sessions of the seminar. In presenting this summary, I will quote, as often as necessary, crucial passages from the texts read and discussed.

LABOR AND CAPITAL AS FORCES IN PRODUCTION (SESSION I)

The evening before the first session of the seminar, the participants gathered for an introductory meeting. At that time, I had the opportunity to make some general remarks about the aim and conduct of the seminar. I will repeat here only four things that I then pointed out.

1. The word "future" in the title of the seminar was not to be interpreted as an interest on our part in predicting what will happen in the years immediately ahead. We were not to be engaged in forecasting events to come. Our concern was rather what should or must happen if the improvements that are needed in both the Soviet Union and the United States are to be accomplished in a sound fashion. If this is not accomplished by Gorbachev and his associates, then it will have to be achieved by their successors. The same holds true for the present and future administration of the government in the United States.

2. The basic terms in all practical problems are ends and means. What ends should be sought? What means should be chosen to attain them? Practicable, not utopian, arrangements and institutions should be the ideal ends sought in both the political and the economic order of affairs, and there should be consonance or harmony between the twin goals. When agreement is reached about the political and economic ideals to be sought, we can then move to the consideration of the means and the arguments pro and con with respect to them.

3. The ultimate question that we would try to answer as we reached the end of the seminar might be phrased in the following manner: Should we be satisfied with the coexistence of diverse polities and economies in the Soviet Union and the United States, or should we hope for their convergence?

In the case of the Soviet Union, should the changes to be made be the reform of institutions that now exist there, or should the changes be more radical than that and amount to a replacement of the existing institutions and arrangements by new ones?

In the case of the United States, should we go much further than we have so far gone in the direction that was first initiated at the beginning of this century by such leaders as Theodore Roosevelt, Woodrow Wilson, Franklin D. Roosevelt, and Harry S Truman; or should we continue to go in the opposite direction that we have followed under the leadership of Ronald Reagan and George Bush?

4. Finally, I pointed out that while the word "democracy" was used as an honorific term by all the participants, its precise meaning was not sufficiently understood. This, I suggested, would become clearer to them when they no longer used the term "socialism" as a term of opprobrium and came to understand that democracy and socialism, far from being incompatible, are really two faces of the same ideal—the political and economic aspects of a justly constituted society, one that would operate effectively to produce the conditions needed to enable all its members to lead good human lives. This point, as will subsequently be made clear, became the controlling insight of the seminar. It not only corrected the current mistaken identification of socialism with communism, but it also helped us to understand why totalitarian communism is the wrong means for achieving democratic socialism.

Like all introductory remarks at the opening of Aspen seminars, these four points probably fell on deaf ears. It would take the next six days of reading and discussion for the participants to achieve the requisite understanding of them. The following session-by-session report of the seminar will show just how it was achieved, with a remarkably high degree of consensus among the participants.

It would be impossible to present this report in the form of the questions asked and the answers given in the course of each two-hour session. Instead, what must be presented is a summary of the main points that were carried away from each session. In this presentation the personal pronouns "I" and "we" will be used—"I" for the things I pointed out in the explication of the texts, "we" for the things that the participants and I were in substantial agreement about as the discussion proceeded.

On the next morning, we began our discussion with Chapter 5 in John Locke's *Second Treatise Concerning Civil Government* (1690). That is the chapter in which Locke advances his quite original labor theory of the right to property, a theory which should never be confused with Marx's labor theory of value. In fact, as I pointed out and we perceived, Locke's labor theory of property contained (more than 150 years before the publication of the *Communist Manifesto* in 1848) a refutation of the central mistake that Marx made in the formulation of the labor theory of value.

The seminar participants were given only Sections 24–29 of Chapter 5 to read, and for our present purposes I am going to quote here only Sections 26 and 27.

> Though the earth and all inferior creatures be common to all men, yet every man has a "property" in his own "person." This nobody has any right to but himself. The "labour" of his body and the "work" of his hands, we may say, are properly his. Whatsoever, then, he removes out of the state that Nature hath provided and left it in, he hath mixed his labour with it, and joined to it something that is his own, and thereby makes it his property. It being by him removed from the common state Nature placed it in, it hath by this labour something annexed to it that excludes the common right of other men. For this

"labour" being the unquestionable property of the labourer, no man but he can have a right to what that is once joined to, at least where there is enough, and as good left in common for others.

He that is nourished by the acorns he picked up under an oak, or the apples he gathered from the trees in the wood, has certainly appropriated them to himself. Nobody can deny but the nourishment is his. I ask, then, when did they begin to be his? when he digested? or when he ate? or when he boiled? or when he brought them home? or when he picked them up? And it is plain, if the first gathering made them not his, nothing else could. That labour put a distinction between them and common. That added something to them more than Nature, the common mother of all, had done, and so they became his private right. And will any one say he had no right to those acorns or apples he thus appropriated because he had not the consent of all mankind to make them his? Was it a robbery thus to assume to himself what belonged to all in common? If such a consent as that was necessary, man had starved, notwithstanding the plenty God had given him. We see in commons, which remain so by compact, that it is the taking any part of what is common, and removing it out of the state Nature leaves it in, which begins the property, without which the common is of no use. And the taking of this or that part does not depend on the express consent of all the commoners. Thus, the grass my horse has bit, the turfs my servant has cut, and the ore I have digged in any place, where I have a right to them in common with others, become my property without the assignation or consent of anybody. The labour that was mine, removing them out of that common state they were in, hath fixed my property in them.

I pointed out, as the discussion of this text began, that the crucial words were "common" and "property." The common included everything in the environment that belonged to no one, but was available to all for appropriation through the labor of hand and mind that anyone mixed with the common to make the product of this mixture that individual's property, to which that individual alone had a right of possession, excluding all others. The examples that Locke gives of primitive acquisitions of this sort were clear to all the participants.

I then concentrated their attention on a portion of the final paragraph of Section 27, which I reproduce here.

> Thus, the grass my horse has bit, the turfs my servant has cut, and the ore I have digged in any place, where I have a right to them in common with others, become my property without the assignation or consent of anybody.

I expanded this one sentence for the participants by the following account of what Locke was, in effect, saying. Let the owner of the horse, grass, turf, and ore be Smith. How did he acquire the horse as his property? By going out into the wilderness, finding, capturing, and taming the horse that thus became, by right of his labor, his private property. Let us suppose that Smith, by his labor, has also staked out his claim to owning a plot of land on which there are grass, turf, and ore. Let us further suppose that, by his own efforts, he has cut down trees, fenced his land, and built some crude farm implements, such as a rake, a shovel, and a plow; and that he has also worked to make a harness for the horse he captured. With all these rightfully acquired possessions, appropriated by his labor from the common, Smith has himself for many weeks produced his own means of subsistence.

Then, one Sunday, while he is standing at his fence, along comes an itinerant, with a bag of personal possessions over his shoulder. Let his name be Brown. Smith asks Brown whether he would like to work for him next week, offering to give him room and board and a share of the wealth produced during the next six days of work. Brown finds the offer a fair one and accepts it, entering voluntarily into a labor contract with Smith. It is this voluntary contract that makes Brown the person referred to in the Locke passage quoted above as "my servant."

The word "my" here does not have the same meaning as

it does in the phrase "my horse" or "my grass." There, "my" refers to private property rightfully acquired by Smith. But Brown is not Smith's private property; nor in fact is the word "servant" satisfactory, for Brown should more properly be described as Smith's employee or hired hand.

During the next week, when Brown works for Smith, his employer decides not to do any work himself. He spends the entire week in his house reading books. All the labor involved in the production of wealth that week is done by Brown's labor on Smith's land, using Smith's horse and other instruments of production (such as shovel, spade, plow, etc.).

At the end of the week, the total wealth produced is, let us say, the quantity X. Smith gives Brown the share of that total wealth that he contracted to give him as Brown's wages for a week of work. Brown departs satisfied with Y, his agreed-upon share. This leaves Smith with Z, the residue of X that is left to Smith after Brown has been paid off.

I then pointed out that the instruments of production used by Brown in working for Smith are capital. We agreed that everything that can be used in the production of wealth, other than labor, is capital. We also agreed that money is not capital, but only an instrument of exchange and a source of purchasing power. Money, in and of itself, is not an instrument of production. We were thus quite clear about the two basic economic terms—labor and capital. We avoided the mistake of calling the labor power of men and women "human capital."

I then asked the group the $64 question. During the week in which Smith did not labor at all, and all the work productive of wealth was done by Brown, did Smith rightfully earn—without laboring—the wealth Z that was left to him after he paid Brown Y out of the total wealth X produced that week? If the answer to that question is affirmative, I said to the group, then a number of things follow that we ought to acknowledge and agree upon.

First, one's own labor power of hand and mind is the only private property that is not acquired. It is each individual's birthright of natural property. This fact makes unjust the ownership and use of human beings as chattel slaves. Only consumable goods and capital instruments can be rightfully owned as private property.

Second, if an individual puts into productive operation the capital he owns, then, even if he does not work himself, that contribution to the production of wealth rightfully earns for him whatever share of the total wealth produced that is not paid to the laborers involved for the work they do. The nonworking capitalist is *not* unproductive. In other words, wealth can be acquired either (a) by working to produce it or (b) by putting the capital one owns into production, or (c) by the combination of both factors. Smith could have labored himself, along with Brown, instead of reading, and then more wealth than X would have been produced, and Smith's share of the total would have been larger than Z.

Third, labor and capital are distinct factors in the production of wealth, and each deserves, by right, that portion of the wealth produced to which each contributes. Labor is the independent factor, in the sense that no wealth can be produced except by some labor input. Capital input by itself will not suffice. But the fact that labor is the independent and capital the dependent factor does not blur the distinct contributions that each makes to the production of wealth.

Finally, the wealth that is rightfully earned by the productive use of the capital one owns refutes the view that what an individual receives from the productive use of capital is "unearned income." The profits or dividends of capital are earned income in exactly the same sense that the wages or salaries paid to labor are earned income.

These insights, I pointed out, challenge the correctness of all the basic propositions in Marx's labor theory of value. If these insights are sound, then it cannot be correct to declare, as Marx does, (a) that all wealth is produced by labor and labor alone, either by living labor or by the labor congealed in machines and other capital instruments; (b) that the portion of the wealth produced taken by the owners of capital is "surplus value"—an "unearned increment" that capitalists *steal* by their "exploitation of labor"; and (c) that capital, certainly the modern form of capital—the machines used in factories after the Industrial Revolution, not the simple hand tools used by laborers before it—cannot be rightfully acquired as private property.

I told the group that we would return to the third point (c) above later when we discussed Marx in the third session, but if we agreed on the first two points—(a) and (b)—we had already discovered serious mistakes in Marxist doctrine that should be rejected.

The seminar next turned to the discussion of a passage from Alexander Hamilton's *Report on Manufactures* (1791). He wrote this as our first secretary of the Treasury. I quote below the paragraphs to which we paid close attention. First this:

> The employment of machinery forms an item of great importance in the general mass of national industry. It is an artificial force brought in aid of the natural force of man; and, to all the purposes of labor, is an increase of hands—an accession of strength, unencumbered, too, by the expense of maintaining the laborer.

I pointed out an error in this statement. The introduction of machinery cannot always be regarded as equivalent to an increase of hands, because in technologically advanced industrial economies, some wealth cannot be produced at all without the use of machines. But at an earlier stage of the Industrial Revolution, it is true that any increase in the production of wealth that results from the use of machinery could have been produced by an increase in the amount of labor employed. In other words, machinery is a labor-saving device. This led us to understand the division of all economies into labor-intensive and capital-intensive.

We concentrated next on the following passage:

> The cotton mill, invented in England within the last twenty years, is a signal illustration of the general proposition which

has just been advanced. In consequence of it, all the different processes for spinning cotton are performed by means of machines which are put in motion by water, and attended chiefly by women and children; and by a smaller number of persons, in the whole, than are requisite in the ordinary mode of spinning. And it is an advantage of great moment that the operations of this mill continue, with convenience, during the night as well as through the day. The prodigious effect of such a machine is easily conceived. To this invention is to be attributed, essentially, the immense progress which has been so suddenly made in Great Britain in the various fabrics of cotton.

The significance of the above, I pointed out, is its indication that with the Industrial Revolution, the total amount of capital employed by a nation became the more productive factor and the total amount of labor became the less productive factor.[1]* We agreed that, were this not so, the factories could not have effectively employed in the spinning industry women and very young children instead of men and, on the whole, a smaller number of workers than had been employed in spinning when that was conducted domestically.

We turned next to the *Preamble of the Mechanics' Union of Trade Associations*, promulgated in Philadelphia in 1827. Here, about twenty years before the *Communist Manifesto* was first published, we find a statement of the labor theory of value—that labor and labor alone produces all the wealth that society consumes. The Philadelphia Mechanics ask:

> Do not you, and all society, depend solely for subsistence on the products of human industry? . . . Do not all the streams of wealth which flow in every direction and are emptied into and absorbed by the coffers of the unproductive [the nonlaboring owners of capital] exclusively take their rise in the bones, marrow, and muscles of the industrious classes [the laborers]?

The laborers are being exploited by capitalists who, being themselves unproductive, get wealth that is an "unearned increment," a "surplus value" stolen from labor. But if this were so, then what the Philadelphia Mechanics should have asked for is all the wealth that labor alone produces. But they did not do that. They asked only for their fair share. I called attention to the following passage:

> . . .It is neither our intention nor desire to extort inequitable prices for our labor; all we may demand for this shall not exceed what can be clearly demonstrated to be a fair and full equivalent. If we demand more, we wrong the society of which we are members, and if society requires us to receive less, she injures and oppresses us.

Their self-contradiction here caused us to ask ourselves whether the Philadelphia Mechanics really affirmed Marx's labor theory of value. I then pointed out other contradictions in the text. The writers observe that the introduction of machinery in the production of wealth has greatly increased the amount of wealth produced and, at the same time, "the demand for human labor is gradually and inevitably diminishing." A diminishing demand for labor with an increased production of wealth must mean that labor cannot be the sole producer of wealth; yet a little later, the writers still refer to "labor (the only source)." Still later, they contradict themselves once again by saying that everyone depends for subsistence "upon the employment of his skill, his labor, or *his capital*." I add the italics to stress the fact that labor cannot be the only source of the wealth produced if some individuals can obtain their subsistence from the employment of their capital rather than their labor power.

The one long text discussed in the first session was the whole of an essay by William Graham Sumner, a professor of sociology at Yale University, entitled "The Challenge of Facts," taken from a book of his, *The Challenge of Facts and Other Essays*, published in 1914. The essay was written at the end of the nineteenth century.

I included this essay in the readings for the first session because I surmised that most of my participants would find

themselves in agreement with it. I was correct in this antici-
pation. The essay is a forthright rejection of socialism. It
begins with the words: "Socialism is no new thing." Later in
the essay are the following passages:

> ... Socialists are filled with the enthusiasm of equality. Every
> scheme of theirs for securing equality has destroyed liberty.
>
> The student of political philosophy has the antagonism of
> equality and liberty constantly forced upon him. Equality of
> possession or of rights and equality before the law are dia-
> metrically opposed to each other.
>
> The newest socialism is, in its method, political. The essential
> feature of its latest phases is the attempt to use the power of
> the state to realize its plans and to secure its objects. These
> objects are to do away with poverty and misery, and there are
> no socialistic schemes yet proposed, of any sort, which do not,
> upon analysis, turn out to be projects for curing poverty and
> misery by making those who have share with those who have
> not.

I pointed out that many writers in the nineteenth century,
John C. Calhoun and Alexis de Tocqueville, for example,
had, like Sumner, thought liberty and equality to be incompatible; but Sumner, more explicitly than they, declares that

> ... we cannot go outside of this alternative: liberty, inequality,
> survival of the fittest; not-liberty, equality, survival of the un-
> fittest. The former carries society forward and favors all its best
> members; the latter carries society downward and favors all its
> worst members.

Before going any further, I explained to the participants
how to correct this great nineteenth-century error. When both
liberty and equality are limited by the restraints of justice,
they are not incompatible. The conflict is between libertarianism, which asks for unlimited liberty, and egalitarianism,
which asks for complete equality and no inequality. It is never
between limited liberty and equality combined with inequality.

The correct principles are: (a) No one should have more

liberty than justice allows, which is to say, no more than individuals can use, without injuring anyone else or the general welfare of society; and (b) No society should establish more equality than justice requires, combining that with as much inequality as justice also requires.

The core of Sumner's rejection of socialism, as he understood it, is his rejection of natural rights, as he understood them. Here are excerpts from the long passage in which that occurs.

> Another development of the same philosophy is the doctrine that men come into the world endowed with "natural rights," or as joint inheritors of the "rights of man," which have been "declared" times without number during the last century. . . .
>
> The notion of natural rights is destitute of sense, but it is captivating, and it is the more available on account of its vagueness. It lends itself to the most vicious kind of social dogmatism, for if a man has natural rights, then the reasoning is clear up to the finished socialistic doctrine that a man has a natural right to whatever he needs and that the measure of his claims is the wishes which he wants fulfilled. If, then, he has a need, who is bound to satisfy it for him? Who holds the obligation corresponding to his right?

Sumner here reveals his misunderstanding of natural rights (which are identical with the rights that were called "unalienable" in the Declaration of Independence and the rights that everyone now calls "human rights"). It lies in his use of the words "needs" and "wishes" or "wants," as if their meaning were equivalent.

Needs are natural desires, the same in all human beings, for they are inherent in human nature; and wants are acquired desires, differing from individual to individual as they are nurtured under different conditions and are affected by different environmental circumstances. We have a natural right only to those things that all human beings naturally need in order to lead a decent human life. This includes not only life and liberty, but whatever else anyone needs in order to engage in the pursuit of happiness, when happiness is understood not as the psychological state of contentment one experiences when one's wants or needs are satisfied, but rather as a morally good life as a whole. Such rights are accompanied by the individual's obligation to make the effort to live well. The obligation to secure these rights falls upon organized society as a whole, since a just government should aim to secure all the natural rights of its citizens.

The first session came to end with almost everyone understanding that natural rights derive from natural needs, among them the need for a decent livelihood without which no one can live a decent human life. That raised a question about the different ways in which the right to a decent livelihood might be secured, and also a question about whether securing all natural rights—economic as well as political— would lead to socialism as well as to democracy.

THE SELF-DESTRUCTION OF BOURGEOIS CAPITALISM AND ITS TRANSFORMATION INTO SOCIALIZED PRIVATE PROPERTY CAPITALISM (SESSION II)

In the afternoon after the session is over, I reflect on the ground covered in the morning and make notes of the main points that I wish to remind the participants to carry over to the following day.

I need not repeat here the full summary presented. For our present purposes only two things should be noted. One is the understanding of democracy and socialism as the correlated political and economic aspects of a justly constituted society.

With constitutional government, political liberty comes into being, but usually only for some, not for all. The United States, for example, was first established as a republic, with political liberty extended only to the small portion of the population that was then enfranchised as citizens. It remained in that condition until the twentieth century, at the beginning of which more than half the population was disfranchised— all the women, most of the blacks, and the poor in those states where there was a poll tax they could not pay. It slowly became a democracy with the Nineteenth and Twenty-fourth amendments, the latter in 1964 when the poll tax was abolished. But if in addition to establishing universal suffrage, a democracy should secure all human rights, then further constitutional or legislative enactments are needed to complete the progress toward the twin ideals of democracy and socialism.

That ideal is political equality, or the equal political liberty for all as required by justice—all with the equal political status and power of citizenship. Justice also requires the political inequality of citizens holding public office for a time, as compared with those not in office. To discharge the responsibilities of their offices, officials must exercise more political power and perform more functions than ordinary citizens. In short, a society is democratic if all, except the few who are justly disenfranchised (infants, the mentally incompetent, and felons), are political haves as citizens, and some —those in public office—have more political power than those not in office.

In the economic order, socialism parallels democracy in the political order. It stands for the ideal of economic equality, as democracy stands for the ideal of political equality. As we recognized in the previous day's discussion of Sumner, among the natural, unalienable, and human rights is the economic right to a decent livelihood.

Postponing for a moment the consideration of the various means by which this right can be secured, the clearest way of stating the parallelism and correlation of democracy and socialism is to say that a society is socialistic to the extent that it achieves in the economic order the same kind of equality that justice requires in the political order and which democracy achieves; all haves (that is, no have-nots, no persons *deprived* of a decent livelihood), but among the haves, some *having more* and some *having less* according to the degree to which they contribute to the economic welfare of society as a whole. (Appendix 3 of the chapter contains a discussion of this subject from a previous book of mine that is now out of print.)

The second thing I stressed at the beginning of the second seminar session was the sharp distinction between the meaning of the word "socialism" as here used and the meaning of the word "communism." It is communism, not socialism, that is incompatible with democracy and with private-property capitalism.

I pointed out that the discussion of the texts assigned for the second session would soon make manifest that, in this century, the private-property, free-enterprise, and market economies of the United States, the United Kingdom, and Sweden were socialized. Another way of saying the same thing is that they all gradually became, in the twenties and thirties, "welfare states." The insights to be found in the *Communist Manifesto* not only led to the Russian Revolution of 1917 and the establishment of totalitarian communism in the Soviet Union. It also contained insights that led to the overthrow of the bourgeois capitalism that dominated Western industrial societies in the nineteenth century and their supplanting by the welfare states or the socialized capitalisms of the societies that became democratic in the twentieth century.

The second session opened with a discussion of those pages in the *Manifesto* in which Marx explains his prediction that the then regnant bourgeois capitalism would sow the seeds of its own destruction. Bourgeois capitalism operated under the governance of Ferdinand Lassalle's and David Ricardo's iron law of wages. The capitalist owners of the factories and employers of labor should seek to maximize their profits by paying labor bare subsistence wages—just enough to keep the laborers alive and able to reproduce the next generation of workers.

Since the owners of capital were the few and the workers

represented the great mass of the population with scant purchasing power, capitalism's increasing production of consumable goods for a dwindling domestic market would lead to overproduction and underconsumption. Though periodically lifted by unmet demand, after temporary failures, capitalism would soon overproduce again, leading to cycles of boom and bust. The final bust would bring about the complete collapse or self-destruction of unreformed bourgeois capitalism. The participants recognized that this was what Marx was saying in the following passage:

> It is enough to mention the commercial crises that by their periodical return put the existence of the entire bourgeois society on trial, each time more threateningly. In these crises a great part not only of the existing products, but also of the previously created productive forces, are periodically destroyed. In these crises there breaks out an epidemic that, in all earlier epochs, would have seemed an absurdity—the epidemic of over-production. Society suddenly finds itself put back into a state of momentary barbarism; it appears as if a famine, a universal war of devastation had cut off the supply of every means of subsistence; industry and commerce seem to be destroyed. . . . The conditions of bourgeois society are too narrow to comprise the wealth created by them. And how does the bourgeois get over these crises? On the one hand by enforced destruction of a mass of productive forces; on the other, by the conquest of new markets and by the more thorough exploitation of the old ones. That is to say, by paving the way for more extensive and more destructive crises, and by diminishing the means whereby crises are prevented. . . .
>
> Owing to the extensive use of machinery and to division of labour, the work of the proletarians has lost all individual character, and, consequently, all charm for the workman. He becomes an appendage of the machine, and it is only the most simple, most monotonous, and most easily acquired knack that is required of him. Hence, the cost of production of a workman is restricted almost entirely to the means of subsistence that he requires for his maintenance and for the propagation of his

race. But the price of a commodity, and therefore also of labour, is equal to its cost of production. In proportion, therefore, as the repulsiveness of the work increases, the wage decreases. Nay more, in proportion as the use of machinery and division of labour increases, in the same proportion the burden of toil also increases, whether by prolongation of the working hours, by increase of the work exacted in a given time, or by increased speed of the machinery, etc.

There are many passages in which Marx describes the utter misery of the working class, those men, women, and children whom he calls the "wage slaves" of bourgeois capitalism. The children went into the factories at a tender age and the rest of their lives was totally consumed by grinding toil—usually twelve hours a day and seven days a week. But instead of quoting these passages, I am going to cite passages written by Tocqueville in 1835 and by the American educator Horace Mann around the middle of the century, in which the condition of the working class is vividly depicted by observers who are far from being Marxist communists. First, the passage in Tocqueville, taken from Volume 2, Book 2, Chapter XX of his *Democracy in America*, entitled "How an Aristocracy May Be Created by Manufacturers":

When a workman is unceasingly and exclusively engaged in the fabrication of one thing, he ultimately does his work with singular dexterity; but, at the same time, he loses the general faculty of applying his mind to the direction of the work. He every day becomes more adroit and less industrious; so that it may be said of him that, in proportion as the workman improves, the man is degraded. What can be expected of a man who has spent twenty years of his life in making heads for pins? and to what can that mighty human intelligence, which has so often stirred the world, be applied in him, except it be to investigate the best method of making pins' heads? When a workman has spent a considerable portion of his existence in this manner, his thoughts are forever set upon the object of his daily toil; his body has contracted certain fixed habits, which it can never shake off; in a word, he no longer belongs to himself but to the calling which he has chosen. . . .

Not only are the rich not compactly united amongst themselves but there is no real bond between them and the poor. Their relative position is not a permanent one; they are constantly drawn together or separated by their interests. The workman is generally dependent on the master, but not on any particular master. These two men meet in the factory but know not each other elsewhere; and, whilst they come into contact on one point, they stand very wide apart on all others. The manufacturer asks nothing of the workman but his labor; the workman expects nothing from him but his wages. The one contracts no obligation to protect, nor the other to defend; and they are not permanently connected either by habit or duty.

The following passage comes from an essay by Mann included in a book of his writings published in 1867.

. . . The British manufacturer or farmer prescribes the rate of wages he will give to his work people; he reduces these wages under whatever pretext he pleases; and they, too, have no alternative but submission or starvation. In some respects, indeed, the condition of the modern dependent is more forlorn than that of the corresponding serf class in former times. Some attributes of the patriarchal relation did spring up between the lord and his lieges to soften the harsh relations subsisting between them. Hence came some oversight of the condition of children, some relief in sickness, some protection and support in the decrepitude of age. But only in instances comparatively few have kindly offices smoothed the rugged relation between British capital and British labor. The children of the work people are abandoned to their fate; and notwithstanding the privations they suffer, and the dangers they threaten, no power in the realm has yet been able to secure them an education; and when the adult laborer is prostrated by sickness, or eventually worn out by toil and age, the poorhouse, which has all along been his destination, becomes his destiny.

With these two passages before us, reinforcing everything Marx has to say about the misery of the working class under bourgeois capitalism, I asked the seminar whether anyone in the room, if he or she could have chosen otherwise, would have chosen to be a factory worker under the conditions that prevailed everywhere in the nineteenth century, in Europe and the United States. These conditions persisted relatively unchanged until the second and third decades of the twentieth century. The answer was a resounding and unanimous negative.

We found evidence of the persistence of these deplorable conditions in Theodore Roosevelt's platform for his Progressive Party in 1912. In it were planks that called for one day's rest in seven for every wage worker, for the prohibition of child labor, for minimum wage standards for working women, for the prohibition of night work for women, for an eight-hour day in continuous twenty-four-hour industries, and for "the protection of homelife against the hazards of sickness, irregular employment, and old age, through the adoption of a system of social insurance."

Everyone recognized that many of the reforms proposed by Theodore Roosevelt were not legislatively enacted until Franklin D. Roosevelt's New Deal in the thirties. I pointed out that Big Steel in Pittsburgh was still operating the mills on two twelve-hour shifts as late as 1928 and that unemployment insurance, old age pensions, and Social Security entitlements came later than that.

We stayed a moment longer with Theodore Roosevelt, turning to his great "New Nationalism" address in Kansas in 1910. He began it by confessing that he would probably be "denounced as a Communist agitator" for talking about the rights of labor as well as the rights of capital and for proclaiming that "the object of government is the welfare of the people." To achieve this goal, Roosevelt insisted that human rights must take precedence over property rights.

... We are face to face with new conceptions of the relations of property to human welfare, chiefly because certain advocates of the rights of property as against the rights of men have been pushing their claims too far. The man who wrongly holds that every human right is secondary to his profit must now give way to the advocate of human welfare, who rightly maintains that every man holds his property subject to the general right of the community to regulate its use to whatever degree the public welfare may require it.

A little later, he pointed out that the economic welfare of the citizens was indispensable to making democracy prosper, for without it most members of the working class were citizens in name only. "We keep countless men," he said, "from being good citizens by the conditions of life with which we surround them."

We turned from Theodore Roosevelt's "socialistic" proposals (socialistic, not communistic) to Franklin D. Roosevelt's establishment in this country of a welfare state by transforming bourgeois capitalism, reeling from the Great Depression, into socialized capitalism. I called the seminar's attention to one other text that had a bearing on FDR's "economic declaration of rights" in his Commonwealth Club Address of 1932, and in his "Economic Bill of Rights," which he delivered in his address to Congress on the State of the Nation in 1944.

That text was Monsignor John A. Ryan's treatise on *The Right to a Living Wage* (1906). This followed in the footsteps of two great papal encyclicals demanding relief for the plight of the working class. Mgr. Ryan made clear that the inventory of natural or human rights was incomplete unless it included the right to a decent livelihood, secured either through earning a living wage or by other means. [2]

The socialization of private-property capitalism (in different ways and in different degrees) in the United States under Franklin D. Roosevelt, in the United Kingdom under Clement Attlee, and in Sweden (or, to put it in other terms, these societies becoming welfare states in the twenties, thirties, and forties of this century) went a long way toward alleviating the misery of the working class. It was clear to all of us that the alleviation or extirpation of that condition had been from the very start the controlling motivation in Marx's thought and program.

A careful reading of the *Manifesto* that he and Engels promulgated in 1848 revealed the steps they proposed for moving toward this objective before what they regarded as the final revolution would (by force, they thought) expropriate the expropriators, that is, take from them the ownership of capital which they used to exploit labor. It also revealed that the economic reforms enacted in the US, the UK, and Sweden involved the erosion of capitalist property rights called for in the closing pages of the *Manifesto*, by means of redistributive taxation, though the Western democracies did not adopt all of the ten measures set forth at the end of the *Manifesto*.

The first step in this direction, according to Marx and Engels, was a step toward democracy, by extending suffrage to the laboring masses. This occurred earlier in England than elsewhere, in the Second Reform Bill of 1867. "The first step in the revolution by the working class," the *Manifesto* declares, "is to raise the proletariat to the postion of ruling class, to establish democracy." Then it goes on to say:

> The proletariat will use its political supremacy to wrest by degrees all capital from the bourgeoisie, to centralize all instruments of production in the hands of the state, i.e. of the proletariat organized as the ruling class, and to increase the total of productive forces as rapidly as possible.
>
> Of course, in the beginning this cannot be effected except by means of despotic inroads on the rights of property and on the conditions of bourgeois production; by means of measures, therefore, which appear economically insufficient and untenable, but which in the course of the movement outstrip themselves, necessitate further inroads upon the old social order, and are unavoidable as a means of entirely revolutionizing the mode of production.

We noted the following points in the foregoing passage. First, Marx and Engels did not realize the significance of the fact that their advocacy of increasing "the total of productive forces as rapidly as possible" contained implicitly an acknowledgment that labor was not the *only* productive force in the economy. They were not advocating an increase in the quantity of the labor force at work, but rather an increase in the capital instruments employed productively. Only by regarding these capital instruments as "congealed labor" could they avoid contradicting their labor theory of value—that labor and labor alone produces wealth.

The second point we noted was that they did not abandon their ultimate revolutionary goal. They still anticipated that the proletariat would "wrest all capital from the bourgeoisie" and would "centralize all the instruments of production in the hands of the state." In other words, private-property capitalism would ultimately be destroyed and would be replaced by state capitalism.

The third point and the one that bears on what actually did take place in the twenties and thirties in the three Western countries above is the step described by Marx and Engels as "despotic inroads on the rights of property." I reminded the seminar that when Marx and Engels refer to "property" or "private property" they are never referring to the ownership of consumable goods, but always to the ownership of the means of production, the private ownership of capital, by individuals or by corporations, as contrasted with its ownership by the state.

Earlier in the *Manifesto*, they had written that the communist revolution could be summed up in a single mandate: *Abolish private property!* But later they describe what has been called "creeping socialism" in terms of inroads on the rights of private property before the ultimate goal is reached by its abolition. While private property still exists in societies that are being socialized economically, that socialization, by means of inroads on the rights of property, involves the erosion of those property rights by the enactment of some of the following ten measures, certainly by numbers 2 and 10, and, in the case of number 3, by the erosion, not the abolition, of inheritance rights.

1. Abolition of property in land and application of all rents of land to public purposes.
2. A heavy progressive or graduated income tax.
3. Abolition of all right of inheritance.
4. Confiscation of the property of all emigrants and rebels.
5. Centralization of credit in the hands of the state by means of a national bank with state capital and an exclusive monopoly.
6. Centralization of the means of communication and transport in the hands of the state.
7. Extension of factories and instruments of production owned by the state; the bringing into cultivation of waste lands, and the improvement of the soil generally in accordance with a common plan.
8. Equal obligation of all to work. Establishment of industrial armies, especially for agriculture.
9. Combination of agriculture with manufacturing industries; gradual abolition of the distinction between town and country by a more equable distribution of the population over the country.
10. Free education for all children in public schools. Abolition of child factory labour in its present form. Combination of education with industrial production, etc.

Such enactments as the inheritance tax, the graduated income tax, ownership by the state instead of private corporations of certain economic agencies, establishment of national banks and credit facilities, establishment of free public schools, abolition of child labor, and the other welfare entitlements by which the national income is redistributed—all these have moved private-property capitalist societies in the direction of socialism.

Creeping socialism as thus accomplished does not, of course, go far enough, in the view of Marx and Engels. It is only a step in the right direction, alleviating the misery of the working class. Marx and Engels have another objective in mind, one that for them is of equal importance. That is the removal of class conflicts and the ultimate establishment of a truly classless society. We found this clearly stated in the last two paragraphs of this chapter of the *Manifesto*.

> When in the course of development class distinctions have disappeared and all production has been concentrated in the hands of a vast association of the whole nation, the public power will lose its political character. Political power, properly so called, is merely the organized power of one class for oppressing another. If the proletariat during its contest with the bourgeoisie is compelled by the force of circumstances to organize itself as a class; if by means of a revolution it makes itself the ruling class and, as such, sweeps away by force the old conditions of production, then it will, along with these conditions, have swept away the conditions for the existence of class antagonisms and of classes generally, and will thereby have abolished its own supremacy as a class.
>
> In place of the old bourgeois society, with its classes and class antagonisms, we shall have an association in which the free development of each is the condition for the free development of all.

I told the seminar that we would return later to these twin objectives of the Marxist revolutionary program: the alleviation or, better, the elimination of the misery of the working class, and the ending of all class conflicts by the establishment of a classless society. At the present stage of our discussion, we would be content to observe that the socialist or welfare measures adopted by various Western democracies, which remained private-property capitalist societies, have moved them toward the ideal of economic equality that is the end at which all the various forms of socialism aim. This ideal, I reminded the seminar, is approached to the degree that any society eliminates have-nots—those totally deprived of the essentials of subsistence, most certainly of a decent livelihood.

Before the second seminar closed, we looked at two more texts. One was Gus Tyler's article "On the Economic Divide" (1988), with special attention to the following paragraph:

> The poorest tenth got 1.1 per cent of the national income in 1977. Tiny as that proportion was, it had shrunk by 1984 and has stayed down so that in 1988 the bottom decile is getting merely nine-tenths of 1 per cent of the national income. This represents a drop of 18 per cent in its share.

In the last decade, the number of have-nots, the seriously deprived, has steadily increased in the United States. For 20 percent of our population, average family income is less than $8,000 per year—substantially below the so-called poverty line, under which people do not have what they need. Not only does this nation now have less economic equality than justice requires, it also has more inequality—a greater inequality between the have-mores and the have-lesses—than justice requires.

I also pointed out that the progress toward equality we have made since the turn of the century is more than phenomenal. It is like the crossing of a great divide. In the United States, as in all other societies before the twentieth century, the political and economic haves were everywhere the privileged few—those who were both citizens and owners of property. The deprived—the have-nots—were everywhere the many. For the first time in the twentieth century, the proportions of the total population have been strikingly reversed. In the societies that have moved toward democracy and socialism, we now have a privileged multitude. The haves, both politically and economically, are the many, and the have-nots, the seriously deprived, are the few.

The other text that we examined came from John Strachey's *The Challenge of Democracy*, posthumously published in *Encounter* in 1963. In it, Strachey points out that, while the standard of living of the workers in the Soviet Union has steadily gone down, the standard of living of the wage earners in the Western democracies has steadily increased. [3] His explanation of this is as follows:

> Why is it that Marx's prophecy of ever increasing misery, which must have seemed thoroughly reasonable and sensible when he made it, turned out to be wrong? I have no hesitation in saying that the explanation is to be found in the increasingly effective use of their democratic institutions by the mass of wage earners of the Western societies. It is democracy which has done it. The Western capitalist employers have not had a change of heart; they still work, and must work, their industries in order to make the maximum amount of profit. They do not like paying higher wages to their workers, or working these shorter hours. By and large they have been impelled to do these things by the wage earners themselves. It is the fact that the wage earners in the democracies have been able to organize themselves, both politically and industrially, that has done the trick. . . .
>
> Slowly, but in the end inexorably, the pressure of the wage earners has driven the governments of the Western democracies to undertake a substantial redistribution of the national income by means of taxation. . . .
>
> Personally I like having a TV set, a motorcar, a washing machine, and the other gadgets of a contemporary home in Western society. For that matter the high standard of life which is being achieved in one Western society after another consists in many other things as well as gadgets; it consists in things like decent housing, more leisure, and a good education for one's children. I want such things, don't you?
>
> The truth is, of course, that these things are enormously important to every wage earner's family. What we can agree is that there is something low and limited about caring *only* for material benefits. If democracy brought *only* washing machines, TV sets, and motorcars, or even good houses, it would be a limited thing. For once one has got these material benefits, one has to learn to use them wisely, and that is even more difficult than getting them. One has to learn that, in the end, their real use is to increase one's freedom to develop as a human being. That is why I suggested that there is a dialectical interplay

between the use of their democratic institutions which the wage earners of the West have been making to get themselves material benefits, and the deeper, and in the end even more important, use of those institutions to increase human freedom. . . .

To face *that* fact would have involved recognizing that Marx's theory of ever increasing misery had proved to be wrong.

This is what I call being blinded by theory. I am not against political and economic theory. On the contrary it is indispensable to form the best theories which we possibly can about the way in which our societies work; otherwise we shall have no guide as to how to change and improve them. But it is essential to recognize that even the most brilliant theories are simply hypotheses designed to account for the observable facts of social life—hypotheses which must be scrapped the moment that these observable facts no longer fit the theories. What oceans of misery the world would have been saved if only the Communists —and everyone else too for that matter—had borne that simple principle in mind. Instead, everybody tends to cling desperately to the theories he has learnt. The Communists have carried this common human error to an extreme; they have been, and remain, "blinded by theory" to the point where in some cases they take no account of the real world at all. The results are disastrous, not only for them, but for all of us, and the greatest example of all is the clinging to the dogma that the wage earners of the Western democracies are sinking into ever increasing misery, when quite obviously their standard of life is steadily rising.

In concluding this report of the second seminar discussion, I must mention an illuminating intervention by my associate, James O'Toole, professor of management in the Graduate School of Business Administration at the University of Southern California. He pointed out the contribution made by Robert Owen in his effort to correct the mistake made by the bourgeois capitalists, in England in the nineteenth century, by their obstinately adhering to the iron law of wages in their treatment of their factory workers.

Owen was himself the owner of a factory in which he demonstrated the economic effectiveness of treating the labor he employed in a quite different manner, paying higher wages, improving the conditions of work in the factories, shortening the hours of work, and consulting the workers about the conduct of the enterprise. All of his recommendations fell upon deaf ears and caused Owen to support the establishment of trade unionism as the only way to bring about the reform of bourgeois capitalism, a reform that he deemed both desirable and necessary for its survival as well as to rectify its injustice.

THE SELF-DESTRUCTION OF COMMUNIST SOCIALISM AND ITS TRANSFORMATION INTO PRIVATELY CAPITALIZED SOCIALISM (SESSION III)

I started the third seminar session with Professor O'Toole's discussion of Owen's attempt to reform bourgeois capitalism. Commenting on Owen's style of industrial management, Prof. O'Toole pointed out that today we recognize Owen's New Lanark as an example of what we have come to call the Japanese style of management. He also said that Marx was quite correct in dismissing Owen as a utopian socialist. Owen was utopian in hoping that the bourgeois capitalists of his day would act in terms of long-term enlightened self-interest instead of being solely motivated by short-term gains in profit for themselves.

I then returned to a matter that had been postponed the day before when we discussed Monsignor Ryan's argument for the natural right to a decent livelihood, obtained either by a living wage or by other means. The question that remained to be answered was: What are all the various means by which this right can be secured?

In the first place, a decent livelihood is either earned or obtained by other means. If it is an earned livelihood, it may be income in the form of wages or salaries, income in the form of the earned dividends from the ownership of productive capital, or it may involve, as we will find Louis O. Kelso advocating in his theory of binary economies, an income derived from the combination of wages and dividends.

In the second place, some portion of a decent livelihood may come not from earned income, but from welfare benefits or entitlements, such as Social Security and Medicare. In addition to these welfare benefits for all, there may have to be special welfare benefits for some, for those who have serious pathological disabilities and for those who, for a time, may be unemployed through no fault of their own. The larger the portion of a decent livelihood that comes from earned income, the less need be provided by welfare benefits. The ideal is a decent livelihood secured for all by means of earned income.

The uneasiness I detected on the faces of the participants caused by these considerations prompted me to add one further point of explanation concerning the difference between political and economic rights. When a government tries to secure or safeguard natural rights that are political in character, it adopts constitutional provisions or legislative enactments that restrain it from invading, transgressing, or violating these rights. For example, the first seven Amendments to the Constitution of the United States protect the individual's natural and unalienable right to civil liberty and freedom of action *from governmental impediments or interference*. The italicized words indicate what the government *should not do*.

When we turn from liberty to a decent livelihood, we see at once the difference between a political and an economic right. In the latter case, securing the right requires positive action and governmental intervention in the economy, not negative action or governmental restraint. That is why securing the right to a decent livelihood has so far involved and will continue to involve legislative enactments, such as minimum wage laws, rather than constitutional amendments of the sort we find in our eighteenth-century Bill of Rights (the first ten Amendments).

These matters being somewhat clarified, the third session

of the seminar began with a consideration of its title: the self-destruction of communist socialism and its capitalization. We saw at once the parallelism of this title with the title of the second session: the self-destruction of bourgeois capitalism and its socialization. The question this led us to ask ourselves was: What basic mistake was made by communist socialism that sowed the seeds of its self-destruction, comparable to the mistake made by bourgeois capitalism that sowed the seeds of its own destruction?

In other words, (1) what mistake did Marx and Engels make that had the same destructive effect on communist socialism that the obstinate espousal of the "iron law of wages" had upon bourgeois capitalism, and (2) what is meant by the capitalization of communist socialism to correct this mistake, paralleling the socialization of private-property capitalism to correct the basic mistake made by the bourgeois capitalists?

Before we attempted to answer these two questions, I reminded the participants of certain points that had been covered in our lexicon of terms. It is necessary to remember that the word "socialism," unmodified by any adjective, signifies an ideal or goal to be sought—a society in which all are economic haves and there are no have-nots. As we have seen, socialized private-property capitalism is one means of moving toward this end. Communist socialism, which is identical with state capitalism, is the means that Marx and Engels proposed for moving toward the same end. Accordingly, the phrases "communist socialism," "Marxist communism," and "state capitalism" all refer to one and the same set of means, quite distinct from the set of means referred to by the phrase "socialized private-property capitalism."

To answer the first of the above questions, we went back to a section of the *Manifesto* that we had not examined before. Here it is.

> The distinguishing feature of Communism is not the abolition of property generally, but the abolition of bourgeois property.

But modern bourgeois private property is the final and most complete expression of the system of producing and appropriating products that is based on class antagonisms, on the exploitation of the many by the few.

In this sense the theory of the Communists may be summed up in the single sentence: abolition of private property.

We Communists have been reproached with the desire of abolishing the right of personally acquiring property as the fruit of a man's own labour, which property is alleged to be the groundwork of all personal freedom, activity and independence.

Hard-won, self-acquired, self-earned property! Do you mean the property of the petty artisan and of the small peasant, a form of property that preceded the bourgeois form? There is no need to abolish that; the development of industry has to a great extent already destroyed it and is still destroying it daily.

Or do you mean modern bourgeois private property?

But does wage labour create any property for the labourer? Not a bit. It creates capital, i.e., that kind of property which exploits wage labour and which cannot increase except upon condition of begetting a new supply of wage labour for fresh exploitation. Property in its present form is based on the antagonism of capital and wage labour.

The abolition of "bourgeois property" (the private ownership of capital, consisting in the means of production that have emerged since the beginning of the Industrial Revolution) leads necessarily to state capitalism. The capital instruments at work must be owned and operated. If not by private individuals and corporations, the only other alternative is collective ownership by the state.

What is the mistake that lies at the root of this radical transference of the ownership of capital to the state? It is the error that we discovered when we read and discussed Locke in our first session. It is the *labor theory of value*, the theory (1) that all wealth is produced by labor, living or congealed labor; (2) that the owners of capital are totally unproductive; and (3) that they exploit labor by taking from it an "unearned increment" or the "surplus value" that labor produces. The profits of the capitalists come from thus exploiting labor; therefore, profit is theft. The following text from the *Manifesto* says all this, though as we saw, it says it not too clearly.

> To be a capitalist is to have not only a purely personal, but a social, *status* in production. Capital is a collective product, and only by the united action of many members—nay, in the last resort, only by the united action of all members of society—can it be set in motion.
>
> Capital is, therefore, not a personal, it is a social, power.
>
> When, therefore, capital is converted into common property, into the property of all members of society, personal property is not thereby transformed into social property. It is only the social character of the property that is changed. It loses its class character.
>
> Let us now take wage labour.
>
> The average price of wage labour is the minimum wage, i.e., that quantum of the means of subsistence which is absolutely requisite to keep the labourer in bare existence as a labourer. What, therefore, the wage labourer appropriates by means of his labour merely suffices to prolong and reproduce a bare existence. We by no means intend to abolish this personal appropriation of the products of labour, an appropriation that is made for the maintenance and reproduction of human life and that leaves no surplus wherewith to command the labour of others. All that we want to do away with is the miserable character of this appropriation, under which the labourer lives merely to increase capital, and is allowed to live only insofar as the interest of the ruling class requires it.
>
> In bourgeois society living labour is but a means to increase accumulated labour. In Communist society accumulated labour is but a means to widen, to enrich, to promote the existence of the labourer.

What is meant here by "accumulated labor"? It is the machinery produced by labor that Marx in other places called "congealed labor." Only by thus calling machinery itself a form of labor can any sense be made of the statement that all wealth is produced by labor and also the statement that the capitalists are unproductive even when they put their capital to work productively.

We saw that the text just quoted contained another fundamental point, also a mistake that underlies the Marxist abolition of the private ownership of capital. The *Manifesto* maintains that capital is collectively produced and collectively operated and, therefore, must be collectively, not privately, owned. What can this mean?

To answer that question, we turned to an essay by Charles Vail, an American socialist, who wrote a pamphlet entitled *The Socialist Movement*, published in 1902. We examined the following passage.

> . . . In the days of individual production private ownership of the tools was necessary to secure to the laborer his freedom and the full product of his toil. But when the method of production was revolutionized and the tools were transformed into social instruments, they were not capable of individual ownership on the part of the laborers. The principle of private ownership, which had hitherto been the means of securing to the laborer his full product, became now the means of his servitude and exploitation. The changed conditions rendered what was once right a decided wrong. . . .

The hand tools that the laborer produces for his own use are privately produced and privately operated and therefore it is right that they should be privately owned. But the industrial machinery the capitalist owns involves many gadgets and elements that have been collectively produced by human society as a whole in the course of its long history, as, for example, wheels, levers, fulcrums, pulleys, screws, nails, leather, rope, and many other technological devices that are embodied in the industrial machinery. They have been collectively produced. The bourgeois capitalist has not paid for them, and, therefore, he has no right to own them. In short, modern industrial machinery cannot rightfully be a private possession.

Just as the mistake made by the labor theory of value in

declaring the capitalist unproductive was exposed in our discussion of Locke, so the mistake of saying that industrial machinery cannot rightfully be private property can be corrected by remembering Locke's point that whatever is in the sphere of the common, or in the public domain, can be privately appropriated. Such private appropriations are protected by patent laws and regulations that usually have time limitations. When the time limit expires, whatever has been protected by patents returns to the public domain and is once again subject to private appropriation.

I presented the following concrete example to the seminar. Jones, a capitalist, is approached by White, an inventor, who offers him the design and blueprints of a new machine that incorporates many things that have long been in the public domain and that, therefore, can be appropriated by him. Jones thinks well of the new machine and offers to pay the inventor a fee for his device and also an annual royalty for a term of years. Jones then hires laborers to produce the machine whose design and blueprints he has bought from the inventor. He pays the laborers off each week for the work they do in building the machine. When they have completed their work, he owns the machine and can put it into productive operation by paying other laborers to operate it.

If there is any injustice in this whole series of transactions, it must be that Jones has not paid the inventor adequately or has not paid the workers fairly. It cannot lie in the fact that what he has paid for is privately rather than collectively owned. It cannot be that it must be collectively owned because it is collectively produced by all the work done by society in the past, and must now be collectively operated.

There was one more text in the *Manifesto* to which I called attention. It follows closely on the texts already quoted. It is as follows:

> You are horrified at our intending to do away with private property. But in your existing society private property is already

done away with for nine-tenths of the population; its existence for the few is solely due to its non-existence in the hands of those nine-tenths. You reproach us, therefore, with intending to do away with a form of property, the necessary condition for whose existence is the non-existence of any property for the immense majority of society.

In a word, you reproach us with intending to do away with your property. Precisely so; that is just what we intend.

The importance of this text, I pointed out to the participants, is that it implies a third remedy, not found in the *Manifesto*, but consistent with its stated object of alleviating or curing the misery of the working class.

The first of the remedies actually proposed by Marx we discussed in the previous session—inroads on the rights of capital, or the erosion of private property rights by the ten measures that the *Manifesto* enumerates in its closing pages.

Marx's second remedy is more drastic. It is the one that we considered earlier in this session—the abolition of the private ownership of the means of production, not just the erosion of the rights of the owners. While the first remedy may only alleviate the misery of the working class, the second, in Marx's judgment, goes much further. It eliminates it, by eliminating the capitalist's exploitation of labor. That is why Marx chose it as the radical remedy for the misery of the working class.

Now here, in the text just quoted, we can see the opportunity for a third and quite distinct remedy, not recognized by Marx, but equally appropriate to his purpose—that is, neither the erosion of private property rights, nor the abolition of private property itself, but the extension of the ownership of capital from the few to the many.

But if the cause of the misery of the working class is the private ownership of capital instruments, then the abolition of private ownership is obviously the cure.

And if the cause of the misery of the working class is the uneroded property rights of the capitalist who, under completely laissez-faire conditions, pays the labor employed a bare subsistence wage, then just as obviously the remedy is to erode those rights, not abolish them.

But if the cause of the misery of the working class is that all or most of the capital available to a society is privately owned by less than one-tenth of the population, then the remedy which fits that cause is promoting the ownership of capital by a much larger proportion of the population.

The open letter written by Louis O. and Patricia Hetter Kelso to Mikhail Gorbachev, included in the readings for the fourth session of the seminar, recommends that he use the third remedy to achieve the reforms for which he is striving.

I told the seminar that we would discover the variety of ways in which the Kelsos think that all capital-intensive economies, that of the United States as well as that of the Soviet Union, can widely diffuse the ownership of capital equities and thus give to many members of society a double income (from earned wages or salaries combined with the earned dividends of capital profits). This is what "binary economics" recommends. A decent livelihood will thus become largely an earned livelihood; it will become less dependent on welfare benefits and entitlements. (See the discussion of binary economics by Prof. O'Toole in Appendix 4.)

To reinforce the critique of the Marxist doctrine that emerged from our close examination of the *Communist Manifesto*, I had included in the readings for the third session the first four chapters of Joseph A. Schumpeter's classic treatment of Marxism, *Capitalism, Socialism and Democracy* (1942). Here the seminar participants would find, I thought, a much more thorough critique, one that went beyond the *Manifesto* to *Das Kapital* and other Marxist writings. I learned, however, that the participants found Schumpeter very rough going. They did not profit from their reading of him as much as I had anticipated.

One more thing remained to be done in this third session. I had assigned for the second session the passage from

Tocqueville that described the misery of the working class as he observed it in America in 1831–32. But I had failed to assign the chapters in *Democracy in America* that were most relevant to the undesirable results of state capitalism under the dictatorship of the proletariat (the Communist party), results that Gorbachev's *perestroika* was trying to undo. To make amends for this omission, I concluded the third session and prepared for the fourth by calling attention to the great, almost indispensable contribution that Tocqueville had made to the solution of the problem with which the seminar began.

The stage is set by one paragraph in which Tocqueville refers to a new kind of oppression—tyranny or despotism—that he fears will develop in any nation that tends toward democracy, which for him means any nation that tries to establish an equality of conditions, especially economic conditions. Here is that paragraph.

> I think, then, that the species of oppression by which democratic nations are menaced is unlike anything which ever before existed in the world; our contemporaries will find no prototype of it in their memories. I seek in vain for an expression which will accurately convey the whole of the idea I have formed of it; the old words "despotism" and "tyranny" are inappropriate. The thing itself is new, and, since I cannot name, I must attempt to define it.

The word that Tocqueville was looking for and could not find became current almost a hundred years later after the Russian Revolution eventuated in the state capitalism of the Soviet Union. It is "totalitarianism." State capitalism or Marxist socialism is totalitarian communism. Totalitarianism comes into existence when all the governing and managing power of a society, both its political and its economic power, is concentrated in the centralized bureaucracy of the state, the *aparatchiks* of the Communist party.

What word names the diametrical opposite of monolithic totalitarianism? It is "pluralism," the kind of political and economic pluralism that preserves the liberties that democratic societies seek to maximize, even as they also aim to maximize, as far as justice requires, an equality of economic conditions.

Tocqueville refers back to the kind of pluralism that existed in what he calls the ancient regime; the aristocratic, feudal society of his own French past. In this feudal society, the many lords, barons, earls, marquises, and dukes were each secondary agencies of government, each with its own domain. The monarch was the sole ruler of the whole country, but his authority and power were checked and diluted by the nobles who were not only his vassals, but also the lords of their own domains.

Tocqueville draws from this historic example of feudal pluralism the lesson to be learned by the democracies of the present. Private associations of all sorts, profit and nonprofit corporations, private business organizations, labor unions, and competing political parties, must play the role that the feudal lords played in the ancient regime. They must function as secondary agencies of government, lessening the concentration of power in the central government. The multiplicity of private associations is the cornerstone of a pluralistic society in which the decentralization of power and authority operates in the balance against its centralized concentration. Abraham Lincoln aptly summarized the pluralistic principle when he said that the government should do for the people only that which the people, individual or collectively (that is, in private associations) cannot do for themselves.

The principle of totalitarianism is exactly the opposite. Everything, except perhaps the private association of the family, is a creature of the state. There is only one political party; there are no private labor unions; there are no private universities or hospitals; there are no private businesses or industrial corporations.

Can private associations exist and operate effectively in the economic sphere without the private ownership and management of capital? Can there be free enterprise and a free market economy without the operation of a plurality of private associations? Can Gorbachev achieve a higher standard of living, especially an abundance of consumer goods, for the people of the Soviet Union without the market economy and the free enterprise that require a plurality of private associations? In short, can Gorbachev achieve the results at which he and his fellow reformers aim without replacing totalitarianism with pluralism and without introducing private-property capitalism to replace state capitalism? [4]

With these questions to be answered the next day, the third session closed.

THE IDEAL OF THE CLASSLESS SOCIETY: POLITICAL AND ECONOMIC EQUALITY (SESSION IV)

In the previous session we had substituted a summary of the development of Marxist doctrine written by Professor O'Toole for Schumpeter's more extensive critique of it. Schumpeter provides us with further critical comments on Marxist errors, in addition to the two basic mistakes made by Marx, the errors we learned from our study of Locke's chapter on property [5]. In Schumpeter's judgment, Marxist communism is doomed to fail (1) because it is conceived in terms of a static, not dynamic, economy, and (2) because it is mainly managerial rather than entrepreneurial. It should be added here that Schumpeter also directs the second of these criticisms against Western private-property capitalism. That has become increasingly subject to the second criticism since Schumpeter's book was published, not to mention leveraged buyouts and junk bond sales.

Some of the participants had already read the dialogue between John Kenneth Galbraith and Stanislav Menshikov (*Capitalism, Communism and Coexistence*, 1988), which had been assigned for the sixth session of the seminar. In this dialogue Galbraith argued, on the one hand, that to achieve the minimal conditions of economic equality in the United States (all haves, no have-nots), private-property capitalism would have to move further in the direction of socialism. Menshikov, on the other hand, expressed the opinion that Gorbachev's reforms could achieve, to some degree, free enterprise and a free market economy, accompanied by a modicum of decentralization, while still remaining what the seminar would recognize as a totalitarian regime, with private ownership of the means of production abolished and with the state the sole owner of capital. It was in these terms that Galbraith and Menshikov agreed in their closing chapters on the future coexistence of the United States and the Soviet Union.

Some of the participants asked why I thought that the position Menshikov advanced was not a feasible one—that achieving free enterprise and a market economy was simply not possible as long as the Soviet Union remained a totalitarian state, as it had to remain as long as its socialistic goals were to be accomplished by state capitalism. I went to the blackboard and put on it the following diagram.

Pluralistic Society with Competing Political Parties	Totalitarian State with One-Party Rule
Decentralized Private-Property Capitalism	Centralized State Capitalism
Private Economic Associations	*No* Private Economic Associations
Free Enterprise	*No* Free Enterprise
Market Economy	*No* Market Economy

I argued that there was no middle ground here—no mixture of free enterprise and a market economy with the nonexistence of private-economy associations and the nonexistence of the private ownership of capital. I also predicted a different future from that predicted by Menshikov—not coexistence, but convergence toward a middle ground of the socialist economies of the Soviet Union and the United States. This called for more than minor reforms of the government and economy of the Soviet Union. It required the replacement of a totalitarian state by a pluralistic society, and of state capitalism by private-property capitalism. [6]

As a preamble to the new turn in the seminar that had been planned for this fourth session, I thought it helpful briefly to recapitulate the ground we had covered in the two preceding sessions.

In the second and third sessions, we had concentrated on only one of the two chief motivations of the Marxist revolutionary program. That was Karl Marx's deep and passionate desire to alleviate or eliminate the misery of the working class under the reign of bourgeois capitalism in England, the United States, and other Western nations.

In the second session, we saw how the alleviation of misery, if not its elimination, was accomplished in the Western nations by the socialization of their economies, adopting in various ways and in different degrees measures for the erosion, not the abolition, of the rights of private property (in other words, inroads on capitalistic profits in order to secure a better standard of living for the working class).

In the third session, we saw how the attempt to eliminate the misery of the working class by abolishing private property and establishing the dictatorship of the proletariat (the totalitarian state with all political and economic control in the hands of the Communist party) had been unsuccessful. It had failed to provide sufficient consumer goods in the marketplace and a decent standard of living for the working class. The fact that their misery had not so far been eliminated or even greatly alleviated was the prime motivating cause of Gorbachev's *perestroika*.

What I referred to above as a "new turn in the seminar" consisted in turning now, in this fourth session, to the second of the two motivations of the Marxist revolutionary program. For Marx and Engels as well as for Lenin, class warfare or conflict in all the societies of the past was a historic social evil that had to be remedied. The only remedy for that evil was the establishment of a truly classless society.

To begin the discussion of this matter, I called attention to the following text in Strachey's *Challenge of Democracy*:

> The first thing to realize is that for Lenin, as for Marx, the division of society into social classes is everything. And when I say "everything," I mean that phrase almost literally. For the Leninist, even more than for the Marxist, nothing in human life really counts compared with this division into social classes. Politics is the struggle for power between these social classes, and power is the power of the state. The state is simply an engine of coercion by the use of which any class which it at the moment in power controls by physical force the class or classes which are not in power. This whole conception derives directly, of course, from Marx's and Engels' formulation of the matter in the *Communist Manifesto* where they wrote that the state is "the executive committee of the ruling class."

The correctness of the Marxist and Leninist assertion that class warfare or conflict has plagued civilized societies from the beginning is amply confirmed by the facts of history. In antiquity, Plato, in his *Republic*, remarked that there have always been two cities, not one, the city of the rich and the city of the poor, and they are forever at war with one another. In the nineteenth century, an American reformer, Orestes Brownson (in an essay on "The Laboring Classes" written in 1840), anticipated by eight years the depiction of class conflict in the *Manifesto*. In our own century, Arnold J. Toynbee in his twelve-volume *A Study of History* singled out two causes for the decline of all historic civilizations: war and class. These are two forms of the same root evil: external conflicts between societies and internal conflicts within each society by virtue of its division into antagonistic classes.

The history of the West records a succession of class conflicts, changing with changes in the economy: chattel slaves vs. masters, dispossessed agrarian workers vs. landlord magnates, plebeians vs. patricians, feudal peons or serfs vs. feudal lords, the industrial proletariat vs. the bourgeois capitalists —in general, the have-nots vs. the haves.

At this point, I found it necessary to digress, reminding the participants of one point that had great relevance to the Marxist-Leninist ideal of a completely classless society. We had agreed earlier that justice calls for the establishment of a society in which all are political haves, all have the status and power of suffrage; and economically, all have the right to a decent livelihood secured. But we also agreed that, in both the political and the economic order, justice also requires that some have more and some have less (based in the political order on the greater political status and power of citizens in public office; and in the economic order on different degrees of contribution to the economic welfare of society as a whole). The ideal, in short, is a nonegalitarian socialism (see Appendix 5).

To try to eliminate such inequality between the have-mores and the have-lesses would be an act of injustice. [7] Hence in a justly constituted society, one class distinction must remain. It would not be a perfectly classless society, for while all would be haves, some would have more than others. Whether this irremovable class distinction engenders a class conflict in society as grievous and bitter as the age-old class conflict between the haves and have-nots was a difficult question. There were differences of opinion that our discussion left unresolved. In any case, we did agree that the ideal to be attained could not be a completely classless society, but rather one that was only relatively classless, with the distinction between the *have-mores* and the *have-lesses* remaining as a matter of distributive justice. [8]

After this digression, I called attention to a few other texts that clearly embrace classlessness as an ideal. One is a single sentence in the essay by Horace Mann that we had discussed earlier. Using the word "property" to signify the ownership of capital, Mann declared: "Property and labor in different class are essentially antagonistic; but property and labor in the same class are essentially fraternal." I have often used this statement by Mann as an endorsement of Louis Kelso's binary economics: that as many persons as possible should become economic haves through two sources of earned income: wages or salaries on the one hand and dividends derived from the profits of capital on the other. Labor and property should be in the same hands. Society should not be divided into non-laboring owners of capital and nonowning laborers.

Exactly the same point is made in the following passage from Strachey:

> What, then, will be the future of the Communist countries? Will they in fact develop into the "classless societies" which their spokesmen hold before them as the goal to be aimed at? I myself believe in the goal of a classless society as strongly as ever I did. It still seems to me that the organization of an economic and social system which does not result in men being separated from each other by the barriers of class—peasants from land-lords, wage earners from the owners of the means of production, educated from uneducated, rich from poor—would be the great-est step forward that humanity could take. That is why I am and remain a socialist.

In the planning that I did to prepare for the seminar, I chose Lenin's Chapter 5 of *The State and Revolution* as the central text for the fourth session. Its analysis and argument was both inspired by and based on Marx's *Critique of the Gotha Program*. Taken together, these two documents con-stitute an essential component of Marxist-Leninist doctrine.

As the *Manifesto* and *Das Kapital* deal with the economic objectives of the revolution that Marx and Lenin spent their lives promoting, so these two documents deal with its political objectives. As the one aims at eliminating the misery of the working class by establishing state capitalism, so the other aims at removing class conflict and establishing the classless society. And as the abolition of the private ownership of the means of production is the crux of the revolution in the economic sphere, so in the political sphere the crux of the revolution is the withering away of the state.

I was disappointed in the result of my choosing Lenin's *State and Revolution* as the central text for the session. The participants did not find what I thought they would in their reading of Chapter 5. They did not understand the significance I attached to this chapter, even when, with the book in hand, I read to them the title of the first part of its first chapter: "Class, Society, and the State: The State as the Product of the Irreconcilability of Class Antagonisms."

I added at once that Marx and Lenin must have had some very special and mistaken view of the nature of the state and of its origin, because though class antagonisms may be involved in all or most historic states, the state as such—the political community or civil society—is not itself the product of class conflict. Since most of the participants had been at an earlier time in one of my Executive Seminars in which we read Aristotle's *Politics*, Jean-Jacques Rousseau's *The Social Contract*, and Locke's *Second Treatise Concerning Civil Government*, they knew that the origin of the state lay in the political nature of man and the human need for political life and liberty, and that it served the purpose of securing these goods as indispensable to the pursuit of happiness or a good human life as a whole. [9]

To explain why I thought these two Marxist-Leninist documents were so important for Mikhail Gorbachev to interpret correctly in his concern with the future of the Soviet state in relation to its origins in the second decade of this century, and to also explain the significance of these two documents for me, I decided to summarize, as briefly as possible, the main points that deserved our close attention.

To this end, the first thing I did was call attention to their dates. Marx's *Critique of the Gotha Program* was written in 1875 and was first published in 1891, at a time when Marx was acquainted with the civil societies of the two most advanced industrial nations, England and Germany, and when he thought of his projected revolution occurring there and not in a backward industrial country such as tsarist Russia. Lenin's *The State and Revolution* was written early in 1917 while Lenin was still resident in Switzerland, six months before the October Revolution that put him and Leon Trotsky in power.

Keeping these dates in mind, we are compelled to ask what vision of the state did Marx and Lenin have at the time they were writing. It could not have been the totalitarian state that came into existence with the dictatorship of the proletariat after October 1917. In the immediately succeeding years, the fledgling Communist party then in power was engaged in two struggles—one against the White Armies of the West who were attempting to undo the revolution, the other the forceful effort to wrest the ownership of the land and of other capital instruments from private capitalists, the "expropriators," and put them into the possession of the state. It therefore had to be the English and German consitutional monarchies, which at that time were oligarchies, not democracies, and in which the ruling class were the bourgeois capitalists of that day. In the populations of these two nations, the ruling few controlled the government, justifying Marx's epithet that the government was nothing but "the executive committee of the ruling class."

In these two nations, as in tsarist Russia, class warfare did indeed exist. The state or its government, controlled by the ruling class, did use coercive force at its disposal to crush the opposition of the disfranchised many—to put down riots and demonstrations, to suppress revolutionary movements, to prevent bomb-throwings and assassinations and to punish those who attempted such extreme measures. Against this background, the following points became clear.

Lenin distinguished between a first and lower stage of the Communist revolution and a second and higher phase. Since for him in the spring of 1917, the revolution was most likely to occur initially in tsarist Russia, not in England or Germany, Lenin described the first phase as a dictatorship of the proletariat (that is, despotic rule by the Communist party in the name of the proletariat) to serve the two purposes already mentioned: to wage war against the capitalist, imperialist nations of the West that would try to counteract the revolution, and to seize by force the private property of the Russian capitalistic class—the landowning *boyars* and the industrial magnates—and to turn over to the Soviet state their capital holdings.

This, in Lenin's view, as it had also been the earlier view of Marx, was only a temporary measure, justified by its pragmatic expediency. While the government of the state was in the hands of the few and coercive force had to be employed by the government to serve its purposes, the dictatorship of the proletariat could not be regarded as the classless society that was the ultimate objective of both Marx and Lenin. Putting the possession of all capital into the hands of the state and all political power into the hands of the Communist party created a totalitarian regime, not the socialistic democracy that Marx and Lenin envisioned.

But this totalitarian regime, they thought, would be only a temporary measure, necessitated by the circumstances that existed in the early years of the revolution. Both Marx and Lenin thought this first and lower phase of the Communist revolution would be succeeded by a second and higher phase. This they described as the classless society that would come into existence when the state withered away—dwindled and disappeared.

In their use of the phrase "the withering away of the state," it is difficult to give a precise denotative reference to the word "state." For Marx, it certainly had to be the bourgeois oligarchies of England and Germany, in which the oppressors were the few capitalists and the oppressed many were the working masses. For Lenin, the reference could also have been the totalitarian state that came into existence with the first stage of the Communist revolution. The totalitarian state in Russia in the third decade of this century resembled the bourgeois oligarchies that Marx had in mind. The class divisions and class conflicts were the same: between the few who were the oppressors; and the many who were oppressed; the few who used the coercive force of the state to impose their will upon the many.

Both Marx and Lenin disclaim the notion that the withering away of the state substitutes anarchy for a government exercising coercive force. But their disclaimers have almost no foundation in their vision of the classless society that will come into existence with the withering away of the state. As they conceive the classless society, the state as such will cease to exist; there will be no government that exercises coercive force to impose its will upon those subject to its power. In any tenable view of the meaning of anarchy, that is anarchy.[10]

The espousal of anarchy is one of two basic mistakes in the Marxist-Leninist doctrine concerning the withering away of the state. They commit a second basic error. That is the extreme egalitarianism in which they clothe the classless society that will come into existence when the state has withered away.

Though they both acknowledge the individual inequalities that exist in any human population, inequalities in endowment and in performance, they do not acknowledge that in a classless society, in which all are haves and there are no have-nots, there will still be a justifiable distinction between those who deserve to have more and those who deserve to have less. They did not anticipate Nikita Khrushchev's amendment of the maxim "from each according to his ability, to each according to his needs," by adding the principle of distributive justice that is expressed in the maxim "to each according to his contribution." [11]

Lenin carefully cautions his readers that he cannot assign a definite time for the transition from the first to the second stage of the revolution—the date when the totalitarian state can be expected to wither away and be replaced by the class-less society. His description of that classless society as a so-ciety that has no "political state," but in which only administrative functions are performed by the people, is con-tained in the closing paragraphs of Chapter 5 of *The State and Revolution*. I quote them below. Readers should note that by the words "Communist society," Lenin means the classless society that comes into existence when the class-divided state withers away (whether that be the constitutional monarchy governed by a bourgeois oligarchy or the totali-tarian state governed by the dictatorship of the proletariat).

Accounting and control—these are the *chief* things necessary for the organising and correct functioning of the *first phase* of Communist society. *All* citizens are here transformed into hired employees of the state, which is made up of the armed workers. *All* citizens become employees and workers of *one* national state "syndicate." All that is required is that they should work equally, should regularly do their share of work, and should receive equal pay. The accounting and control necessary for this have been *simplified* by capitalism to the utmost, till they have become the extraordinarily simple operations of watching, re-cording and issuing receipts, within the reach of anybody who can read and write and knows the first four rules of arithme-tic. . . .

From the moment when all members of society, or even only the overwhelming majority, have learned how to govern the state *themselves*, have taken this business into their own hands, have "established" control over the insignificant minority of capitalists, over the gentry with capitalist leanings, and the workers thoroughly demoralised by capitalism—from this mo-ment the need for any government begins to disappear. The more complete the democracy, the nearer the moment when it begins to be unnecessary. The more democratic the "state" consisting of armed workers, which is "no longer a state in the proper sense of the word," the more rapidly does *every* state begin to wither away.

For when *all* have learned to manage, and independently

are actually managing by themselves social production, keeping accounts, controlling the idlers, the gentlefolk, the swindlers and similar "guardians of capitalist traditions," then the escape from this national accounting and control will inevitably become so increasingly difficult, such a rare exception, and will probably be accompanied by such swift and severe punishment (for the armed workers are men of practical life, not sentimental intellectuals, and they will scarcely allow any one to trifle with them), that very soon the *necessity* of observing the simple, fundamental rules of every-day social life in common will have become a *habit*.

The door will then be wide open for the transition from the first phase of Communist society to its higher phase, and along with it to the complete withering away of the state.

Lenin did not live to see how the totalitarian state developed under the despotic rule of the Communist party when first Joseph Stalin and then Leonid Brezhnev became its chairman. The pragmatic necessity for the dictatorship of the proletariat, to expropriate the capitalists and to safeguard the Soviet state against the White armies, had disappeared. Like any other nation, the Soviet Union needed a large military installation for its national security, but that could have been managed without resorting to totalitarianism in the organization of the state or despotism in the operation of its government.

It is reasonable to ask whether Lenin would have regarded the totalitarian state as it developed after his death, together with its despotic control by the Communist party, as a class-divided society that should wither away, to be replaced by the classless society that, for Marx and for him, was an ultimate objective of the Communist revolution.

Would he not have recognized that the bureaucrats of the Communist party had become what the Yugoslav writer Milovan Djilas called "the new class," a class that oppressed the working class, the disenfranchised masses, as grievously as the bourgeois capitalists had oppressed the proletariat at an earlier time? If the answer to these questions is affirmative, then we must conclude that Lenin would have called for an end to the prolonged first phase of the Communist revolution.

What should replace the despotic rule of the Communist party? Certainly not a government that eschews the use of coercive force to enforce its laws. Even in a classless society, there will always remain a criminal element against whom the government must exercise coercive force. The notion that in a classless society the criminal element in the population will disappear is contrary to all recorded facts. In the Western societies that have approached, but not yet fully realized, classlessness, a criminal class still remains.

The notion that when the Communist revolution reaches its second and higher stage, a new type of man will emerge and there will be a whole population without any criminal class, is a utopian fantasy of the most extreme sort.

That being so, whatever society and government emerges in the Soviet Union to replace the totalitarian state and despotic rule by the Communist party, that state and government will have to exercise coercive force against criminals. It can do so without any loss of liberty, the view of Marx and Lenin to the contrary notwithstanding.

The replacement of the totalitarian state by a socialistic democracy that is pluralistic in its economic and political structure depends upon more than the correction of the errors made by Marx and Lenin in their theory of the first and second phases of the Communist revolution, leading to the ultimate establishment of a classless society. As the participants and I agreed earlier, state capitalism must be superseded by privately capitalized socialism; for without privately owned capital, the private associations indispensable for free enterprise, a free market economy and competing political parties, cannot exist or operate.

When I finished this detailed commentary on Lenin's *State and Revolution*, the fourth session of the seminar concluded with the consideration of an interesting point made by Strachey in his *Challenge of Democracy*. He asked about the role of political parties in a relatively classless society, and observed that in the divided societies of the past, opposing parties represented the opposed interest of conflicting classes. The conflicting classes had different political and economic ends in view and so the opposition of the political parties that represented their interests was about conflicting ends. But in a society without class conflicts, there can be no opposition about ends, but only about the means by which the ends agreed upon by all should be achieved. Here is Strachey's statement of the matter.

What would be the probable character of the differences which would divide the political parties of a society which was both democratic and classless (which no major society in human history has yet been)? Perhaps one may catch a hint of what they might be from a remark which an eminent Indian official made to me the other day. He said that in present-day India what they needed was a "6 per cent party" and "an 8 per cent party." What he meant was that the true issue in Indian public life today was the speed at which India should push forward her economic development. Should she aim at raising her Gross National Product by say 6 per cent a year or by 8 per cent a year? This was the really crucial issue. . . .

This is the sort of economic issue over which rival political parties in a classless society would contend, once they were free to do so. But economic issues are not everything. Indeed in the highly developed societies they will be increasingly overshadowed by other issues. Such issues will be such things as these: how much eduation are our children to have, and what is to be its character—predominantly humanistic or predominantly scientific, or in practice, of course, what blend of the two? Or again: what is to be the attitude of the state to organized religion, favorable, hostile, or neutral? Is complete national independence and sovereignty to be maintained at all costs or should there be federations and mergers with other suitable nation-states? Or finally, how much control from a world organization can be accepted? The moment one thinks of it, one sees that there will be plenty for rival parties to dispute about in classless societies.

CONCLUSION: THE SOLUTION
OF THE PROBLEM

The preceding sections have not given an exhaustive account of all the turns and twists in the seminar. What has been selected for presentation in this report has been controlled by the central focus of this chapter: the problem posed by William Pfaff with which the chapter began and which instigated the plan of the seminar in the first place. In my judgment, we have now either reached or closely approximated a solution to that problem.

Before I restate the problem and propose what I think is its solution, I wish to call attention to the essay by Professor O'Toole which was the centerpiece of the fifth session of the seminar. I have already commented on the book by Galbraith and Menshikov that had been assigned for the sixth session. I have given our reasons for maintaining that the future of private-property capitalism in the West and state capitalism in the Soviet Union lies not in their coexistence, but in their convergence toward a common set of economic arrangements.

What I now wish to report is the culmination of the discussion in the fifth session of Professor O'Toole's essay, entitled "From Marx to Madison: Socialism's Cultural Contradictions."[12] That is best summarized in the essay's closing paragraphs:

> ... Pluralism thus becomes the only effective mechanism for reconciling the adversarial issues found in a modern society— conflicts between those who seek greater political and market freedom and those who seek equality and economic security, between those who want greater industrial efficiency and economic growth and those who desire a higher quality of life.
>
> All the great domestic political and economic issues facing any advanced nation—including the Soviet Union—can be mapped as conflicts between groups with these different values and goals. The genius of Western democracies is that they have

arrived at ways of getting as much of all of these values as possible. A pluralistic society attempts to satisfy all competing interests. Because no system is perfect, all the various constituents in a democratic society will never be fully satisfied. Yet, because the system treats the values of all the constituents as legitimate, democracy is the only condition that modern men and women accept as just. . . .

But the only way to find the centre is through the turbulent, conflict-ridden pluralistic process. The citizens of Western nations have learned to pay the price of political turbulence, flux, and tumult in order to achieve the continual economic renewal, social justice, and institutional legitimacy that emerge from Madison's miraculous process. Now the question is whether the entrenched leaders of the Marxist states will accept the unpredictability and uncontrollability of democracy in order to overcome the technological stasis, social injustices, and institutional illegitimacy of their societies. They will not *want* to do so—that is certain—but, ultimately, they may be *forced* to accept democracy as the international cultural revolution creates irresistible pressures for change.

To proceed now with the solution of the problem that initiated the seminar, let me quote the summary statement of it given in the first section of the chapter: In what limited respect should the Communist party be retained and continue to function in the Soviet Union, and what principles or propositions in Marxist-Leninist doctrine should be retained while others should be rejected?

The answer to the first interrogative clause is immediate and obvious. If political pluralism is to be achieved as the needed replacement for monolithic totalitarianism, the Communist party, if it remains at all, must become merely one of several competing and opposing factions in the political arena. This has now been decreed, and seems likely to happen.

The second interrogative clause also has a quick answer, one that was given in the first section: The solution of the problem cannot be found in terms of all or none, but rather in terms of partial retention and partial rejection. The Marxist-Leninist doctrine is not wholly true and sound, but neither is it wholly false and unsound.

That quick answer now needs to be spelled out in some detail. What are the correct and sound elements in the Marxist-Leninist doctrine that Mikhail Gorbachev should retain and to which he should appeal in his effort to persuade the people of the Soviet Union to adopt the policies of *perestroika*? What is fallacious and unsound in the Marxist-Leninist doctrine that Gorbachev should unhesitatingly reject and be able to give clear reasons for rejecting?

In its sessions the seminar succeeded, I think, in putting its finger on the points that have to be rejected by Gorbachev if he is to succeed in raising the standard of living of the great mass of the Soviet people by filling the marketplace with a more plentiful supply of consumer goods; and also if he is to succeed in giving the Soviet people the political liberty that is in increasing demand throughout the world and has already produced radical changes in Hungary, Poland, East Germany, Romania, and Czechoslovakia. Gorbachev's success in these efforts still leaves him with a problem that may cause his downfall—the problem of the growing ethnic nationalism and demands for independence in the Baltic provinces, in the Ukraine, Georgia, Armenia, and so on. But the remarkable succession of events that occurred with startling rapidity in the summer of 1989 plainly show that when the power of the Communist party is drastically reduced or completely overthrown, as it was in the above four satellites of the Soviet Union, socialist democracies tend to emerge in place of totalitarian despotism.

In all but the recent decade of the last seventy years, the world has seen, in the Soviet Union and in the United States, a dogmatic, quasi-religious devotion to doctrinal extremism. The extreme right wing of the Communist party in the Soviet Union, the faithful zealots of the party line, swear their allegiance to a literal interpretation of the words of Marx and Lenin as if they spoke the truth in every respect. The zealots treat the writings of Marx and Lenin, all composed before the advent of the Russian Revolution, as if they were sacred Scripture, in the same way that fundamentalist Christians quote the Bible. There is the unvarnished literal truth, infallible, incorrigible, and final.

The extreme right wing of the large conservative faction in the United States, the fanatical anticommunists of the McCarthy era and ever since, reject Marx and Lenin as wholly wrong, mistaken in every respect. There is no truth at all to be found in their writings. The fact that the constituents of this faction have not read the basic Marxist and Leninist documents, the fact that they could not give anything like an accurate account of their content, does not deter them from rejecting the caricature of what communism stands for which they suppose these documents to contain. They simply do not know what motivated Marx and Engels to propose revolutionary measures in the first place, nor do they recognize that we in the United States have adopted many of these measures in making the economic improvements that have occurred in this country.

In between these two extremes is a middle ground to be occupied by those, in the United States and the Soviet Union, who are or can be persuaded that political and economic problems are never likely to be solved by proposals that are either wholly true or wholly false.

In my long experience of conducting Aspen seminars, in which the *Communist Manifesto* is read and discussed, I have always begun by saying that Marx is more right than wrong, but that his correctable errors are of the first importance in our effort to get at the truth. I have had no difficulty in persuading the participants to read and discuss the *Manifesto* with that in mind.

From the evidence of what has happened in Hungary, in Poland, in East Germany, in Romania, and in Czechoslovakia, it can be fairly assumed that a large portion of the people of the Soviet Union are similarly persuadable. The unpersuadable zealots in the Communist party, who adhere to the party line with religious fervor, are likely to remain a problem that Gorbachev must deal with. He must choose between scuttling them or being himself scuttled by a popular uprising against them.

What is the retainable validity in the Marxist-Leninist doctrine, its unrejectable insights and proposals?

The first things to be mentioned are the two prime motivations of the revolutionary proposals by Marx and Lenin. Can anyone gainsay the truth in the insight that the misery of the working class in the nineteenth century and the mistreatment of proletariat labor by the bourgeois capitalists of that era and in the first decades of this century was a problem that justice required mankind to solve? Can anyone gainsay the truth in the insight that class divisions, class conflicts and warfare, which have been going on in civilized societies from their beginning, are a social evil that prudence required mankind to remedy? Must not everyone who answers these questions affirmatively also acknowledge their indebtedness to Marx and Lenin for devoting all their efforts to putting these matters at the top of mankind's agenda, as well as indebtedness to them for whatever is sound in their proposals for dealing with them?

That Marx was right in predicting the self-destruction of bourgeois capitalism by its adherence to the iron law of wages is a matter of historical record.

That he was also right in his proposals of two measures for the alleviation of the misery of the working class—by inroads on or the erosion of the unregulated rights of the private owners of capital and by the widest possible diffusion of the private ownership of capital—is also attested by the successful adoption of these two measures in the economic reforms which have occurred in this century in the United States, in the United Kingdom, and in Sweden.

These reforms have not yet gone far enough to create the economic equality that is the goal of socialism, a society in which all are economic haves and there are no economic have-nots. They have been accomplished in different ways and in different degrees in all the democratic societies in which all (with justifiable exceptions) are political haves and there are no political have-nots. But in these societies, the apparent motion is toward the realization of the Marxist-Leninist ideal of a classless society.

These are the points that Gorbachev can certainly stress in claiming that *perestroika* is faithful to the teachings of Marx and Lenin. They are also the points with respect to which he should be able to win the support of the Western societies that have reformed private-property capitalism and have established welfare states.

What, then, in Marxist-Leninist doctrine must be rejected as mistakes to be corrected if *perestroika* is to serve the ends Gorbachev has in mind for it? We have discovered all of them in the course of the preceding sessions of the seminar. Let me list them in the order in which we discovered them.

1. Marx's labor theory of value, the theory that labor, living labor or the labor congealed in machinery, produces all the wealth a society consumes and uses; and that the private owners of capital who derive income without working for it are totally unproductive.

2. Marx's assertion that capital instruments cannot rightfully be owned and operated by private individuals or corporations and, therefore, that capital must be owned and operated by the state.

3. As an inexorable consequence of the state capitalism that Marx advocated, the establishment of a totalitarian state, in which all political and economic power is concentrated in the central government, called by Marx "the dictatorship of the proletariat," as carried on by the despotic regime of the Communist party.

4. The Leninist doctrine of the withering away of the state (either the bourgeois oligarchy in the West or the dictatorship of the proletariat in the Soviet Union) on the march to the establishment of a classless society. This

has not yet occurred in Russia and is not likely to occur there or elsewhere except by steps in the direction of political and economic justice that eliminate political subjugation and economic deprivation and that institute pluralistic societies that are both democractic and socialistic.

5. The utopian fantasy of a society existing without any government at all, one that exercises coercive force to maintain peace and harmony and to prevent and punish criminal conduct; in short, the espousal of philosophical anarchy implicit in Lenin's doctrine of the withering away of the state.

6. Finally, the Marxist-Leninist misunderstanding of what justice requires with regard to equality and inequality, political and economic. Not only does it require that all should be haves, but it also requires that some should deservedly have more and some have less.

When the six mistakes in Marxist-Leninist doctrine are corrected, what is the positive picture that emerges?

The verdict of history, looking back at the rise and fall of communism in the twentieth century, will be that communism chose the wrong means to establish socialism as a desirable goal. This will be seen as the reason for its miserable failure and its total rejection.

When a relatively classless society and a nonegalitarian socialism has come into existence, both East and West, it will not be thought that communism projected a wrong goal for the social revolution it initiated—socialism conceived as a society in which the right to a decent livelihood is secured for all and all economic have-nots have been eliminated. It will be recognized that socialism as a desirable end could not be achieved by communist means—the abolition of the private ownership of capital, replaced by the totalitarianism of state capitalism. [13]

The positive side of the picture can be further stated as

follows. Human beings have natural needs that should be fulfilled, and they have innocuous wants that also deserve fulfillment. A society that aims at nonegalitarian socialism serves basic human needs by securing the right to a decent livelihood for all. Private-property capitalism, not state capitalism, is the effective means for producing enough consumable wealth and providing a decent standard of living to satisfy all the reasonable wants of its members.

In conclusion, one question that may arise in the minds of readers deserves an answer. If it is true that the recorded history of civilizations is a history of class conflicts and class warfare, is not the forthcoming desirable establishment of classless societies the end of history? [14]

To answer that question, let us assume that all the present threats to the viability of this planet are removed by drastic measures for protecting the environment from irreversible lethal changes. Let us assume that mankind has centuries of time ahead for the continuance of life on earth.

On that assumption, here is the answer. With the establishment of classless societies, the first great epoch in human history will come to an end—the epoch that began with the rise of cities and the emergence of civilized life, enduring from 6,000 years ago to the present. The second great epoch of civilized life on earth will then begin when the first classless societies are established in the next century or two.

The end of class conflicts is not the end of history, though it is the end of one historical epoch. The future holds a second in store, for as long as mankind continues to live on earth, human circumstances will continue to change.

ENDNOTES

1. The equivalent of the addition of machinery to an increase of hands has another profound significance. When I

asked the participants whether the addition of power-driven machinery to the productive forces at work resulted in (a) making the economy more productive, or (b) making the laborers that worked with the machinery more productive, or (c) both in differing degrees, they argued for some time about these three alternatives. I then pointed out that if an addition of machinery was equivalent to an increase of hands, then the correct answer must be a, not b or c, because one laborer's productiveness added to the productiveness of another laborer does not result in the latter's becoming more productive.

2. The economic components of a decent livelihood, obtained by a living wage together with other sources of income, including welfare benefits, are: ". . . a decent supply of the means of subsistence; living and working conditions conducive to health; medical care; opportunities for access to the pleasures of sense, the pleasures of play, and aesthetic pleasures; opportunities for access to the goods of the mind through educational facilities in youth and adult life; and enough free time from subsistence-work, both in youth and in adult life, to take full advantage of these opportunities." M. J. Adler, *The Common Sense of Politics* (1971), p. 25.

3. Strachey makes the following comparison of the condition of workers in Western democracies and of workers in the Soviet Union:

> Compare the position of a wage earner in a factory which is owned by a Western-type, private, profit-making, joint-stock company, but who possesses full democratic voting and trade-union rights, with the position of a wage earner in a Communist-type state-owned factory, without the right to choose either the kind of government which he prefers or to organize a political party of his choice, or to form his own trade union, or to strike for better pay if he thinks he can get it. Which of the two men has the better chance of getting for his own consumption a high proportion of the values which he produces? I have no doubt that experience has now shown that the wage earner with dem-

ocratic rights, even if he works in a privately owned factory operated for profit, has the better chance.

Readers should be informed that Strachey was at one time the leader of the Communist party in Great Britain. *The Challenge of Democracy* is, in a sense, a retraction of Strachey's pro-Communist apologia in an earlier book, *The Coming Struggle for Power* (1932), in which he predicted the triumph of Soviet Communism throughout the world.

4. At the beginning of this section, we asked what is meant by a phrase implied in the title of the third session: the capitalization of communist socialism. We now have the answer. The capitalization of socialism results from replacing state capitalism with private-property capitalism. The socialization of private-property capitalism and the private-property capitalization of socialism are two faces of the same movement toward an economy that is both just and expedient, that is, effective in the production of a decent standard of living for all.

5. The two basic mistakes are the labor theory of value and the notion that modern industrial capital cannot rightfully be a private possession.

6. Even as we talked, Hungary, Poland, Czechoslovakia, and Romania were moving in that direction during the summer of 1989; and now, as I write these words in the autumn of 1989, the mass protests in East Germany and the mass exodus to the West betoken the same direction of change there.

7. At this point, I digressed to report Nikita Khrushchev's amendment of the Marxist slogan "From each according to his ability and to each according to his needs." That the common needs of each should be served is certainly a principle of justice, for natural rights have their basis in inherent natural human needs. But Khrushchev went a step further. He added a second principle of justice: "to each according to his contribution." Applying this principle would

obviously create a class distinction between the have-mores and the have-lesses.

8. I should record here, but cannot report in detail, a fairly extended discussion of the ways in which class conflicts arising from this one remaining class distinction might be ameliorated, as, for example, by reducing the gap or chasm that exists between those who have more and those who have less, especially in the economic dimension. This holds true for the Soviet Union as well as for the United States.

9. Many of the participants had also read Chapters 5 and 6 in my book *A Vision of the Future* (New York, 1984), the first on "State and Society," the second on "Government and Constitution." I recommended to them that, for the present purpose, they also read an earlier book of mine, *The Common Sense of Politics*, especially Chapter 6, "The Necessity of Government," and Chapter 7, "Concerning the Goodness of the State." I pointed out that Part Three of that book was concerned with a new political ideal, one that had emerged in the nineteenth century and for which we are indebted to Marx—the idea of the classless society.

10. In *The Common Sense of Politics*, Chapter 8 deals with "the anti-political philosophers," in whose number are Marx and Lenin as well as such self-confessed anarchists as Kropotkin and Bakunin. One section of that chapter argues, successfully I think, against the utopian fantasy that a peaceful and harmonious society can exist without government, one which, if it is constitutional government, must exercise, in the words of the great German jurist Hans Kelsen, a monopoly of authorized force. I append here that section as whole.

> The limited power of human reason is a case in point, and one that has a direct bearing on the question about the necessity of government. No matter how free it is from the pressures and prejudices of conditioning circumstances, the finite intelligence of man does not enable him to know with infallible certitude the answers to all questions, especially not the solutions to the problems that confront him in the sphere of action. Hence even

if men were to be as fully rational as they might be under the best of circumstances, disagreements would still arise among them concerning the solution of problems that confront them when they try to live together socially and act in concert to achieve any common purpose.

Carry this one step further and suppose that the emotions or desires of men were completely controlled by reason or intelligence, so that men would never come into conflict except as a result of the inability of reason to reach agreement about all practical matters. It would then still remain true that the authority of government would be indispensable for social life; for, as we have seen, authority is needed to decide matters about which reasonable men can disagree. If each individual were to retain the complete autonomy of heeding no voice except that of his own reason, his being able to act cooperatively with others would come to an end the first time that the group fell short of unanimity about the solution to a problem.

The situation just imagined is, of course, plainly contrafactual. Reason is not only fallible and uncertain in its judgments about practical matters; it is also severely limited by the independent and often contrary impulses of desire or emotion, which it cannot control. Man is not a purely rational being but a rational animal, with appetites and drives that can impel him to act against the counsels of reason and can even subvert or color the judgments of his intelligence. This is a species-specific property of human nature, not a product of conditioning circumstances.

Given any social environment imaginable, even one completely devoid of all the institutions within our experience so far, men would still be so constituted that they would come into conflict with one another as the result of clashing drives or desires, and not merely because reason is unable to achieve unanimity about all practical matters. This being the case, government, with the authority to adjudicate disputes and to enforce the judgment of a tribunal, is indispensable to a peaceful resolution of the conflicts that would arise in any imaginable society, man being what he is or even what he might be under the best of circumstances.

It is human nature that makes government necessary, not

the institution of private property as the anarchist claims. To whatever extent he agrees with the political philosopher that social life is better for man than the life of the isolated individual and that peace is better than war or violence, he has accepted premises that work against his contention that government must be abolished for the benefit of man or for the improvement of the human condition.

What fundamental tenets are shared by those who, however else they differ, call for the abolition of government and of the state as we know it?

1. They hold that the maximization of freedom requires the complete autonomy of the individual, each heeding only his own private judgment, each obeying himself alone.

2. They hold that the maximization of equality involves the sovereignty of the individual, no one in any way being subject to direction or dominance by anyone else.

3. Therefore, they hold that government, being incompatible with the autonomy and sovereignty of the individual, necessarily prevents the maximization of freedom and equality.

4. Denying or dismissing the distinction between de jure and de facto governments, they regard government as nothing but an instrument of coercive force, enabling those who hold the power of government to tyrannize over or subjugate others. Since coercion, like aggression or violence, is inherently evil, government itself is inherently evil.

5. Repudiating the state which involves one or another form of centralized government, they assert, on the positive side, that men can live peacefully and fruitfully together through purely voluntary and undirected acts of cooperation; and they envisage this as happening with the maximum of decentralization and fluidity, the cooperation occurring in small leaderless groups or with leaders emerging and changing from moment to moment as the occasion warrants.

6. They anticipate the objection that their vision of the anarchic society does not fit the nature of man, by denying that man has a fixed nature independent of social and cultural conditioning. They hold, on the contrary, that man as he now is and as we now know him is the product of the historic institutions of the state and government; and that, with the destruc-

tion of the state and government, a *new* man—or man as he *can* be—will emerge.

This doctrine contains an admixture of truth and error. Let me try to make the separation which will eliminate the error and preserve the truth. I start with the denial of human nature.

It is true that many human traits are a product of nurture or a selective development of human potentialities by conditioning circumstances; but it is not true that man as a species has no genetically determined properties that will persist as long as the species persists, without being affected by the changing external circumstances of the physical or social environment. To suppose that, apart from a conditioning environment, man is a wholly plastic or indeterminate blank, to be given this or that determinate character by the circumstances under which he lives, is to regard man as unlike any other species of living organism.

11. This error of extreme egalitarianism is the fatal flaw in the doctrine that Chairman Mao thought was based on the teachings of Marx and Lenin. It was what led to the Cultural Revolution that China, after ten years of unspeakable horrors and disasters, finally abandoned.

12. The essay was published as a feature piece in Encyclopaedia Britannica's *Book of the Year 1989.* I disagree with Professor O'Toole on only one point. I think that Tocqueville is a much better, more penetrating exponent of democratic pluralism than Madison. As any reader of *Federalist No. 10* can find out for himself, James Madison, like many others of the Founding Fathers, was no democrat. They were proponents of liberty, *not* equality. (On this point, see Part 4 of my commentary on the Constitution, *We Hold These Truths* [1987], which is entitled "The Emergent Ideal of Democracy.")

Madison regarded the plurality of factions in society as the cause of many mischiefs, but as long as liberty is preserved, factions cannot be eliminated. However, their effects can be controlled. In *Federalist No. 10*, Madison argues for those measures in the Constitution that he thinks will serve to control the worst effects of factions. They are the constitutional provisions that place dominant political power in the hands of the landowners and manufacturers. These provisions made our eighteenth-century constitution antidemocratic; they have since been amended as, in the course of time, our Constitution gradually became democratic. In my judgment, O'Toole's essay would be more accurate by dropping Madison out of the picture, even at the expense of abandoning its catchy alliterative title.

13. The second of the two seminars here being reported ended on August 25, 1989. Eight months later, a third seminar on the same subject was held in the first week of May 1990, at the Aspen Institute at Wye, in Queenstown, Maryland.

In view of the extraordinary events of the intervening eight months, in the Warsaw Pact nations in Eastern Europe and also in the Soviet Union, the discussion proceeded along somewhat different lines. The basic changes that in the earlier seminars we thought should happen to realize the hopes of *perestroika* had in fact begun to happen and were continuing to do so. The changes in the East appeared to be on a line of convergence with the political institutions and the economic arrangements of the West. Toward the end of the third seminar, the participants reached a substantial agreement about this convergence. I would like to report the main points of that agreement.

We began by a common understanding that technological advances always consisted of new machines, improvements in old machines, or some new devices, including machines for storing, retrieving, and processing information. All technologically advanced economies in varying degrees are capital-intensive economies in that degree. In consequence, they should also become homogeneous in their political institutions and economic arrangements, if political and economic justice is to be achieved and, at the same time, these societies are to become economically efficient and prosperous.

This homogeneity contrasts strikingly with the political and economic heterogeneity among these nations until the last eight months. In regard to what details will this new homogeneity develop?

1. All will aim at democracy and socialism as ideals to be realized: haves without have-nots in both the political and the economic order.
2. None will be state capitalism: none will be completely centralized economies.
3. None will be totalitarian regimes: all will be pluralistic in their political institutions (free elections with contending parties) and in their economic arrangements (competing private corporations and other agencies owning capital, operating in a free market).
4. All will be mixed economies with a private and public sector, with a tendency to increase privatization of the economy.
5. All will be regulated market economies; none will be laissez-faire. All will have commercial as contrasted with state banks; all will have regulative central banks; all will have regulated stock markets for the purchase and sale of stocks representing shares of equity in capital holdings.
6. The factors of supply and demand will be operative in all, and so in all there will be problems of inflation, variable interest rates, unemployment, and profitable vs. unprofitable ventures.
7. In all, more and more persons or families will have income derived both from the earnings of labor and also from the earnings of the capital they own.
8. In all, the division in kind between the haves and the have-nots will gradually disappear, but there will always remain the division in degree between those who have more and those who have less, and these societies will, therefore, be nonegalitarian democracies and so-

cialisms. All will also, therefore, have the problem of reducing the gap that separates those who have much more than enough from those who have barely enough.

9. In all, there will be a portion of the population that may turn out to be unemployable because of deficiencies in native ability or deficiencies in education, or both.

10. In all, some welfare entitlements will remain, not only because of the existence of unemployables, but also because earned income will be insufficient to provide all the goods and services comprising a decent livelihood to which everyone has a natural right.

11. From all of these societies, unsocialized bourgeois capitalism and Marxist totalitarian communism will have completely disappeared.

12. Because of their political and economic homogeneity, these societies will tend to form political and economic unions that can be described as unions of socialist democratic republics in which a multiplicity of joint enterprises crossing national boundaries will exist and between which customs and immigration barriers will cease to exist.

Using names that are now employed in the United Nations, the homogeneous societies referred to above are, for the most part, the states of Western and Eastern Europe, the Soviet Union, the United Kingdom, Canada, Australia and New Zealand, the United States, and Japan.

With the heterogeneity that existed until 1990, the nations just named divided into what journalists called the "First World" and the "Second World," using the phrase "Third World countries" for the rest of the countries represented in the United Nations.

We should now use the phrase "First World" to cover what, before the last quarter of 1989, was called the first and second world, the political and economic homogeneity of which is imminent, reserving the phrase "Third World" for the less technologically advanced and less industrialized countries that represent the have-not populations. Revising this endnote in the late summer of 1990, we must now use the phrase "Second World" for the despotically ruled, oil-rich Arabic and Islamic nations of the Near East. The conflicts and tensions between the First and Second worlds, rooted in racial and ethnic animosities as well as in control of the world's petroleum, are so threatening to the peace of the world that amelioration of the conflict between the first and the Third World—between the have and the have-not nations—will have to be postponed.

Point 7 in the foregoing enumeration bespeaks the triumph of Kelsonian binary economics over the errors of Marxism. Binary economics recognizes that capital as well as labor are productive forces and proposes that earned income be derived by as many as possible from two sources, not one—from both the wages of labor and the dividends due privately owned shares of capital.

To maximize the present tendencies toward the homogenization of the First World, certain words and phrases must be washed clean of their unfavorable connotations (that is, the opprobrious affects attached to them), such as "privatization" and "private ownership" in what were formerly the Warsaw Pact nations and in the Soviet Union; and such as the word "socialism" in the United States, the United Kingdom, Canada, and Australia.

To that end, the Western countries named above must understand that the socialism to be realized is nonegalitarian; that in all societies of haves without have-nots, some will justly get more and some will justly get less.

The Eastern countries named above must also be assured that Locke's principle of limitation upon the right of appropriation will apply to private-property capitalism—that it will be so regulated that no one will be permitted to acquire so much capital at any time that nothing is left in the Gross National Product for others to acquire enough. Since the size of the GNP is never likely to be infinite, enough must be left by those who can rightfully take larger slices out of it for everyone else to appropriate smaller slices.

14. The phrase "the end of history" is the one used by Francis Fukuyama, the deputy director of the Policy Planning staff of the U.S. State Department, as a title for a mistitled, misguided article that was published in *The National Interest* (Summer 1989) and excerpted in the *New York Times* (August 27, 1989, IV, p. 5). It caused a flurry of discussion that it did not deserve, discussion that was as misguided as the article itself.

Appendix 1. The Reading List

Session I. Labor and Capital as Forces in Production

John Locke	*Second Treatise Concerning Civil Government*
	Preamble of the Mechanics' Union of Trade Associations
Alexander Hamilton	*Report on Manufactures*
William Graham Sumner	*The Challenge of Facts*
Mortimer J. Adler	*A Vision of the Future*

Session II. The Self-Destruction of Bourgeois Capitalism and Its Socialization

Karl Marx and Friedrich Engels	*Manifesto of the Communist Party*
John A. Ryan	*A Living Wage*
Theodore Roosevelt	*The New Nationalism*
	The Progressive Party Platform of 1912
Alexis de Tocqueville	*Democracy in America*
Charles H. Vail	*The Socialist Movement*

Franklin D. Roosevelt   *The Commonwealth Club Address*
Henry A. Wallace   *An Economic Bill of Rights*
Gus Tyler   *On the Economic Divide*
John Strachey   *The Challenge of Democracy*

Session III. *The Self-Destruction of Communist Socialism
            and Its Capitalization*

Joseph A. Schumpeter   *Capitalism, Socialism and
                               Democracy*
Karl Marx and
  Friedrich Engels   *Manifesto of the Communist Party*
John Strachey   *The Challenge of Democracy*

Session IV. *The Ideal of the Classless Society: Political
            and Economic Equality*

Horace Mann   *The Importance of Universal,
                               Free, Public Education*
John Strachey   *The Challenge of Democracy*
Mortimer J. Adler   *A Vision of the Future
                               Six Great Ideas*
V. I. Lenin   *The State and Revolution*
Louis O. Kelso and   *Open Letter to Mikhail
  Patricia Hetter Kelso   Gorbachev*

Session V. *The Emergence of a Homogeneous World Economy*

James O'Toole   *From Marx to Madison:
                               Socialism's Cultural
                               Contradictions*
Gus Tyler   *The Rise and Fall of the Great
                               Powers*

Session VI. *Conclusion: Coexistence or Union?*

John Kenneth Galbraith and   *Capitalism, Communism and
  Stanislav Menshikov   Coexistence*

Appendix 2. The Dictionary and Thesaurus of Basic Terms

The definitions and synonyms proposed below to rectify the rampant ambiguities do not beg any of the questions that confront us nor prejudice the positions we may take on any of the issues with which we shall try to deal. All the definitions are in accord with twentieth-century facts.

CAPITALISM   Used descriptively, this word refers to a capital-intensive vs. a labor-intensive economy, or a technologically advanced industrial economy. In this meaning, the economy of the Soviet Union is capitalistic as well as that of the United States. In this meaning, the economy of Tibet is not capitalistic.

PRIVATE-PROPERTY CAPITALISM   A capital-intensive economy in which capital instruments or instruments of production (all the nonhuman factors in the production of wealth) are privately owned and operated by individuals and by corporations as private associations. This is also called free enterprise and free-market capitalism. Here there are private capitalists as well as workers who are not employed by the state. In varying degrees, this is also decentralized capitalism and may involve some mixture of state ownership and control of capital resources with private ownership and control of capital resources. This is why it is sometimes called a *mixed economy*.

MARXIST COMMUNISM   A capital-intensive economy in which all capital instruments are owned and operated by the state. Private ownership of the means of production is abolished. Except for the family, there are no private associations. It is both state capitalism and a totalitarian state, with almost complete centralization in both the economic and the political sphere. Here the state is the only capitalist, and all workers are employed by the state.

SOCIALISM   The goal common to all forms of socialism can be stated as the participation by all in the general economic welfare of the society in which they live. Such participation consists in being able to earn a decent livelihood to which everyone has a right, though some who are unable to do that through no fault of their own should receive welfare benefits from the state.

Often misused as a synonym for Marxist communism (*see above*), this misuse must be corrected. There are many forms of socialism; Marxist communism is only one of them. All forms of socialism tend to concur in the ultimate economic goal, differing from one another in the means and methods by which they seek to achieve that goal.

A society achieves the goal of socialism to the extent that it has no seriously deprived members or economic have-nots. All are economically equal insofar as all are economic haves at the baseline of a minimum decent livelihood. Among the haves, some will have *more* and some will have *less* in proportion to the degree of their contribution to the production of wealth and the general economic welfare of the society. A synonym for any society that is, in one way or another, socialistic is a welfare state.

POLITICAL DEMOCRACY   A constitutional form of government, with universal suffrage, and thus with all having the right to be governed with their own consent and all having political liberty. In addition to universal suffrage (restricted by the disfranchisement only of infants, hospitalized mental incompetents, and imprisoned felons), a democracy secures for all its citizens their natural, human, and unalienable rights. It is also a form of representative government in which there are free elections for public office in which at least two parties are contestants.

CLASSLESS SOCIETY   As contrasted with all the class-divided societies of the past, a future classless society (since none exists at present) is a society in which only differences in degree prevail and there is no division of society into classes that are different in kind, not in degree. In such a society all are political and economic haves and none (with justifiable exceptions) are political and economic have-nots. A classless society combines democracy in the political sphere with socialism in the economic sphere, but not if the socialism takes the form of Marxist totalitarian communism.

FORMS OF CAPITALISM   One form is what Marx called "bourgeois capitalism." This is the laissez-faire capitalism in which capital is owned by much less than 10 percent of the population, and in which nonunionized labor is paid a subsistence wage. It is unsocialized capitalism.

In contrast to bourgeois capitalism, the socialized capitalism of the welfare state or mixed economy achieves the socialist goal with varying degrees of success. Though Marxist communism (state capitalism) is a form of socialism, it differs from socialized private-property capitalism on many points of justice and expediency. It also differs with respect to private ownership of capital, with respect to free associations and free enterprise, and with respect to its efficiency in producing consumable goods that are elements in the standard of living.

The various subforms of socialized capitalism differ from one another with respect to the number of workers who benefit from the earnings of capital, either directly or indirectly; with respect to the standard of living they are able to maintain; and with respect to their efficiency in the production and distribution of wealth.

ADDENDA   To socialize an economy is to decrease the number of economically deprived persons or families, where deprivation means *having less than the minimum* needed for a decent livelihood (not to be measured in terms of money, but in terms of economic goods and services).

To capitalize an economy is to increase both the amount of capital it has available for use in the production of wealth and also the number of its members who are owners of capital and derive either all or a portion of their income from the earnings of capital.

Appendix 3

NOTE: The following discussion of economic equality and welfare, democracy and socialism is taken from Chapter 12 in my book *The Common Sense of Politics* (1971), no longer in print.

I

In the preceding chapter, I argued for the proposition that economic deprivations can prevent men from being good citizens but should not be made the reason for depriving them of citizenship. I turn now to the other face of that same proposition, which declares that economic equality is indispensable to the effective operation of political equality; or, in other words, that economic and political democracy must be conjoined in order to realize the ideal of the just state and just government.

While the democratic constitution creates a de jure government that, in terms of purely political institutions, is perfectly just, it does not by itself create a perfectly just state; nor is democratic government itself perfectly just unless it establishes economic as well as political equality. If democracy is conceived as doing political justice and only that, then that is not enough. With economic justice overlooked, it cannot do complete justice. Worse, in the absence of economic justice, political democracy is itself an illusory achievement.

Economic justice and equality are, in principle, akin to political justice and equality. To understand this is to understand how economic and political democracy involve parallel institutions. As the politically democratic state is the politically classless society, so the economically democratic state is the economically classless society. As the politically classless society is one in which there is no division between a ruling class and a subject class, that is, those who are citizens with suffrage and those who are wards of the state, so the economically classless society is one in which there is no division between haves and have-nots, that is, between those who have the economic prerequisites for citizenship and for the pursuit of happiness and those who are deprived of them.

We are thus led to the conclusion that political democracy cannot be effectively established unless government so controls and regulates the economy that economic inequalities do not make a travesty of the political equality that is instituted by universal suffrage.

Before going on to the question of what controls and regulations are needed to achieve economic equality, it is necessary, first, to be sure that we understand economic equality as a realizable, not utopian, ideal. It is utopian to the extreme of being manifestly absurd if it is conceived as consisting in an arithmetically determined, quantitative equality of economic goods or possessions. While that is beyond any possibility of achievement, and, in addition, may for many reasons be inherently undesirable, there is nothing impracticable about the ideal when it is conceived, in qualitative terms, as consisting in every man's having all the economic goods and conditions that he needs in order to make a really good life for himself.

I have elsewhere enumerated the economic goods and conditions that are components of a really good life. While that enumeration may not be exhaustive, it suffices to delineate the range of goods required for an effective pursuit of happiness:

A decent supply of the means of subsistence; living and working conditions conducive to health; medical care; opportunities for access to the pleasures of sense as well as to the pleasures of play and aesthetic pleasures; opportunities for access to the goods of the mind through educational facilities in youth and in adult life; and enough free time from subsistence work, both in youth and in adult life, to take full advantage of these opportunities.

Unless the individual has either income-producing property or purchasing power through other forms of income (wages, salaries), he will not have the economic goods he needs for the pursuit of happiness—things that are goods not only because they maintain his life and health, but because they facilitate his acquirement of other goods, especially the goods of leisure, the goods of mind and character that are related to the exercise of suffrage. Since every man is under a moral obligation to make a really good life for himself, and since this underlies his basic natural right to the pursuit of happiness, a just government and a just state are under the reciprocal obligation to promote every man's pursuit of happiness by doing what they can to facilitate or ensure the possession of the requisite economic goods by all. They discharge this obligation by whatever measures or institutions promote the general economic welfare in such a way that every man has *at least the indispensable minimum* of economic goods that he needs for a good life. When this is the case, then all men are economically equal—equal in the sense of each *having* what he needs. They are all haves; none is a have-not, an economically deprived person, prevented by economic deprivation from leading a good life.

2

The foregoing exposition calls for three comments. First, the economic equality that consists in *all men having* and *none being deprived* of the requisite economic goods is established when every man has at least the *indispensable minimum* he needs, not when every man has the *identical amount* of economic goods or possessions. This is tantamount to saying that two men are economically equal if both have the indispensable minimum, though one has considerably more than the other. In relation to the pursuit of happiness, the man whose possession of economic goods exceeds the indispensable minimum by a vast amount may suffer serious moral and other disadvantages, disadvantages almost as severe as those suffered by the economically deprived.

I have explained elsewhere how a life may be ruined by an excess of good fortune as well as by an excess of bad fortune. A superfluity or abundance of goods can militate against success in the effort to make a good life. It takes an almost heroic strength of character to resist the seductions of ease and affluence. Hence it might not be utterly far-fetched to think that a just government, in discharging its obligation to promote the pursuit of happiness by all, should take measures to limit the possession of economic goods to a *reasonable maximum*, even as it should take measures to ensure the possession of economic goods to an *indispensable minimum*. However, the protection of rights is one thing and the enforcement of virtue is another. The latter is not the province of government.

In any case, the difference in the degree to which individuals possess economic goods when all have at least the indispensable minimum may result in an inequality of power that jeopardizes their political and their economic equality. The possession of great wealth, vastly in excess of the indispensable minimum and greatly exceeding the amount possessed by most men, in addition to endangering the pursuit of happiness by the few who have such vast estates, confers inordinate power on them which they may be tempted to use in ways that militate against the common good. Hence justice may require the setting of a reasonable maximum to protect the common good against the eroding effects of self-serving interests, but not to protect individuals from the misfortune of excessive wealth.

Second, the foregoing enumeration of economic goods, even if not exhaustive, includes more than is needed for good citizenship, though not more than is needed for a good life. Of the goods enumerated, I would select and stress the following as being of critical importance for an intelligent and effective exercise of suffrage and for active participation in political life: first and foremost, a decent supply of the means of subsistence; that, supplemented by opportunities for access to the goods of the mind through educational facilities in youth and adult life, and sufficient free time from subsistence work, not only to take advantage of these opportunities, but also to engage in political activity. These, taken together, would provide the economic conditions indispensable to political participation. Hence, in relation to citizenship, men who have these indispensable economic goods are, for political purposes, economically equal. To which the proviso must be added that no one should be permitted to accumulate wealth to an extent that confers an inordinate power to serve private interests in contravention of the common good.

Third and last, the foregoing enumeration of economic goods omits or glosses over one consideration that must be taken into account in relating economic to political equality. I said earlier that the individual may have the economic goods he needs for the pursuit of happiness *either* through his possession of income-producing property (his ownership of capital, the means of production) or through his having, through other means, equivalent purchasing power to obtain these economic goods. From the point of view of the good life, the difference between having income-producing property and having its equivalent purchasing power through other forms of income is negligible if both provide the indispensable minimum of economic goods needed for the pursuit of happiness. But from the point of view of economic equality in relation to political equality, the difference may be far from negligible.

The difference between owning income-producing property and receiving an income from any other source is the difference between being independent of and being dependent on the will of others for one's means of subsistence. This remains true in some measure even when the wage earner's interests are secured or protected by welfare legislation and by the power of labor unions. It is relevant to recall at this point that the philosopher Immanuel Kant made economic independence—independence of the will of others in gaining one's livelihood—an essential condition for active citizenship. Those whom he regarded as, in one way or another, economic dependents, he relegated to passive citizenship or subjection. Hence a politically significant economic inequality may still exist in a society in which some of its members, usually a relatively small number, derive their income from their ownership of the means of production, while the rest derive their income solely from the wages of labor, even though both groups are equal in all other respects, that is, they have at least an indispensable minimum of other economic goods . . . .

4

. . . State capitalism, or communism, as two leading ex-communists—John Strachey and Milovan Djilas—have observed, substitutes a new class of concentrated "owners" and operators of capital for the concentrated private ownership that existed under bourgeois capitalism. The new class comprises the bureaucrats of the state, in whom economic power is not only concentrated but also united with political power. In consequence, a communist society, so long as its government remains a dictatorship of the Communist party in the name of the proletariat, is hardly a classless society, either economically or politically. Though it may be a welfare state, it also tends to be a totalitarian state, in which there is and can be little or no political liberty, even though it is nominally a republic with a constitution and with citizenship.

We are, therefore, left with only two economic systems as ways of achieving the economic welfare and equality for all that is indispensable to political equality and freedom for all. One is the mixed economy; the other, universal capitalism. Both are socialistic in their aims, and both are opposed to bourgeois capitalism and to state capitalism (communism) as means.

The mixed economy has the advantage of so far appearing

to be a feasible economic system. In contrast, the feasibility of universal capitalism must remain an open question until it is tried and tested. In principle, however, universal capitalism is designed to achieve a greater measure of economic equality, though perhaps not a greater measure of economic welfare, for all. In the mixed economy, the division between owners and workers still persists, with a small portion of the population having a degree of economic independence that the rest do not possess. In addition, the mixed economy can operate to achieve general economic welfare for all, and some measure of economic equality, only by making the central government the agency for redistributing wealth, so that those without income-producing property nevertheless have sufficient purchasing power. In consequence, it tends to concentrate economic and political power in the hands of the central government and verges toward the totalitarianism of state capitalism.

On these counts, the untested possibility which I have called universal capitalism is to be preferred. It is in no way inimical to political democracy, as state capitalism certainly is, and as the mixed economy might become. It would appear to be the economic system best able to achieve the combined ideals of economic and political democracy—the economically and politically classless society.

If universal capitalism should turn out not to be feasible, and if no fifth alternative can be devised, then the mixed economy, with all its inherent conflicts, would appear to be the only system that can achieve some measure of economic welfare and equality, and achieve it in a manner that is compatible with the preservation of political liberty. Should the mixed economy be our only available and feasible means, then the process of socialization must be carried further to eliminate poverty, to ensure the indispensable minimum of economic goods for all, and to set a reasonable maximum for the acquirement of wealth. In addition, a working balance of power must be maintained between the private and public sectors of the economy to prevent an excessive concentration of economic power in the hands of the central government, while at the same time giving the central government the authority it needs to regulate the private sector for the general economic welfare and the common good.

Appendix 4

NOTE: The following commentary on binary economics and the diffusion of private ownership of equities in capital, relevant to current economic reforms in Eastern Europe, was written by Professor James O'Toole in the Graduate School of Business Administration at the University of Southern California in Los Angeles.

REMAKING EASTERN EUROPE'S ECONOMIES À LA KELSO'S AND ADLER'S "UNIVERSAL CAPITALISM"

In their influential 1958 book *The Capitalist Manifesto*, Louis Kelso and Mortimer Adler advocated "a capitalistic redistribution of wealth to preserve our free society." Some twenty years later, the Congress enacted their proposal, in part, as Employee Stock Option Plan (ESOP). Today, a few reformers in Eastern Europe and the Soviet Union appear to be reexamining Kelso's and Adler's "universal capitalism" in their search to create economic systems that are both free and fair. Ironically, rigid ideological thinking in Washington and on Wall Street may hinder the application of this creative solution to their difficult problem. For example, a Bush Administration official recently surveyed the condition of Eastern Europe's state-owned enterprises in which he found outmoded technology, obsolete products, unskilled management, dispirited workers, and the absence of development capital —and concluded that the task of remaking the economies of the Soviet Bloc was as hopeless as "turning geldings back into stallions."

Certainly, the administration is not alone in this depressing conclusion. The Friedmanite gnomes of Wall Street also argue that it is impossible to turn the existing command-and-control structures into modern, market-driven economies; hence, they conclude that the only practical course is to impose an astringent shock of undiluted market deregulation coupled with an immediate sell-off of state-owned enterprises to domestic entrepreneurs or foreign speculators. Of course, they recognize that this will create massive unemployment, high inflation . . . and subsequent political unrest. But they trust that this volatile situation will be only temporary, thus avoiding the kinds of tyrannical military "solutions" that have been imposed countless times in similar situations in Eastern Europe in the past.

Unfortunately, there are major obstacles in Eastern Europe to the three standard, Wall Street–approved approaches to transforming state-owned systems into market economies based on private ownership.

First, Western-style "privatization" is a pipe dream. Selling off state-owned industries to domestic capitalists is impossible for the simple reason that there are no capitalists or capital to speak of in Eastern Europe.

Second, selling nationalized enterprises to foreign investors is a non-starter because (a) few foreign companies are interested in purchasing marginally profitable state collectives, and (b) Eastern Europeans are reluctant to sell their few productive business to foreigners.

Third, there is little enthusiasm anywhere in Eastern Europe for the "cold turkey" and "get tough" free-market prescriptions now being offered by the American financial community (for example, closing down all currently unprofitable state-owned industries and eliminating the costly welfare benefits that are the East Bloc's single social accomplishment). Even the most resolute anticommunists like Lech Walesa are unwilling to swap Marx for Michael Milken and Lenin for Milton Friedman.

Given this reluctance to leap from the frying pan of Marxist communism into the fire of survival-of-the-fittest capitalism, Americans must begin by acknowledging that, if we wish to have any influence at all on the future of Eastern Europe, our traditional free-market solutions may need some creative modifications. Our search for fitting solutions must begin by seeing the world through Eastern European eyes. First, we must recognize that nearly everyone in the East Bloc desires the freedom, efficiency, and material benefits derived from market economics, yet, at the same time, few have any appetite for the unemployment, homelessness, and poverty amid plenty that arise from unrestrained Reaganism and Thatcherism. Eastern Europeans admire much about America and Britain, yet relatively few of them wish to emulate us. Instead, most prefer the "softer" social democratic systems found in Scandinavia, West Germany, and Austria (welfare states which, on most "hard" economic indicators, are increasingly outperforming the the relatively unfettered free-market systems found in the US and the UK).

Clearly, most East Europeans see things a little differently than we do. After all, these are countries now led by idealistic playwrights and shipyard electricians, as opposed to the practical lawyers and MBA's who dominate the U.S. national administration. For example, while recently undertaking research in Hungary. I admit to having come across a handful of highly vocal Friedmanite economists (whom the American press never tire of interviewing), yet the recurrent theme one hears in the living rooms and coffee shops of Budapest is sung in a different, nonideological key. Here is how a Hungarian entrepreneur—call him Imre—explains how Eastern Europeans hope life will be after communism:

> Under the Soviet system, no one gets rich. To us, that is stupid. Under American capitalism, some get very rich, but others remain very poor. We don't think that is fair. But in Finland and Sweden, everybody gets rich. Now, to Eastern Europeans, that sounds smart and fair!

To Americans, that may also sound a bit utopian. But, according to Imre, it also explains why America is not as influential as Western Europe in the current efforts to redesign the East Bloc economies.

> We have a complex problem here in Mitteleuropa that will require a creative solution. But you Americans try to solve problems with ideologically "correct" solutions. While the Russians are getting better about looking to Marx for the "answers" to every problem. Americans are getting worse about adhering to the gospel of Adam Smith. One thing we have learned during these miserable last forty years is that creativity and ideology are incompatible.

What does Imre mean by a "creative solution" to the economic crisis in Eastern Europe?

> There are several ways we could go. For instance, we could take all of Hungary's numerous and diverse state-owned businesses and turn them into public enterprises, each of which would issue shares of common stock. Then, the government could issue a diversified portfolio of these stocks to every Hungarian citizen, with perhaps 20 percent of each portfolio in shares of the company where the citizen works.

But wouldn't that be giving the companies away?

> Not at all. Marxist constitutions claim that the people own the means of production. So this would merely bring the rhetoric of "social ownership" into reality. The people really do own those enterprises, so it is in no way a gift if they can now buy and sell them. In fact, it would simply grant title to property that is already theirs but which the state had appropriated and misused.

Imre argues that, in this fashion, there would be a more equal distribution of wealth in Hungary than in any nation in the world, communist or capitalist. And not only would this meet the people's desire to create a just system out of the ruins of communism, it would create irresistible pressures for industrial efficiency:

> Since shareholders would want their companies to be profitable in order to pay high dividends and wages—and for the stock

to increase in value—the owners and workers would demand that their companies be well managed. Thus, by making everyone a capitalist, we remove the problem of social tension that would be created if only some people benefited from the transition to a market economy; and, at the same time, we would gain the support of everyone for efforts to increase efficiency —even if that meant creating some unemployment or closing some factories, neither of which would be politically acceptable to our people under the envy-creating scenarios we are being fed from America.

But how does the Hungarian government make money on the deal, so they can pay back their enormous foreign debt? "Simply by taxing the corporations, workers, and owners— just as in America!" And what happens to the goal of equality when the people start to sell their shares? Imre suggests that there might be a short-term moratorium on the sale of shares while a stock exchange was formed and people were educated about the realities of stock ownership.

Then, we must recognize that people are not equal. Some will sell their shares and lose money, others will buy and gain. All the government can do is give them the same starting opportunities—which is something that you still fail to do in Britain and America. Under this system, everyone would be given equal wherewithal to start: after that, it would be up to them what they make of it. However, most people are conservative in this part of the world, and would likely hold their shares—at least for long enough for our industry to have become competitive internationally, and for our emerging entrepreneurial sector to have grown large enough to take the burden of growth off the formerly state-owned enterprises. When that happens, we'll be affluent enough that our people will be able to tolerate the inevitability of a little inequality.

It is clear that Imre has in mind other countries besides Hungary for his proposal:

Poland, Czechoslovakia—even the Soviet Union itself! Perhaps we should call the system People's Capitalism to make it more acceptable to those who have grown up under socialism. And you can call it a giant ESOP to make it palatable in America! But, then, this would be a truer capitalism than you achieve with your ESOPs, wouldn't it? It would be capitalism for all, and not just a nice pension plan for a few workers. You Americans claim that capitalism is good for the rich, so wouldn't capitalism enjoyed by everyone be an even better system? If we were to succeed in creating a system that is both free and fair, wouldn't it be ironic if, someday, America might even imitate us?

Of course, there are countless "Imre's" in Eastern Europe, men and women using their new freedom to find creative solutions to their imposing problems. The issue for Americans is whether we will play a meaningful role in this significant process, or be seen as irrelevant. Will the opportunity to help shape the "New Europe" pass us by because we were too obsessed with trying to reconstruct ideologically "correct" Wall Street stallions?

Appendix 5

NOTE: The following statement of the ideal of the classless society is taken from Chapter 13 of my book *The Common Sense of Politics* (1971), no longer in print.

I

We have seen why a just state must be both politically and economically classless; for the division of a population into a ruling and a subject class, or into haves and have-nots, is an unjust treatment of equals. With this understood, we pass to the question whether a just state must also be socially classless; and as soon as the question is asked, we are aware that it is both different from and more difficult than the problem of political classlessness and the problem of economic classlessness.

From the point of view of justice, the only political class division that is significant is that between a ruling class and a subject class; the only economic class division that is significant is that between men who have the prerequisites for citizenship and the pursuit of happiness and those who are deprived of them. But when we approach the question of social classes from the point of view of justice, we can think of no class division that has parallel significance. On the contrary, we are confronted with an innumerable variety of social class distinctions, none of which seems to be relevant to the basic problems of a normative political philosophy.

Our problem, therefore, must be restated as follows. Are there any other class distinctions, over and above the two just mentioned, of significance from the point of view of perfecting the justice of the state and of government?

The answer to that question, in principle, is contained in the notion of factions. When social classes are opposed in their interests and when this opposition converts them into political factions, then the existence of such classes as factions in conflict becomes significant from the point of view of justice. To explain their significance, I am going to use as my model the economically based class distinction between the rich and the poor, the haves and have-nots.

From the beginning of political history in the West, right down to the present, the basic class conflict in society has been between these two factions. Karl Marx did not discover class conflict in the nineteenth century. Plato, in the fifth century B.C., observed that there are always two cities, not one, the city of the rich and the city of the poor, and they are forever at war with one another. The discussion of revolution in Aristotle's *Politics* centers mainly on this class conflict. When we come down to the eighteenth and nineteenth centuries, we find the same predominant concern with the conflict between these two factions in society. James Madison's discussion of this problem in the famous tenth *Federalist Paper* will help us to relate class conflict to a principle of justice other than the principle of equal treatment for equals.

2

Madison made two assumptions that had the look of truth in his day, but no longer need be granted. The first was that factional conflict cannot be eliminated from society, certainly not the conflict between the rich and the poor. The second was that the ever-present conflict between these two factions is a conflict between the few and the many, the rich being the minority and the poor the majority.

Though Madison himself did not use the phrase "tyranny of the majority," he had that notion in mind when he sought to protect the minority faction against self-interested legislation on the part of the majority faction. That phrase was later introduced by Alexis de Tocqueville and John Stuart Mill; and the same essential point is involved in one of the major objections raised by the philosophical anarchists against the state and government, namely that it always involves the tyranny of a faction—in their view, always a minority faction. From the point of view of justice, it makes no difference whether the tyrannical faction is a majority or a minority. What makes the faction tyrannical is the same in both cases.

As we observed earlier, tyranny, in the strict sense, is the government of persons as if they were things, thus reducing them to the status of slaves totally without rights. When we speak of factional tyranny, we are not using the term "tyranny" in this strict sense but are extending it to cover any exercise of power for the self-interest or good of the party in power, rather than for the common good of the community and all its members. Hence when the faction of the rich has predominant power in the state and exercises it for its own self-interest, rather than for the common good, we have the tyranny of a minority. Similarly, when the faction of the poor comes into power through being a majority of the electorate, and exercises its power in self-interested ways that do not serve the common good, we have the tyranny of a majority.

Factional tyranny, thus defined, involves the injustice that consists in acting for a special interest as against the common good.

The factional tyranny that chiefly concerned the conservatives or the reluctant democrats of the late eighteenth and the nineteenth century (Madison, Tocqueville, John C. Calhoun, and Mill) was the tyranny of a majority—the masses that were just then beginning to achieve political power through the extension of the suffrage. Assuming, as Madison did, that factional conflict could never be eliminated, they tried to devise ways of circumventing its injurious effects. Upon examination, their proposals turn out to be nothing but ways of circumventing the will of the majority, for good or ill.

The Federalist's advocacy of representative government as against direct democracy, and the proposal of such things as the Electoral College and the indirect selection of senators, were aimed at restoring the power of the minority to check that of the majority. Calhoun's proposal of a concurrent majority would, if adopted, have had a similar effect, for it would give a nonconcurring minority the power to interpose a nullifying veto on the will of the majority. Mill's proposal of plural voting and of minority representation were aimed in the same direction.

From the point of view of justice, the problem of factions cannot be solved by such proposals, which do no more than try to shift power from the majority to the minority, or at least to restore a balance of power in which each can check or stalemate the other. On the supposition, which must be allowed, that one faction is no less self-interested than the other, and, therefore, no less inclined to tyrannize over the other, justice is not served by any of these proposals. I submit, therefore, that the only way to solve the problem of factional self-interest and the tyranny in which it is likely to result is to eliminate factional conflict itself by abrogating the class divisions from which it arises.

To say this is to challenge Madison's assumption that factional conflicts cannot be eliminated from society. The conflict between the rich and the poor certainly can be. As I pointed out earlier, that assumption may have had the look of truth in Madison's day, but the socialist revolutions and movements since his time support the contrary view, for there is now at least a reasonable hope that the ideal of economic equality can be realized. With that, the factional conflict between the haves and the have-nots can be eliminated from the socialist, democratic republic just as the conflict between a ruling minority class and a subject majority class has been eliminated by the democratization of the constitution.

3

The principle we have learned is that the tyranny, or injustice, that is the almost inevitable result of factional conflict cannot be remedied by shifts in power from one faction to the other, but only by eliminating conflicting factions from society, as they are eliminated in two important respects by the establishment of political and economic equality for all.

In addition to the two factional conflicts just considered, are there others? Are there social—not political, not economic—class distinctions that create factional conflicts that must also be eliminated to rectify the ever-threatening tyranny of one faction over another?

Racial and ethnic class distinctions suggest themselves at once. There may be others, but the consideration of these two will suffice to exemplify what is meant by saying that the socially classless state is one in which there are no factions of this type. As long as racial and ethnic class distinctions persist, factional conflict between the racial or ethnic majority and one or another racial and ethnic minority is likely to occur; and if it does, the tyranny of the majority is a likely result.

The socially classless state will come into existence only

when all social class distinctions that might generate factional conflicts and factional injustice have been eliminated. Since the ideal at which we are aiming is the perfectly just state, or the best possible society, the elimination of the factional injustice that is the ever-threatening result of factional conflict must supplement the elimination of the injustices that are rectified by democracy and socialism.

At one time it was thought impossible to eliminate the injustices just mentioned by achieving a politically classless and economically classless society. Revolutionary historical changes have altered our view of what is possible. Even if the ideal of the politically and the economically classless society is not yet fully realized, its realization can be projected from steps in that direction which have already been taken.

The possibility of eliminating the factional conflicts that arise from racial and ethnic and, perhaps, other social class distinctions is not, of course, as clear. What is clear, however, is that their elimination is necessary for the sake of justice; and if we are given to believe, as I for one am, that the necessary must be possible, such faith is at least the first step in the direction of making every effort to create the socially classless state by eliminating all social class distinctions that generate factional conflicts.

4

I would like to add two comments. The first concerns the notion of social equality. We have seen that political and economic equality can be defined with precision. Can we define social equality with a comparable degree of precision? I think it is possible to do so. Individuals are treated as socially equal when they are treated as having the worth or dignity that is inherent in being a person, not a thing. Their social equality is violated only when they are subject to discrimination on the basis of one or another social class to which they happen to belong. Discrimination among persons is justified only by their individual inequality in native endowment and personal attainment.

The elimination of all social class distinctions—not just those that generate factional conflicts—is probably impossible and clearly undesirable. Social equality can be established simply by not allowing such nonfactional class distinctions to become the basic for a discriminating treatment in favor of one human being as against another.

The second comment I would like to make concerns the notion of "the establishment" that has such currency today, at least in speech. The term is, for the most part, used invidiously or dyslogistically, to refer to a dominant faction exercising its power tyrannically in a self-interested fashion and, therefore, in contravention of the common good. Thus used, the term "establishment" connotes a source of injustice. In the eighteenth and nineteenth centuries, the establishment that revolutionary movements sought to overthrow was a minority faction of the ruling and propertied few. Today, the establishment that the new left seeks to overthrow is a majority faction which, in their view, oppresses racial minorities and ignores the injustice being done to those still impoverished. The achievement of a truly classless society, with all factional conflicts eliminated, is the only way in which the injustices done by factional establishments, whether they are minority or majority establishments, can be rectified.

The ideal of a truly classless society takes two forms: the one proposed by the anarchist or antipolitical philosopher, the other by the political philosopher. For Mikhail Bakunin or for Marx, as for the extremist of the new left in our own day, the truly classless society can come into existence only with the destruction of the state and of government. The new left often has this in mind when it speaks of destroying the establishment. For the political philosopher, the ideal of the truly classless society cannot be achieved except through perfecting the justice of the state and of government—the establishment that the anarchists wish to destroy.

I, therefore, purpose to use the word "establishment" in a noninvidious way to refer to all the institutions of the state and of government, through which justice must be done to realize the ideal of a truly classless society, with liberty and equality for all. These are the institutions that must be established to create the truly classless society; and, therefore, I think it proper to refer to the ideal at which political philosophy now aims as the ideal of the classless establishment.

5

We have come to an understanding of the ideal that now seems possible of attainment—the best society that the perfection of our institutions can achieve. At this point in history, as at any other, our vision of the possible cannot avoid being limited by the experience on which it is based; but it is, nevertheless, a larger vision than was vouchsafed our ancestors.

Reviewing the careers of historic civilizations, Arnold Toynbee has observed that they have all been beset by the twin evils of class and war. While that is still true of all existing civilizations, we are living in the first century in which the eradication of these evils appears to be a practicable possibility, not a utopian dream.

This is the first century in which world government has been envisaged as a practicable remedy for the international anarchy that is identical with a permanent state of war between sovereign states. It is not their nationalism or the fact that they are national states, but rather their sovereign independence that puts them at war with one another—the cold war of diplomacy, espionage, and terrorism, or the hot war of bombs and bloodshed. It is also the first century in which the injustices of slavery, serfdom, subjection, poverty, and racism can be and have been considered eliminable, not merely for some favored segments of humanity but for all mankind.

I have used the term "classless" to describe the ideal of a society from which all factional conflicts have been eliminated; and I have shown that, in order to provide the maximization of liberty and equality for all, the classless society must be achieved not through the destruction of the state and government, but rather by perfecting the justice of our social, economic, and political institutions. The classless society thus conceived—or, as I have called it, the "classless establishment"—is an ideal that is new in the history of normative political theory. Its newness is certified by the recency of the judgments that democracy and socialism are not only possible but desirable.

To be sure that this is not misunderstood, let me recall that by democracy I mean the democratic constitution of a republic in which there is no division of the population into a ruling and a subject class; and that by socialism, I mean the economic counterpart of political democracy, achieved by the participation of all in the general economic welfare so that there is no division of the population into haves and have-nots. The socialist, democratic republic is only a first approximation of the new ideal of a classless society. A fuller realization of that ideal calls for the elimination of other class divisions, based on racial, ethnic, or other discriminations that create factional conflicts and result in injustice to one or another segment of society.

Though the ideal now envisaged as possible is new, it is subject to one qualification that is not new in principle. Yet our understanding of the principle *is* new. The just state and just government are not ultimate ends to be achieved for their own sake. The best society that is capable of institutional achievement is only a means to the good life for human beings. Our moral obligation to do whatever can be done to bring it into existence derives from a more fundamental moral obligation—the obligation that every man has to make a good life for himself.

The truth of this basic normative insight was imperfectly

understood when, in earlier periods of history, it was thought to be impossible to universalize it—that is, to extend its application to all men, all without exception, not just the privileged few or even the privileged many. This gives us the measure of the imperfection of the ideal that earlier centuries aimed at, for the best society that they could conceive, even when they conceived it properly as a means to the good life and not as an end in itself, provided the external conditions of a good life for only a portion of the population, usually considerably less than all.

"All"—when what is meant is *all without exception*—is the most radical and, perhaps, also the most revolutionary term in the lexicon of political thought. It may have been used in the past, but it was never seriously meant to include every individual member of the human race, not just the members of one's own class, or even one's fellow countrymen, but every human being everywhere on earth. That we are now for the first time in history beginning to mean all without exception when we say "all" is another indication of the newness of the emerging ideal of the best society, the institutions of which will benefit all men everywhere, by providing them with the conditions they need to lead good human lives.

Local or parochial justice and local or parochial peace are, therefore, not enough. Worldwide justice and worldwide peace are not embellishments of the ideal; they are of its essence. If we think of the socialist, democratic republic as something to be achieved in this country or that, we are not thinking of the ideal to which we should now be committed; we should think instead of a worldwide union of socialist, democratic republics that would be a world state and a world government, establishing justice and preserving peace on a global basis. This and this alone is the proper and adequate representation of the ideal to which we should now be committed, because we can no longer justify aiming at less, on the ground that only parochial goals are practically achievable. On the contrary, as I hope to show, the goal of a good society is no longer achievable within parochial limits but only on a worldwide basis.

Understanding the best possible institutions as means rather than as ends, and the best possible society as a means to the good life for all, still further enlarges our conception of the ideal at which we should aim. More is required than the maximization of liberty and equality for all; even worldwide justice and worldwide peace are not enough; for all these things could conceivably be accompanied by conditions that would militate against or prevent the achievement of the ultimate end—the pursuit of happiness by all. Wealth must be produced in a sufficient quantity to provide every man with more than the bare necessities of life, and it must be produced in such a manner that every man, in addition to having the requisite physical comforts and conveniences, also has ample free time in which to improve the quality of his life by engaging in the pursuits of leisure and enjoying the pleasure of play. Even this is not enough, as we have now come to realize with justified anxiety, if we allow the over-population of the earth and the deterioration or destruction of the life-sustaining and life-enhancing biosphere to occur.

Hence our conception of the best society must include considerations, both economic and ecological, that have never heretofore been regarded as essential to the ideal that men have projected for realization.

TWO

A Disputation on the Future
of Democracy

At the Aspen Institute, July 1977

Moderator: BILL MOYERS

Participants: MORTIMER J. ADLER
President
Institute for Philosophical Research

MAURICE CRANSTON
Professor of Political Philosophy
London School of Economics

ANTHONY QUINTON
President, Trinity College, Oxford

BILL MOYERS:

The surroundings are not medieval but the intent is, although a very modern spirit broods over these proceedings —the spirit of John Adams, who, as many of you know, had considerable doubts about the longevity of the experience of which he was a founding partner. Not long after the Revolution of 1776, John Adams in a letter had ominous things to say about the future of democracy. No democracy ever lasts very long, he said; democracies soon commit suicide.

On a more prosaic level, we may recall the story of the young girl who one day came in to her mother and said, "You know that vase that has been so long on our mantel?" "Yes," her mother said, "that vase has been in this family for generations." "Well," said the girl, "this generation just dropped it."

There is a widespread opinion that this generation is dropping the vase of democracy. And that is one of the questions in dispute today and tomorrow.

These proceedings are medieval in intention, because a disputation, as Mortimer Adler has informed all of us, was a frequent intellectual exercise at some of the great medieval universities—Paris and Oxford, in particular. These disputations were more than debates. In the kind of debate to which we have become accustomed in this country, there are verbal jousters trying to score points against one another. That is not what we are going to be doing in this discussion. Rather, we are going to be listening to a dispute about the answers to some questions which have been propounded about the future of democracy in the world as we have it, and as it seems likely to develop—a dispute in which persons who hold differing views of the future of democracy will speak, taking the time necessary to illuminate and expand upon the rationale as well as the purpose of their arguments.

Mortimer Adler will begin and will finish this afternoon what he has to say in his prepared remarks. Maurice Cranston will then take the remaining part of the afternoon session to respond to Mr. Adler's argument. And tonight Anthony Quinton will lead off with a presentation of his own response to everything that has up to then been said. Then there will be a discussion among the three participants toward the end of the session this evening.

Mortimer Adler:

Thank you, sir. Mr. Moyers, Mr. Quinton, Mr. Cranston, ladies and gentlemen.

The questions to be disputed are three. First: *Should* democracy as a form of government everywhere prevail? Second: *Can* democracy survive where it now exists in some degree of approximation, can the ideal be more fully realized where it now is imperfectly approximated, and can it be instituted where it does not now exist? Third: *Will* democracy survive, become more perfectly achieved where it now exists, and be adopted and perfected where it does not now exist?

In reply to these questions, I will undertake to defend the following theses: First, that democracy should prevail everywhere because it is the only perfectly just form of government and, as such, the political ideal that should be universally realized as fully or perfectly as possible. Second, that democracy can survive where it now exists and be perfected there, and that it can be adopted and perfected everywhere else. Third, that what is possible will probably come to pass—not in this century, but in a future not too remote, on the one assumption that civilized life itself will be preserved on this planet through the solution of problems that now threaten it.

Let me begin with a definition of terms. By "democracy," in a narrow sense, I shall mean a form of government, and so I will always indicate this narrow sense by using the phrase "political democracy." Political democracy is government of, by, and for the people. Let us consider the meaning of these three prepositional phrases:

Of the people. Democracy is constitutional government, government with the consent of those capable of giving their consent and capable of participating in self-government. A political democracy is always a republic, but it is never merely a republic.

For the people. Democracy is government that secures all

the natural, human, or moral rights to which human beings are entitled.

By the people. Democracy is a republic in which universal suffrage has been established, a republic in which all human beings (with the exception of infants, feebleminded, and insane) are equally citizens, equally constituents of government, and equally participants in self-government; but not all exercising equal political power, because only some are citizens holding and exercising the political power that is vested by the constitution in certain public offices.

In short, political democracy as an ideal is constitutional government with universal suffrage and with a constitution that secures all inherent and unalienable rights, called in various writings "natural" by Adler, "human" by Cranston, and "moral" by Ronald Dworkin.

By democracy in a broader sense, I shall mean a society all of whose social institutions and economic arrangements support and facilitate the form of government that I have called "political democracy." I will use the phrase "democratic society" to refer to democracy in this broader sense of the term. The ideal of political democracy will be approximated or imperfectly realized in any society that is not democratic. On the other hand, political democracy itself is the indispensable first step toward a democratic society, and tends toward it to the extent that it extends its constitutional charter of human rights beyond the preservation of political rights to the establishment and furtherance of economic rights. The relation between political democracy and a democratic society—the first an indispensable means to the establishment of the second; the second an indispensable means to the fulfillment and preservation of the first—is of critical significance in our consideration of the future of democracy.

Before I attempt to argue in defense of my three theses, permit me to reflect on some relevant historical considerations.

Political democracy as defined is not yet a century old. It

did not exist anywhere in the world prior to the twentieth century. And in those countries in which political democracy came into existence in the twentieth century, it is still very imperfectly realized—the ideal is only approximated to some degree.

In the ancient world there were three basic political conflicts: first, that between the Greeks and barbarians, in which the principle of constitutional government was opposed to oriental despotism; and, second, that among the Greek cities themselves, in which there was opposition between two forms of oligarchical constitution. These were called by the Greeks "oligarchy" and "democracy," but both were oligarchies because both involved slavery and other unjust exclusions from citizenship.

In a later, the Roman, phase of the ancient world, the first of these two oppositions repeats itself—the conflict between despotism and oligarchy, in terms of the monarchy which preceded the republic and, later, in terms of the empire which succeeded it.

In the medieval world, the major tension was between purely royal government (or absolute kingship) and government both royal and political, but apart from a few free self-governing cities there were no republics in the medieval world, and the few that existed were oligarchical in constitution.

In the modern world there have been two movements. First, the gradual dissolution of royal authority, which turned more and more despotic in the fifteenth and sixteenth centuries, thus causing republican revolutions that began by setting up limited monarchies and then predominantly constitutional governments. Second, beginning no earlier than the nineteenth century, the gradual amendment of republican constitutions by extensions of the suffrage and by correction of various forms of oligarchical injustice, both with respect to citizenship and officeholding.

What is our situation in the present day? For the most part, the people of the world live under despotisms of one sort or another, domestic or colonial. A comparatively small part of the human race enjoys the blessings of constitutional government—the liberty of life under law which is due every being who by nature is rational, free, and political. Where constitutional governments exist, many of them still remain operative vestiges of oligarchy, whether overt or concealed. Few, if any, are by explicit enactment perfectly democratic in constitution; and where these are democratic on paper or in constitutional principle, they are seldom even remotely democratic in actual practice.

In the hundred years since John Stuart Mill wrote *Representative Government*, a small number of political democracies have come into existence for the first time in history, most of them since the turn of the century and most of them in Europe or North America. This is not to say that the ideal polity has been actually and fully realized on earth in our time. Far from it! What came into existence in our time were legal enactments that established the form of democratic government in a small number of political communities. In most cases—most notably, perhaps, in the United States—the discrepancy between democracy on paper and democracy in practice was vast at the beginning and has nowhere yet become negligible.

The first exposition and defense of political democracy as an ideal—as the only perfectly just form of government— occurred in the middle of the nineteenth century and is to be found in Mill's *Representative Government*.[1]* It is the most recent truly great book in political theory—a work that stands in the line of Plato, Aristotle, Aquinas, Marsilius, Hobbes, Spinoza, Montesquieu, Locke, Rousseau, Kant, and Hegel. It was published in 1861, a little more than a hundred years ago. Addressing itself, as a treatise in political philosophy should, to the question about the ideally best form of government, it answers that question by a fully reasoned and

* Endnotes for this chapter are on page 186.

critically cautious defense of the proposition that democracy is, of all forms of government, the only one that is perfectly just—the ideal polity.

In the sphere of political action, as distinct from that of political thought, Mill did have some predecessors, such as Colonel Thomas Rainborow and Sir John Wildman among the Levellers in Cromwell's army; Nathan Sanford and John Ross in the New York Constitutional Convention of 1821; Robert Owen in the formation of the community at New Lanark and similar communities elsewhere. But in the sphere of practical politics, Mill is the first to advocate the enfranchisement of women and hence the first to conceive universal suffrage as including the other half of the population.[2]

At the time that Mill wrote *Representative Government*, democracy in his sense of the term—constitutional government with universal suffrage operating through elected representatives—did not exist anywhere in the world. Republics there were and constitutional monarchies, but all of them were oligarchies of one type or another: the ruling class—the enfranchised citizenry in the republics, or the citizenry and the nobility in the constitutional monarchies—comprised only a small fraction of the population. The rest were disfranchised subjects or slaves.

We should certainly not allow ourselves to be distracted or confused by the fact that the Greeks invented the name "democracy" and used it, either invidiously for mob rule as Plato did, or descriptively as Aristotle did for a form of government which, as contrasted with oligarchy, set a much lower property qualification for citizenship and public office. The democracies of the ancient world differed from the oligarchies only in the degree to which participation in government was restricted by property qualifications for citizenship and public office—which could result, as it did in the case of Athens, in the difference between a democracy of 30,000 and an oligarchy of 500. However significant that difference must have seemed to the 30,000, it could hardly have had much meaning for the 90,000 disfranchised human beings, who, in Aristotle's terms, were useful parts of the political community, but not members of it.

We have no reason to complain about how the Greeks used the word "democracy." But it is disingenuous, to say the least, for contemporary writers to use it as a synonym for "popular government," and then make that term applicable to any form of government in which some portion of the population—the few, the many, or even all except infants, idiots, and criminals—participate somehow in the political life of the community.

By that use of the term, anything other than an absolute monarchy is a democracy in some degree—more or less, according to the proportion of the population that forms "the people," the ruling class. According to such usage, democracy in Mill's sense of the term is merely the limiting case in the spectrum of popular governments, the case in which "the people" is coextensive with the population, excepting only those who, as Mill says, are disqualified by their own default. We are then compelled to say that the Greek oligarchies were simply "less democratic" than the Greek democracies; and that modern democracies became more and more democratic as the working classes and finally women were granted suffrage. It would take the semantic sophistication of a six-year-old to recognize that this is a use of words calculated to obscure problems and issues rather than to clarify them.

It can be said, of course, as it has been, that democracy in Mill's sense represents an ideal which, through the course of history, diverse forms of constitutional government have been approaching in varying degrees; and that to whatever extent they are popular—to whatever extent "the people" is an appreciable fraction of the population—they are entitled to be called "democratic" by virtue of their tending to approximate the ideal. But to say this is worse than confusing.

While it may be poetically true to describe the course of history as tending toward democracy as the political ideal, it is simply and factually false to attribute that tendency to our ancestors as if it were the manifestation of a conscious intention on their part. Democracy, in Mill's sense, was not the ideal to which the past aspired and toward which it strove by political revolutions or reforms. With the possible and qualified exception of Immanuel Kant, no political philosopher before Mill ever argued for the inherent or natural and equal right of every human being to be a citizen actively participating in the government of his or her community. None regarded it as an ideal; none, in fact, even contemplated the possibility of a genuinely universal suffrage.

The prior uses of the term "democracy," both descriptive and denigrative, should not prevent us from perceiving what is genuinely novel in the political conception for which Mill appropriated that term. It involves an adequate appreciation of the full extent to which universal suffrage should be carried on the grounds of a right to participate in government, a right inherent in every human being. Hence it regards constitutional government with truly universal suffrage as the only completely just form of government—the ideal polity.

In what follows, I shall be exclusively concerned with this new conception which, under any other name, would be exactly the same. Since no other name, nearly as appropriate, is available, I shall use democracy in Mill's sense of the term, hoping that the reader will remember why, when the term is used in that sense, nothing prior in theory or practice can be called "democracy" or "democratic." Anyone, of course, is privileged to use words as he pleases, but that privilege does not justify obfuscation or confusion in their use.

For the most part, taking the planet as a whole, political democracy, even in very imperfect realization, is the exception rather than the rule. Even where it does exist, it is not yet accompanied by a society that is democratic. Though there are intimations of a democratic society in the process of coming to be, a democratic society does not yet exist anywhere. If some approximations of it exist here and there, these are even more exceptional than the imperfect realizations of political democracy now in existence.

Let me repeat what I have already said: democracy does not yet fully exist in practice. It is still an imperfectly realized ideal; yet it is thoroughly practicable, in no way utopian. Of all the forms of government traditionally recognized, it is the only one which has no past. All the others have pasts that teach us not to wish a future for them and to wish that democracy would replace them wherever they still exist, precisely because it corrects in principle and will remedy in practice their fundamental injustices and faults. Democracy belongs entirely to the future, but the future will belong entirely to democracy only if we can completely overcome the various obstacles to its existence, preservation, and growth.

Argument for Thesis I: that political democracy should prevail everywhere because it is the only perfectly just form of government

I begin with a question of fact. Is man by nature a political animal and are all men by nature intended to participate in self-government; or are some men by nature intended to rule and some intended to be ruled by others, without their consent or participation?

To this question, my answer is an affirmation of the proposition that man is by nature political, and a qualified affirmation of the consequent proposition that (with the exception of infants and those with pathological mental disabilities) all men are capable of participating in self-government, and should, therefore, by right be enfranchised citizens of a republic, through which status they have the political liberty to which they are by nature entitled.

This answer involves a repudiation of Aristotle's view (shared less openly by many others) that some men are intended by nature to be self-governing citizens with political liberty, whereas others by nature are intended to be ruled, if not as chattel slaves, then at least as subjects (as children are ruled by their parents for their own good), without a voice in their own government.

To accommodate modern ears, I have translated Aristotle's remarks about natural slavery into the proposition that some men are intended by nature (that is, by their endowments at birth) to be governed for their own good, and for their own good should be deprived of any voice in their own government.

If this proposition is true, then political democracy can hardly claim to be the ideal polity. It has no special justice in excess of that possessed by a constitutional oligarchy, administered for the benefit of those subject to its rule. In fact, it might even be said to involve a certain injustice, insofar as it gives political power to those who should not have it—all those who are not by nature fit for suffrage. Only if all men are by nature political animals—only if all are naturally endowed to live as free or self-governing men—do all have the right to be enfranchised citizens and the duty to participate in government. Only then is democracy, of all forms of government, supremely just.

This is not the place to argue the factual truth of the central proposition or of its contradictory. But we ought to spend a moment considering what the best form of government would be if only some men are by nature political animals. Would the "some" be a small or a large proportion of the population? Would they be the few or the many? Undoubtedly, the few. These, then, would comprise a political elite, a cadre of officials, a professional bureaucracy that should govern the rest of the people for their own good. So far we have a benevolent despotism; but if we now add that the government should be duly constituted (should be constitutional or limited rather than absolute—a government of laws); that, except for the political distinction between the official ruling class and the rest of the people, an equality of social and economic conditions should prevail (all men should share equally in the general welfare that the government aims to promote); and that the government should safeguard, equally, the private rights and liberties of each individual or family; then what we come out with is the kind of government recommended by certain recent commentators on the political scene, such as Bertrand de Jouvenel, with a fondness for Gaullism, or Walter Lippmann, with a nostalgia for Platonism.

Such a form of government can appropriate to itself the name "democracy" by appealing to Alexis de Tocqueville's sociological (rather than political) conception of democracy as a society in which a general equality of conditions prevails. Equality of conditions can, as Tocqueville recognized, tend toward completely centralized totalitarian government, more oppressive than any ancient despotism.

However, if a community retains the limitations and checks of constitutional government, and if the general welfare that is promoted by the government includes the protection of the private rights and liberties of the people, then, perhaps, it does deserve to be called, as de Jouvenel calls it, a "social democracy." Nevertheless it is not a political democracy; for while the community enjoys government *of* and *for* the people, government *by* the people has been replaced by the rule of a professional bureaucracy (which, it is hoped, comprises the few who are by nature competent to govern).

A "social democracy," thus conceived, might very well be the best—the most just—form of government if it were true that only some men are by nature political animals. But if the contradictory proposition is true—if all are political animals—then a merely *social* democracy involves the same essential injustice that is to be found in any benevolent despotism.

As Mill helps us to see, what is pernicious about the idea of the good and wise despot—in all the forms that it has taken from Plato to Charles de Gaulle—is not the myth that any one man or any few actually have the superior qualities that merit putting the government entirely in their hands. Granted such men can be found, the point is rather that letting them rule, with wisdom and benevolence, reduces the rest of the population to a perpetual childhood, their political natures stunted rather than developed. By the standards of wisdom, efficiency, or competence in government, political democracy may not compare with the excellence in government that can be achieved by a specially qualified bureaucracy. But if all men deserve political liberty because they have a right to a voice in their own government, then government by the people must be preserved against all the tendencies now at work in the opposite direction, and for one reason and one alone: its superior justice.

With this one factual proposition affirmed—that man is by nature political—and with the affirmation of the principle that political justice consists in securing natural rights, the argument that democracy is the only perfectly just form of government proceeds as follows.

Tyranny, or government solely in the interest of those holding and exercising political power, is absolutely unjust, being a violation of the rights of the ruled and a transgression of the common good of the people as a whole. Strictly speaking, tyranny is not a distinct form of government but a perversion, in different ways, of the three genuinely distinct forms of government—despotism, oligarchy, and democracy. Despotism and oligarchy are more susceptible to tyrannical perversion than democracy, though both may avoid tyranny, as is the case when the absolute power of a despot is benevolently exercised. The benevolence of a despotism, however, in no way minimizes the intrinsic injustice of absolute rule.

I shall not deal here with other perversions of government beyond making the simple observation that oligarchies can suffer degeneration into despotisms, and democracies can decline into oligarchies or despotisms. The line of political progress is in the opposite direction, usually by means of revolution: despotism overthrown in favor of republican or constitutional government; oligarchical constitution gradually amended in the direction of democratic universalism.

Despotism, which is government without the consent of

the governed, may be either tyrannical or benevolent. If benevolent, with some concern for the common good and for the rights of the ruled, it has a degree of justice to this extent.

Constitutional government, or government with the consent and participation of either some or all of those who are capable of giving their consent and participating in government, is more just than the most benevolent despotism by virtue of acknowledging a right that benevolent despotism denies: the right of human beings, all or some, to participate in self-government.

Constitutional government with an unjustly restricted franchise (restricted by unjust discriminations in terms of race, sex, property, and so on) is less just than constitutional government with a justly extended franchise—universal, with only the previously mentioned exceptions. Constitutional government with an unjustly restricted franchise is oligarchical. Constitutional government with a justly extended franchise is democratic.

The three distinct forms of government—despotism, oligarchy, and democracy—are not coordinately divided. Because both are constitutional or political government, both oligarchy and democracy are divided against despotism, which is nonconstitutional, absolute government. Within the generic sphere of constitutional government, oligarchy represents every species of unjust constitution; democracy, the one species of just constitution.

As the foregoing analysis reveals, there are three principles or elements of political justice:

1. Government is just if it acts to serve the common good or general welfare of the community and not the private or special interests of those who happen to wield political power. By this principle, tyrannical government, exploiting the ruled in the interests of the rulers, is unjust; and by the same principle, a benevolent despotism can be to some extent just.

2. Government is just if it is duly constituted; that is, if it derives its power from the consent of the governed. The

powers of government are then de jure powers, and not simply de facto: we have a government of laws instead of a government of men. By this principle, constitutional governments of all types have an element of justice lacked by all absolute governments. By this criterion, an absolute monarchy, however benevolent the despotism, is unjust.

3. Government is just if it secures the rights inherent in the governed, that is, the natural, and hence the equal, rights which belong to men as men. Among these rights is the right to liberty, and of the several freedoms to which every man has a natural right, one is political liberty, the freedom possessed by those who have some voice in the making of the laws under which they live. When political liberty is thus understood, only men who are citizens with suffrage enjoy political liberty. The unenfranchised are subjects who may be ruled paternalistically or benevolently for their own good, but who are also unjustly treated insofar as they are deprived of a natural human right. By this principle, constitutional oligarchies are unjust, and only constitutional democracy is just.

The last of these three principles is the critical one, the one that is essential to democracy. With the exception of tyranny, other forms of government may have certain aspects of justice, but only democracy, in addition to being constitutional government and government for the common good, has the justice which derives from granting every man the right to participate in his own government. This right needs a few more words of explanation.

Like every natural right, this one is rooted in the nature of man. Its authenticity rests on the truth of the proposition that man is by nature a political animal. To affirm this proposition is to say, first, that *all* men, not just some men, should be *constituents* of the government under which they live and so should be governed only with their own consent; and, second, that they should be citizens with *suffrage* and be thus empowered to *participate* in their own government. (I have stressed all the crucial words in this interpretation of the proposition's meaning.)

From this it follows that democracy is the only perfectly just form of government. Anyone who understands the basic terms of this analysis can work out the demonstration for himself by applying, at every step, two principles: that all human beings are by nature political animals; and that justice consists in treating equals equally and in securing for all equally their natural or human rights. Wherever any normal, mature man is treated as a slave, as a subject of despotic rule, or as a political pariah excluded from citizenship, there, absolutely speaking, injustice is being done.

Two infirmities are inherent in all forms of government, but they are remediable to some extent in political democracy, whereas they are not remediable at all in the other forms of government. Therefore, even with these infirmities in mind, political democracy is to be preferred to all other forms of government.

The two infirmities inherent in all forms of government are clearly stated in Mill's *Representative Government*. One is *incompetence* on the part of those who exercise political power (whether it is exercised by an absolute ruler, a despot, a ruling class in an oligarchy, or the predominant majority in a democracy). The other is the *tyranny* of those who exercise political power (whether that is the tyranny of a non-benevolent despot, of the ruling class in an oligarchy, or of the majority in a democracy).

No other form of government is to be preferred to democracy because of these infirmities, for all other forms of government are subject to the same infirmities, and they are not remediable in other forms of government, whereas remedies can be found for them in political democracy.

The remedy for the incompetence of the rulers in a political democracy is the education of the people for their duties as citizens and as public officials. I shall return to this point later in dealing with the more perfect realization of the ideal of political democracy.

While advocating the extension of the suffrage to the laboring classes (because it was clearly unjust "to withhold from anyone, unless for the prevention of greater evils, the ordinary privilege of having his voice reckoned in the disposal of affairs in which he has the same interest as other people"), Mill feared that the enfranchised masses would exercise their newfound power in their own factional interests and would tyrannically subjugate the upper-class minorities to their will. He also feared that the judgment of the uneducated would prevail, by sheer weight of numbers, over the judgment of their betters, to the detriment of the community as a whole.

The marked inequality of conditions which, in Mill's day, separated the working masses from the upper classes and brought them into a sharp conflict of factional interests led Mill, the proponent of democracy, to have the same fears about it that led others to oppose it. Let it be said in passing that the remedies—proportional representation and plural voting—which Mill proposed as ways of safeguarding democracy from its own deficiencies would have nullified democracy in practice, if they had been carried out. To be in favor of universal suffrage (which makes the ruling class coextensive with the population), while at the same time wishing somehow to undercut the rule of the majority, is as self-contradictory as being for and against democracy at the same time.

This is not to say that the problems which concerned Mill were not genuine in his time. Those problems—especially the problems of factions (the age-old conflict between the haves and the have-nots) and the problem of an uneducated electorate—can be solved, but not in the way that John Stuart Mill, James Madison, or John C. Calhoun proposed. They can be solved only through the development of a general equality of conditions. This, by gradually substituting a classless society of haves for a class-divided one, will tend to reduce and ultimately to eliminate the conflict of economic factions. By gradually giving all equal access to schooling and enough free time for leisure and learning in adult life, it will also enable every educable human being (all except the incurably feebleminded or insane) to become educated to the point where he or she can be as good a citizen—as sensible in the exercise of his or her suffrage—as anyone else.

All men are not equally intelligent at birth; nor will all ever become equally wise or virtuous through the development of their minds and characters. These ineradicable inequalities in human beings do not in themselves undermine the democratic proposition that all normal men are educable enough to become good citizens. To think otherwise is to revert to the aristocratic proposition that some men are so superior to others in natural endowment that they alone are educable to the extent required for participation in government. I am not saying that the problem of producing a sufficiently educated electorate (when it is coextensive with the population of the community) has yet been solved. It certainly has not been, and we are still a long way from solving it. I am only saying that the changes which have taken place since Mill's day—especially the technological advances which have brought affluence and ample opportunity for learning and leisure in their wake—give us more hope that it can be solved than Mill could possibly have summoned to support his wavering democratic convictions.

The remedy for the tyranny of the majority does not consist in the measures Mill proposed, such as proportional representation or plural voting. It consists rather in the constitutional enactment of all natural or human rights, and in the judicial review of legislation. The second of these remedies permits unjustly oppressed minorities to appeal to the courts for a redress of their grievances by upholding their constitutional rights against unconstitutional legislation enacted by a tyrannical, or self-interested, majority. Even when this remedy is not fully and effectively operative, a tyrannical democracy is preferable to a tyrannical oligarchy or a tyrannical despotism by virtue of the fact that in the latter two instances of tyrannical rule the tyrannically ruled is a majority, not a minority. Hence more human beings are unjustly treated; more injustice is done.

The opponents of Thesis I are challenged to come up with an alternative form of government that they can defend as more just than political democracy—more just, not more efficient or expedient under certain circumstances. This challenge applies to an opponent who holds the view that democracy should not prevail, even if it can or will. Or, if not that, then at least such opponents are challenged to propose a second-best form of government which they are willing to recommend as substitutable for political democracy *if* they think democracy cannot and will not survive or prevail, even though they acknowledge it to be, in principle, more just than any other form of government. This challenge applies to an opponent who holds the view that democracy should prevail, but that it cannot or will not.

Confronted with adverse views about the viability of democracy, held by those who regard themselves as realists, I am impelled to ask certain questions.

Let me begin by assuming the truth of the realist's denial in its most extreme form; in other words, let us assume the *impossibility* of government by the people in any sense which tends to realize, in some degree, the ideal of democracy. What then?

First, must we not conclude that the ideal is a purely visionary, utopian one, not based on men or conditions as they are or even might be? For if it were a practicable ideal, based on things as they are or might be, how could it be impossible of realization—in the strict sense of impossible?

Those who thus eliminate democracy as a practicable ideal must therefore be asked whether they have any genuinely practicable (that is, actually realizable) political ideal to substitute for it. If they say no, they must be further asked whether the reason is that they reject normative political thinking entirely and so refuse to take the question seriously.

However, if they concede the possibility of sensible and

reasonable talk about good and bad forms of government, and hence are seriously concerned with thinking about the best of all possible (that is, realizable) forms, then they should either have some alternative to democracy as the ideal polity or be in search of one. In either case, they must be asked to state the standard, principle, or norm in terms of which they would propose a particular form of government as best, or better than some other. Justice? Wisdom? Efficiency? Strength?

If they appeal to any standard other than justice, or do not include justice among the principles to which they appeal, I must remind them that democracy is said to be the best form of government only in terms of justice, not in terms of wisdom, efficiency, strength, or any other criterion, and so they have failed to find a substitute for democracy.

My question, I must remind them, is not about democracy in any sense of that term but about democracy as defined: constitutional government with genuinely universal suffrage, operating through elections and elected representatives, with majority rule, and under conditions of social and economic as well as political equality. Do they regard democracy thus defined as the ideal polity, and if they do, do they hold it up as the ideal by reference to principles of justice?

If they answer this compound question with a double affirmative, then there is only one further question to ask. Let me assume they take the view that the difficulties confronting democracy—if not now, then certainly in the future—are likely to be so great that, even if they are not, absolutely speaking, insurmountable, we may nevertheless be unable to overcome them in any really satisfactory manner. Hence, they may say, we should prepare ourselves for this eventuality by thinking of a second-best form of government, one which, while less just, would be more workable because it would get around the difficulties now besetting democracy. My question to them is: What form of government would that be?

I do not know whether there is more than one possible

answer to this question; but I do know, and have already mentioned, one alternative to democracy that is espoused by those who wish to discard government by the people while retaining government of and for the people. I am even willing to concede that if political democracy should prove to be impossible, then so-called social democracy may very well be the best form of government that can exist. But I am not yet willing to yield—and I see nothing in the contemporary discussion of the difficulties of democracy that requires me to yield—on the proposition that all men are by nature political.

I must, therefore, repeat what I said earlier; namely, that, men being what they are, "social democracy" is a poor second-best, for it imposes upon the many who are disfranchised the essential injustice that characterizes any benevolent despotism. Hence, until insurmountable difficulties force us to surrender all hope for the future of democracy, we should be loath to settle for anything less than the best form of government that befits the nature of man.

Argument for Thesis II: That political democracy can survive and be perfected where it now exists in some approximation of the ideal, and that it can be adopted where it does not now exist and, after being adopted, can be perfected there.

What are the obstacles that must be overcome for the survival and perfection of democracy where it now exists in some degree of approximation, and for the adoption of democracy where it does not now exist and for its subsequent perfection there? They are threefold.

The first is the obstacle presented by the difficulty of instituting a system of public education which would be adequate to the needs of a political democracy, and which would remedy or remove one of the infirmities inherent in democracy—the incompetence of the people, and especially of the ruling majority.

This obstacle to the realization of democracy in practice

is necessarily an accidental one. It does not, it cannot, lie in the essence of a rational, free, and political nature. But that nature needs training—the formation of good habits—for it to realize the perfections of which it is capable. Democracy demands a higher degree of human training than any other form of government, precisely because it depends upon the reasonableness of free men exercising their freedom politically. The obstacle here is not human nature but our various educational failures. I shall discuss only one of these failures, the failure of our educational institutions in the sphere of specifically intellectual training.

That failure is measured by the educational requirement of democracy. The essence of the democratic constitution is universal citizenship. Hence all men must be educated for citizenship. But this is not simply a quantitative matter.

The problem is not solved by erecting and financing a school system ample enough to take in all the children. We have almost done that in this country during the last fifty years, but even if we had done that completely, even if all children not committed to asylums for feeblemindedness went through our American schools and colleges, American education would still be serving democracy miserably. The reason is simply that American education is predominantly vocational rather than liberal. It is based on the thoroughly undemocratic prejudice that more than half the children are not intelligent enough for truly liberal education. (Need I add that more than half the educators do not know what a truly liberal education is?)

Vocational education is training for a specific job in the economic machine. It aims at earning a good living, not living a good life. It is servile both in its aim and in its methods. It defeats democracy in the same way that economic servitude does. To exercise the freedom of democactic citizenship, men must not only be economically free, they must also be educated for freedom, which can be achieved in no other way than by giving every future citizen the maximum of liberal education. Put concretely, that means schooling for every boy and girl from kindergarten through college, with a curriculum from which every vestige of vocationalism has been expunged.

In a just economy, the costs of this education would be met in such a manner that no child would be deprived because of poverty. In a just economy, vocational training, thrown out of the schools, would be undertaken by industry through a system of apprenticeships. Training for a specific job should be done on the job, not in the schools.

But, it will be said, liberal schooling for all is impossible for other reasons. I know this from the sad experience of having talked about American education to teachers and laymen in large groups all over the country. The real reason, they say, that we have to train the majority of children vocationally is that only the fortunate few who have superior mental endowments are capable of receiving liberal education. The so-called educators have no facts to support this statement, but the fact that they make it shows that they understand neither democracy nor education.

If a child has enough intelligence to be admitted in maturity to citizenship, which means enough intelligence not to require hospitalization, and enough intelligence to become a parent, govern a family, and earn a living, then that child has more than enough intelligence for all the liberal education we can find time to give him in ten or twelve years of schooling.

Let me state this in the form of a dilemma: either a child has enough intelligence for liberal education through the Bachelor of Arts degree, or he does not have enough intelligence for democratic citizenship.

Deny the validity of this dilemma, and you make a mockery of democratic citizenship. A citizen is not a political puppet pushed around by propaganda. He is a free man, exercising a critical and independent judgment on basic questions affecting the common good. Not all men have the talents required for high public office, but all normal men do have sufficient mentality for the primary and basic office in the democratic state, which is citizenship. They have the power, but it must be trained, and that training, the development of a free and critical mind, is one of the essential aims of liberal education. It can be accomplished by the discipline of the mind in its essential functions of reading and writing, speaking and listening—all the arts of thinking, not merely speculatively or privately, but practically and socially.

Our oligarchical ancestors understood this. Whether in Greece and Rome, or in this country during its formative period, they knew that citizenship required liberal schooling; they knew why education had to be liberal in order to prepare for citizenship; they knew that intellectual discipline was prerequisite for freedom of mind and freedom in action. So far they were right, but they made one fatal error. They identified the propertied classes with the intellectually elite. They restricted citizenship to the wellborn and disguised their oligarchical injustice under the aristocratic pretension that only the few, the same few, had enough wit to be educable and so deserve citizenship.

They were hypocrites, but so are we if we continue to think, as most Americans do, that the equality of citizenship belongs to all, but not equality of educational opportunity. Admitting all children to school is not enough. We must give them all the same kind of education; not liberal education for the few and vocational training for the many. To say this does not mean that we should try to give each child the same *absolute* amount of education, for each can receive only according to his capacity. It does mean that each child has a sufficient capacity for liberal schooling, even as he has enough intelligence for citizenship, and that each should receive the same *proportion*, namely, as much as he can take, which is much more than we have ever tried to give.

So far we have failed, partly because our educators are antidemocratic, harboring all the prejudices of oligarchy and the delusions of aristocracy, and partly because we have not yet even tried to solve the technical problem of constructing and administering a liberal curriculum for all the children. This last fact, by the way, explains the popularity of vocationalism with the educational profession. Not knowing how to universalize liberal education—not wanting to think about it because it is so difficult a problem—they conceal their ignorance and sloth behind the untruth that the failure is God's rather than man's. The Creator may have intended man for freedom, but, paradoxically, He did not endow the majority with enough mind to be educated up to it.

We may constitutionally grant all normal men the status of citizenship. We may even achieve the economic reforms necessary to emancipate them from servitude and to secure them from poverty. Progressive industrialization and technical progress may provide all men with sufficient leisure. But unless we educate all men liberally for citizenship, they will not be able to discharge the duties of that high office, and democracy will exist only on paper, not in practice.

Liberal education cannot be completed in school. We grasp the essence of such education only when we understand it to be preparation for more education, more liberal education throughout an entire life. Unless liberal schooling is followed by adult liberal education, it will be to no purpose. Habits fail from disuse; the intellectual virtues cannot be kept alive without continuous exercise. Universal adult education, liberally conceived, should, therefore, not be an afterthought. It is an essential part of democracy's educational requirement. Without it, the mind of the citizen will go to sleep, and a sleeping citizen might just as well be a dead one.

One word more about education. Liberal education cultivates all the intellectual virtues except prudence. Like the moral virtues, prudence cannot be taught in school, or by teachers out of books anywhere. Prudence is a habit formed only by the exercise of practical judgment, and practical judgments can be truly made in a practical manner only by those who have the responsibility for action. Deprive men of citizenship and they will not develop the virtue of political prudence, which is the habit of judging rightly about means to the common good. The sort of education, then, which is requisite for political prudence comes from political action itself, from active participation in the political life. This means that there is no way of fitting men for citizenship without first making them citizens.

A second obstacle to the survival and perfection of democracy is the obstacle presented by social and economic inequalities that impede the effective operation of the political equality that democracy confers upon all who are citizens. Even though oligarchy is removed from the constitution, it still exists in practice to whatever extent the wealthy are able to exercise undue influence on the government, but principally in terms of the economic servitude of the working classes in an unsocialized capitalistic economy. Political democracy will not work in practice unless it is accompanied by economic democracy in the organization of industry and by economic justice in the regulation of all matters that affect subsistence, employment, and economic security.

Let me make the essential point here in another way. Defending the exclusion of the nonpropertied, laboring classes—the proletariat—from citizenship, John Adams enunciated this principle: "No man who is economically dependent on the will of another man for his subsistence can exercise the freedom of judgment requisite for citizenship." The principle is completely true. No man who is subservient to the arbitrary will of another man for his economic livelihood can act as that other man's equal politically. This is just as true of wage slaves under unsocialized capitalism as it was so obviously true of chattel slaves or serfs under feudalism.

But the principle being true, Adams drew the wrong practical conclusion from it by advocating an oligarchical constitution, excluding the economically dependent (the unpropertied) from citizenship. He sought to adapt the polity to an unjust economy, making the polity thereby unjust. If we are democrats politically, we must proceed in exactly the opposite direction. We must reform an unjust economy to make it fit a just polity, and that reform plainly means the further reform of capitalism as we know it.

What does that mean positively? Communism? I hardly think so, for when men are subservient for their subsistence to the will of the state, they are no more economically free than they are under private capitalism. Political democracy is as incompatible with communism as with bourgeois or unsocialized capitalism. The answer, I think, lies in a departure toward the mean away from both extremes, toward the achievement of socialistic objectives by capitalist means, that is, by the widest possible diffusion of the ownership of capital.

One further point must be considered here. There are those who think that the inferior social and economic conditions of certain countries justify for the time being inferior forms of government (such as benevolent despotism or a benevolent oligarchy). I argue that the establishment of political democracy is, in the temporal order, antecedent and prerequisite to the establishment of the social and economic conditions of a democratic society, even though the establishment of a democratic society is requisite for the perfection of political democracy where it exists in some degree of approximation to the ideal.

The mistake that is made here turns on a misuse of the distinction between two ways of considering the diverse forms of government, namely, *absolutely* and *relatively*. Relative justification is by reference to contingent and limited historic conditions. In this manner, a form of government which is not the best absolutely, nor free from essential injustice, may be justified as the best that is practicable for a given people at a given time. Absolute justification is by reference to the nature of man as a rational, free, and political animal; to the nature of the political community as an indispensable means to the good life; and to the nature of government as organizing and regulating the community so that it may serve effectively as a means to this end.

The absolute consideration does not neglect the range of

individual differences within the human species, any more than it ignores the differences between the normal and the abnormal, the mature and the immature. It does, however, abstract from those defects or inadequacies which are due not to nature, but to nurture—to failures of education, to deficiencies of experience, to economic impediments, to restricted opportunity, to cultural limitations of all sorts.

My reply to those who appeal to the relative mode of justification is as follows. One way of getting a people to breast the currents of their own political life is to throw them into the water all at once, not to immerse them gingerly by degrees. Industrialization and economic revolutions will accelerate everywhere the emancipation from peonage and serfdom. We can also expect the processes of education to be vastly augmented everywhere. Political prudence is acquired only through practice. If a people are to be educated up to the responsibilities of politically mature men, they must be given the opportunities for political experience through self-government. Let me repeat once more: there is no way of fitting men for citizenship without first making them citizens.

The distinction between an absolute and a relative consideration of the forms of government has been traditionally used to justify inferior forms of government for inferior peoples, or peoples living under inferior economic or cultural conditions. We must now use it in the opposite way: to demand that inferior conditions be remedied so that the best form of government absolutely is also the best relatively for every human group.

The third obstacle to the survival and perfection of democracy is the obstacle presented by the anarchic world of sovereign nations in perpetual war with one another, cold or hot, and by the violence or terrorism abroad in the world that is generated by injustices that cannot be redressed by national governments as they are now constituted.

If the obstacle is the anarchy of separate sovereign states, the remedy is the formulation of a single worldwide political community through federal union, thus establishing for the first time effective world government and positive law, replacing alliances, leagues of nations, and the reign of international law which has always been, and must always be, devoid of the sanctions requisite for government.

War, upon which other forms of government thrive almost in direct proportion to their intrinsic injustice—war, the heady wine of tyranny—weakens and enervates democracy. Despite the international anarchy, democracy may come into being locally through just domestic institutions, but it can never really flourish and grow to full maturity in practice if it is continually beset by war or the threat of war in interstate affairs.

Political history teaches us that the best republican institutions of the ancient world were overturned by dictatorships arising to meet the needs of efficiency in war. The events of our own age confirm the insight that due process of law, which is the essence of constitutionalism, and the public debate of public issues, which is indispensable to democracy, must be abandoned or abridged under the exigencies of war.

Furthermore, international anarchy, which is identical with the permanent existence of a state of war between sovereign states (whether carried on quietly by the diplomats or noisily by the generals), necessitates not only the maintenance of permanent military establishments but also the separation between a government's domestic and foreign policies. Both of these factors operate against democracy. By its very nature, foreign policy expresses calculations of expediency, not determinations of justice. The necessarily Machiavellian character of foreign policy cannot help infecting domestic legislation. What is worse, foreign policy cannot be popularly determined, as domestic policy can be, because it must be secretly fomented and stealthily executed by all the deceptions of diplomacy. Foreign policy is necessarily the prerogative of the executive branch. Any check on foreign policy by the legislature or by popular referendum hamstrings a government in foreign affairs. But the supremacy of the legislature should be unexceptional and inviolable in popular or democratic government. The processes of government cannot be perfectly democratic if they are forced to include foreign affairs as a major concern of the common good which cannot be openly submitted to the people or settled by due process of law.

Hence we see that the international anarchy, misnamed "the society of nations," works against democracy in any state where it may arise, because it perpetuates war, keeping the nations forever embroiled in fighting, or, what is as bad, in foreign affairs. This was true before August 6, 1945; it is much more urgently true now in the light of all that the explosion at Hiroshima portends. The atomic warfare of the future puts a life-or-death premium on secrecy in preparation and surprise attack. In every war, the initial advantage is to dictatorships rather than democracies, because they can proceed without popular discussion or consent; but in the next war the initial advantage will also be the final one.

The ideal of democracy and the ideal of world peace are separate in thought, but not in practical realization. The one is the ideal of perfection in human government, responding to the political nature of man; the other is the ideal of perfection in human association, responding to the social nature of man. The world political community has always been implicitly the ultimately perfect society, for nothing else can abolish war and perfect human life. The unity of peace which is the common good of all mankind cannot begin until the specious society of nations is transformed into a worldwide society of men. Until all men are citizens of the world, none will enjoy fully the citizenship granted by local and isolated democracies. Without unlimited fraternity, liberty and equality cannot reach their proper limits.

We should, perhaps, consider other threats to the survival and perfection of democracy where it now exists and to the spread of democracy to countries where it does not now exist:

scarcity of food, energy, and other resources; population increase; environmental pollution; nuclear warfare. With respect to all of these, my argument turns on the measures that I think are feasible ways of overcoming the three major difficulties already set forth.

Argument for Thesis III: that political democracy, supported and facilitated by a democratic society, will prevail everywhere and will survive and prosper

The essence of my argument is that justice, together with the fullest degree of liberty that justice allows and the most complete equality of conditions that justice requires, will prevail in the long run.

My reason is identical with John Locke's: that men will not long suffer injustice without seeking redress.

My further reason is that liberty and equality (both limited by justice) are goods that men will not relinquish if there is any way of achieving them.

My final argument is that there is no alternative to the democratic government of a democratic society that men will long accept and endure.

BILL MOYERS:

Well, we have certainly had a clearly defined and precisely defined subject put before us. And now that that has been done, we will begin with a response or a challenge to Mr. Adler from Maurice Cranston.

MAURICE CRANSTON:

If I have understood him correctly, Mr. Adler has put three main theses: the first that democracy should prevail everywhere; second, that democracy can survive where it now exists, can be perfected there, and can be adopted and perfected everywhere else; and third, that what is possible will probably come to pass in a future not too remote.

Now I agree with Mr. Adler's thesis in the first paragraph that democracy ought everywhere to prevail, though I don't wholly share his view that it is the only perfectly just form of government. I do consider it perhaps the least unjust form of government, and that's my reason for supporting what is perhaps the major part of his argument. I agree with Mr. Adler, too, that democracy can survive where it now exists, but not with his thesis that democracy can be perfected there; and still less do I share his belief that democracy can be adopted and perfected everywhere else. And I cannot agree with Mr. Adler's third thesis that democracy will be adopted and perfected in a future not too remote, where it does not now exist.

Now perhaps I ought to follow him into stipulating the definition of terms because I want to use words slightly differently from the ways in which he himself used them in his presentation. I intend to use the expression "constitutional democracy" in a way which corresponds fairly closely to his use of the expression "political democracy." I do not want to take up his expression because it would, I think, hinder rather than help the development of my own argument. I am, nevertheless, happy to follow Mr. Adler in using the expression "democratic society," though perhaps in a different way from the way in which he uses it, and I'd further agree with him that democratic government (if he would allow that small alteration or modification of the terms I quote from him) can only be imperfectly realized in any society that is not a democratic society. But I don't believe that democratic government is itself the indispensable first step toward democratic society. The relationship between the two is more complex, I think. Sometimes it's a democratic society which precedes the democratic government, and to explain this I must follow Mr. Adler into the realms of history.

But first perhaps I ought to sketch out what seems to me

to be the central problem of democracy. No one, I think, is likely to disagree that political democracy is government of, by, and for the people. And I think there's not likely to be much controversy about the other standard definitions: that monarchy is government by one, and oligarchy government by a few. The difficulty, it seems to me, about the concept of democracy is that whereas it's easy enough to understand how one man can govern a large number of men, and how a group of men can govern a large number of men, it's hard to imagine how a large number of men can govern themselves. For while one man has one will, and a smaller group of men may be united by a common will, how can a large number of men stand to themselves as rulers when a large number of men have, taken together, a vast number of differing and probably conflicting, competing wills? How can people turn themselves into "a people" with a single will of its own? How do people transform themselves or become transformed into "a people"?

Now of course this is not the problem only of democracy, it is also a problem posed by the republican ideal, something to be dated from ancient Rome, even as democracy is something to be dated from ancient Greece. In the republican ideal, sovereignty is transferred from the king to the people. This is what I think the Romans believed themselves to be doing when they dismissed their kings and set up a republic. The Roman kingdom was a collection of people brought together in common allegiance to a single king. Their identity as Romans was thus created by the office of kingship and the existence of a kingdom. After the kings had been dismissed, Roman society continued to exist as virtually a kingless kingdom. Indeed, that is substantially what their republic meant to them. Kingship or sovereignty was removed from the king and dispersed among the people, vested in the people, who in turn set up political institutions to formulate laws and conduct the administration of their political society.

But such a republican ideal is far from being democratic.

What we should call government, as distinct from sovereignty, was undertaken by officeholders, enjoying, presumably, the tacit consent of the people. Unlike the Roman kingdom, where everybody was a subject, the Roman republic instituted distinctions between citizens and noncitizens, distinctions between various classes; but in theory, at any rate, the citizens were the people, and the republic was the people's own state. The republican ideal is thus one which is inclined to magnify the state, but it doesn't offer to the ordinary man, even perhaps to the ordinary citizen, much actual participation, beyond the occasional opportunity to vote in plebiscites devised by the dominant group of officeholders. According to the republican ideal the nation is sovereign over itself, but since it has to accomplish this rather paradoxical feat through the institutionalization of leaders, in the real world (and I have to confess to trying to be somewhat of a realist, when I can be) the republican ideal has more often than not actualized itself in the form of an elaborately ritualized despotism.

Now the democratic ideal is different from this. It does not merely transfer sovereignty from the king to the people; it calls upon the people to govern themselves. Since it demands more, it's hardly surprising that the democratic ideal has been even less effectively actualized in the real world than has the republican ideal. Mr. Adler says that "political democracy" as he defines it is not yet a century old. And if I may substitute the term "constitutional democracy," I would agree with him, that it is something dating, more or less, from the nineteenth century. But I don't want to call this "political democracy," because there are other types of political democracy which seem to me to have earned the right to this name, and their history is much older.

Mr. Adler does not, it seems to me, admire very much the democracy of ancient Greece. He protests that the difference between an oligarchy and a so-called democracy in Athens was a matter of numbers. A difference between a ruling minority of 500 and one of 30,000. A difference, he says, that would hardly have mattered much to the 90,000 disfranchised. Now it is a fact that Athenian democracy has always had a bad press. Not only Plato, with his hideous picture of the democratic man, but practically all the philosophers and historians from whom we derive our knowledge of ancient Athens were hostile toward democracy. To understand it better, we need, perhaps, to engage in the exercise proposed by A. J. M. Jones in his book on *Athenian Democracy*—that of reconstructing our conception of Athens by treating the testimony of hostile witnesses with considerable reserve and piecing together evidence that we can ascertain from other sources. Of course Mr. Adler is right to remind us that Athenian society was made up of citizens and outsiders, and one can readily see why he will not admit that there was ever rule by "the people" in a city where only one-third of the inhabitants were counted, for political purposes, as people.

But I think we ought not, perhaps, to take an excessively twentieth-century view of all this. Even in the nineteenth century, champions of democracy in western Europe were content to state their demand for universal suffrage as a demand for a vote for every registered male resident on the tax rolls. The idea of extending the suffrage even to women never came into the heads of most of them. The disfranchised persons in Athens about whom Mr. Adler worries so much were not systematically excluded; they were simply not thought of as being qualified to participate.

During the democratic phase of Athenian history, the citizens who did rule themselves did so in a manner which is highly instructive and, I think, rather wonderful. They met en masse to make laws, to decide about peace and war, to name generals and ambassadors, and even to try legal cases, which last, perhaps, was rather unwise of them. But they didn't set up institutions as the Romans did and entrust officeholders with decision making. They debated and decided among themselves. Crude common sense prevailed, no doubt, more often than sophisticated statecraft, but that is what we should expect of an assembly where the citizens were, for the most part, uneducated and so necessarily outnumbered the educated.

This evidence of democratic wisdom is conspicuous again in the other form of democracy of which Europe has had some long experience—that of the Swiss cantons. Mr. Adler does not as much as mention it. And here he is in the company of most worldly historians who consider anything Swiss to be too boring to mention. But perhaps up here in this mountain altitude and amid this scenery we may allow ourselves to look at the Swiss experience. Tacitus thought Swiss democracy was a typical barbaric form of government, which could be practiced by tribes in their forests but was not fitted to a civilized, urban society who knew the meaning of the word "law." And this brings us, I think, to a point stressed by both Jean-Jacques Rousseau and Thomas Jefferson: that direct democracy, if we may use this expression to distinguish the Swiss and Athenian kind from the constitutional modern kind, went together with a simple agricultural society; and it is very difficult for a democracy of that kind to exist in a modernized, industrialized society. Rousseau, I think, argued that the reason why Athenian democracy collapsed was that the society, the culture of Athens, had become too sophisticated; and certainly Jefferson wanted to maintain the agricultural nature of American society in order to protect what he understood as democracy. Now, unlike Mr. Adler, I don't think we run the risk of being distracted and confused by thinking about conceptions of democracy older than our own contemporary understandings of constitutional democracy. In fact, I believe that the considerations of the problems posed by these older systems enable us to reach a fuller understanding of the strengths and the weaknesses of constitutional democracy, which was quite rightly the main focus of Mr. Adler's paper.

I imagine that Swiss democracy derived from that older

tradition of tribal government, in which instead of being ruled by a single chief, certain Alpine communities decided to rule themselves by meeting en masse and voting on important questions. We needn't perhaps quarrel with Charles Montesquieu's suggestion that geography influences political arrangements and hence that the contours of the Alpine valleys enabled the inhabitants to resist conquest by alien kings and emperors and so to acquire the habits of independence and liberty. These Swiss were fairly few in number, they were fairly equal in their rank and possessions, and perhaps fairly equal in their intelligence or lack of intelligence. Their backwardness prevented the emergence of a sophisticated medieval ruling class. And the interesting thing is that once they had established their political democracy, the inhabitants of the Swiss cantons became the most passionately conservative people in Europe.

What we think of in the West as democracy—constitutional democracy—is, I think, usually a liberal idea. In Switzerland, where direct democracy has had so long a history, democracy is a conservative idea. And Swiss history has perhaps been a constant struggle between the backward cantons in the Alps against the centralizing, modernizing, progressive champions of parliamentary institutions who emerge in the cities of the plains. It would perhaps be not too much of a distortion to suggest that the past 150 years of Swiss history has been a history of conflict, perhaps not even yet settled, between two types of democracy: direct democracy in the remote cantons, and constitutional democracy in the big cities.

Now, whereas Mr. Adler has set out to defend only one type of democracy, constitutional democracy, I think it is perhaps necessary to say something in defense of more than one type. Direct democracy, where it still exists, is old, and constitutional democracy, as Mr. Adler very rightly reminded us, is new. Now how did it come into existence, this constitutional democracy? Well, in my own country, the United Kingdom, it came about by stages. The Glorious Revolution of 1688–89 set up a constitutional government; Parliament began progressively to dominate the king; and the extension of the suffrage by a series of enactments, which finally extended the suffrage to all persons over eighteen, has now produced in England a democratical sort of system. I would be very reluctant to say that England—or the United Kingdom—is a democracy, if only because the House of Lords is still an important part of Parliament, but I will leave that aside for the moment and simply say that British constitutional democracy is basically democratized constitutional government.

The United States is, of course, different. If we look at the discussions which took place in the early years of this nation, there is a clear consciousness of two particular characteristics of the American situation. The first, so well expressed by Alexander Hamilton, is that the Americans' whole understanding of political values and the rights and liberties, and what these concepts meant, derived from the experience of having been part of English political culture. The second, the awareness, so eloquently expressed by Jefferson, was that American society had come to be significantly different from English or European society. Americans had forgotten feudalism and acquired in the New World a democratical way of life; what I would call democratic society arrived before democracy. When Alexis de Tocqueville came to America in the middle of the nineteenth century, he found something which existed nowhere in Europe, except in Switzerland, a democratic sort of people trying to democratize and, in many cases, successfully democratizing institutions which had been set up by rationalistic liberal constitutionalists in the eighteenth century. For in the event, neither Hamilton, the conservative disciple of David Hume, nor Jefferson, the Rousseauesque romantic champion of democracy, had his way. It was the ideology of Locke and Montesquieu (both good enough liberals, but neither of them certainly a democrat) which formed the American Constitution, and it was the continuing democratic character of American society which demanded that the government should become more and more democratic, that the political system should more and more reflect the democratic nature of American society.

Now perhaps we could say that the Americans' constitution was, from its early days, intensely republican. That is to say, it was much concerned to invest the sovereignty in the people, whereas the English were always content to let sovereignty repose in king and Parliament. But the American constitution was not in itself, I think, in the early days, particularly democratic. To this extent, government in America needed to be democratized almost as much as government in England needed to be democratized. The most striking difference between the two, perhaps, is that American society, being already democratic, brought about that reform with a clear purpose in mind—and of course much sooner—whereas the democratization of Great Britain has come about in a series of steps, none of which I think was directed toward one single coherent end, but as a series of measures which accumulated in such a way as to produce, progressively, democratization of the British constitutional system. There was no clear understanding or desire for democracy, I think, in England, as there was in America—not, at any rate, before the 1914–18 war.

Mr. Adler says that democracy does not yet fully exist in practice anywhere. And here again, I entirely agree with him. But because I agree with him I want to do one thing which he discourages us from doing, and that is to use the word *democratic* in such a way as to allow us to say that some Greek states were more democratic or less democratic than others, some more oligarchic or less oligarchic than others.

The situation seems to me to be that precisely because democracy does not yet fully exist in practice, we have some hesitation in applying the word to any existing system, and therefore, the adjective "democratic," which allows for degrees and even styles of "democraticness" (if you will forgive an ugly word), is very useful. The worst of all ways of dealing with this situation seems to be that employed by C. B. Macpherson in his book entitled *The Real World of Democracy*, where he notes that since most nations of the world claim to be democratic nowadays, we might agree to say there are three different sorts of democracy: communist, the Third World, and capitalist. Therefore, we're all democrats; we must only admit to being democrats of different styles.

This I think is a very bad way of dealing with the problem of democracy, although of course I suppose it might be said that Professor Macpherson has converted the entire world to democracy by a stroke of the pen, rather than by embarking on the Third World War. Unfortunately, by making the word "democracy" describe everything, it describes nothing.

The crucial question that seems to emerge from these considerations is, are there any tests for the authenticity of a claim to be democratic? Some people would want to say, and some people do say nowadays, for one sees it very often asserted in the more advanced American publications, that only direct democracy is the genuine thing; and, although I don't share this view, I can understand why people say it, because direct democracy does really seem to offer every single person a place and a voice in the proceedings of government. And I think that belief owes a great deal to Rousseau, who picked it out as being a distinctive characteristic of democratical sorts of societies. Indeed, Rousseau carried the argument further and maintained that representative government was some kind of a fraud; parliamentary government was a fraud because genuine representation not only did not take place but wasn't possible; no man could represent another, and therefore to have democracy you must abolish representation and let every man speak for himself.

Now of course it is a very difficult question to decide, how can any one man represent another in politics. I can represent you if I'm a lawyer in a court case, and I can represent my country if I'm an ambassador elsewhere, but how can I represent the inhabitants of a constituency, say, of 30,000 persons? It is a very difficult problem to solve. But it seems to me, although this is a serious problem for constitutional democracy, direct democracy has to face almost the same problem of representation. We don't know exactly how the popular assemblies of ancient Athens conducted their business, but Swiss democracy still continues to this day in such cantons as Glarus and Appenzell, where we may witness what the *Landesgemeinden* do, when the people meet in them from time to time, to legislate in person. I am sorry that my political science friends who are doing political research on political experience in so many other places tell us very little about this Swiss institution, which is such a fascinating feature of existing modern political life. It strikes me, at any rate, when I have watched these people meeting en masse—the entire adult male population of Glarus or Appenzell—I have noticed that some people do all the talking and others do all the listening, although everyone has the same right to speak as well as his right to vote. I have a very strong suspicion that it was the same in Athens. In other words, the naturally assertive or naturally eloquent persons got up and talked, and they commanded the tacit consent of people who agreed with them, and so they became in effect the spokesmen, in other words, the representatives of certain points of view. Even if that representation is not institutionalized in the simple, direct democracy, it must, I think, be there—not a logical necessity but a natural necessity, based on the limitations of time and the character of human assemblies and all the rest of it. Therefore, it seems to me that you cannot claim, as some of our romantic friends do claim today, that direct democracy offers every person a kind of immediate participation in political government which indirect or constitutional democracy forbids him. It offers, perhaps, a close and more intimate relationship. But representation, plainly, is there in direct democracy as it is in avowedly representative democracy of the constitutional kind; and therefore I think that each type of democracy has somehow to solve the problem of representation. I myself don't know how to solve it; it seems to me one of the perennial puzzles of politics: how can one man represent another?

And of course, if we think how representation is supposed to take place in the modern world, if we look at the actual voting systems which are employed in constitutional democracies, we find, again, that they all tend to make it very difficult for the whole variety of opinion in a country to achieve adequate organization, adequate expression, and so forth, and that therefore the extension of the suffrage from the smaller group of property owners to everybody over the past hundred years has tended at the same time to offer people a vote and also to deprive them of anything to vote for; to create a situation in which political parties themselves lose their own coherence; so the vote you're given is often not much use to you, except as a sort of protest vote. While everybody's in a position to vote against the existing administration, the individual is very hard pressed to find a party which really corresponds to his own aspirations and which has any chance of acceding to power. This is a dilemma, in particular, of countries like my own, the United Kingdom, where many people feel they would like to vote for a policy, but they don't recognize, in the existing parties, anything which represents the sort of thing they want to say. So people feel cheated by a system which has given them the vote. They are no longer in the situation which was enjoyed, in the nineteenth century, by the natural liberals and natural conservatives, who could vote for a liberal or conservative party that represented, on the whole, their point of view.

The extension of democracy has, in a sense, made it much more difficult for constitutional government as such to operate effectively. In fact it seems to me the constitutional government itself is a very delicate mechanism, and it becomes more delicate when it becomes democratized. And it's for these reasons, then, very briefly, that I cannot share the optimism of Mr. Adler about democracy. In fact I feel extremely pessimistic, today, about the prospects for constitutional democracy, in both the immediate and the more distant future.

I shall not develop any arguments in favor of democracy, because I think the case has already been extremely well put by Mr. Adler in his remarks. Indeed, it's really rather extraordinary to find a philosopher who speaks in favor of democracy, because most philosophers since Plato have been hostile toward democracy, and even Mill himself, whom Mr. Adler quoted as the champion of democracy, is the champion of a kind of democracy that some of you would not recognize. For Mill wanted to give an extra vote to the educated class and most of the power to a cultivated bureaucracy, and things of this kind, which I myself might be quite happy to see take place, but which some of you here might regard—very reasonably—as being somehow not quite democracy.

Now of course most philosophers, most intellectuals, prefer enlightened despotism—not only Plato, but even second-grade intellectuals like Voltaire, Bentham, Mrs. Webb, Bacon himself, all thought there should be government by an educated elite who understood things. Naturally, if you think that knowledge is what you need to govern, and that knowledge is something acquired by scientific method, you cannot have rule by the people; the people know nothing about science. Therefore, as Sir Henry Maine pointed out in the nineteenth century, to be a champion of scientific government means you cannot be a champion of democracy. And indeed I could quote numerous other authors who think in this way. So that if we put Mr. Adler on a list of philosophers who were in favor of democracy, you would find him in very slender company indeed.

Let me turn to the question of liberty. I think it is perfectly true that you can't have democracy without liberty, but I think you can have liberty without democracy—and indeed I think our ancestors had it. In England and in Holland they had it, and in certain parts of France. They certainly had liberty there without democracy, and in some of the Italian republics they also had liberty without democracy. It is a good thing that it is possible to have liberty without democracy, because if it were not possible, the world would have had considerably less liberty than it has had, and we should have learned much less than we have learned about what it means to be free.

It is true that constitutional government without democracy—which was the idea of course of John Locke, and of the Whigs in England, of Louis-Philippe of France, and of Hamilton here in America—is an idea rather out of favor nowadays, but it was on the achievements of this system of constitutional government without democracy—freedom without democracy—that constitutional democracy itself was built. The great virtue of this constitutionalism was its respect for the rights of man. It was, no doubt, a very aristocratic kind of liberalism; it was certainly aristocratic in the important sense that it was opposed to monarchy, opposed to the pretensions of the king to rule; and it was aristocratic in another sense, that it tended to look down its nose on ordinary people. But on the other hand I suppose those aristocrats had a protective feeling as they looked down their noses; they felt that they were defending not only their own class interest against the king but the people as a whole against the king, and I think to a great extent this claim was justified.

Now the only objection that I myself can find against liberal constitutionalism of this aristocratic kind is that it simply is not democratic enough for a society which is itself becoming more and more democratic. Everybody today is literate, and what is less important, everybody has become a taxpayer, and it is very unjust surely that a taxpayer, and a literate taxpayer at that, should be excluded from the voting role. Moreover, as a result of certain changes in the family structure, married women have been allowed to own property, which used not to be the case, so that many of them have become taxpayers, too. And since they've been allowed to own property and pay taxes, it's surely absurd they should not be given a vote. I don't think I myself would have been a very passionate suffragette or suffragist in 1800, but I think I would have been by 1910. Obviously circumstances alter things. In modern industrial society, any form of government except democracy is almost impossible to justify.

Mr. Adler put a case for considering democracy the most just form of government so fully and systematically that I don't think I need to repeat it. Perhaps I should take up my remaining minutes by speaking on the more depressing topic of the future—of democracy in the stricter, as it were temporal, sense. First of all, constitutional democracy is only one of several ideas which compete in the modern world for public favor. If it is, as Mr. Adler insists, something new, it's not the only new thing in the air. It has rivals which seem to be increasingly popular. For example, we have the new and potent ideologies of nationalism, populistic despotism, and totalitarian socialism. And all these systems, of course, may pay their lip service to democracy. Eastern Germany calls itself The German Democratic Republic; the populistic despotisms of Colonel Qaddafi and other Arab states tend, on the north shore of Africa, to advertise themselves as democratic peoples' republics. The claims of such populistic regimes are clearly derived from the old republican ideal. This ideal, of which I spoke as being characteristic of ancient Rome, has, in the modern world, become almost as important as the democratic ideal, but it is an ideal which is threatening, and has in many cases totally squashed, the democratic ideal.

Let me put to you in a crude form the argument for republicanism in this particular sense. First of all, in a republic, the state belongs to the people. Second, the more active and more powerful such a republican state becomes, the more it gives effect to the will of the people. Third, the more the people's will is fulfilled, the more their freedom becomes real; therefore, the more active and powerful the state becomes, the more freedom the people have. This is the kind of argument that is extremely widespread in modernity. But such typical republican reasoning comes into conflict with democracy, because it collides with the liberal tradition of constitutional thinking. For according to the liberal tradition, the constitution is there to ensure that the state does what it has to do, and no more. A state is needed to protect the rights of the citizens, who have called the state into being, but its activity must be carefully circumscribed to ensure that it does not itself trespass on those citizens' rights. The state, from this liberal constitutional perspective, is seen as both a necessity and a danger. I need not say this to an American audience, because it is natural for you to think in that way, is it not? But it is otherwise with the continental governments. We cannot say of them that the state does not impinge upon the liberty of the individual unless it is necessary to do so, for the better protection of the people's own rights. Liberty is the silence of law, as Thomas Hobbes put it, but law has also to enlarge liberty, as John Locke put it. So you see, a marvelous combination of law and liberty is called for in the liberal constitutional tradition.

Now, we in the English-speaking world have lived with this understanding of constitutional government for generations. And it has only recently been called into question by etatist ideologists of the left, who seek to enlarge the state so as to revolutionize the material conditions of social existence. But in continental Europe, notably since the emergence of neo-Roman ideals at the time of the French Revolution, the yearning for a powerful people's state, for all-pervasive republican institutions, has taken deep roots, and it is there, I think, that we see one of the great dangers to the future of democracy.

Bertrand de Jouvenel, in his book, *Sovereignty*, did make one very important point, I think, that when the idea of sovereignty was transferred in France from the king to the people, it was made absolute. All the limitations on sovereignty which medieval tradition had imposed on the sovereignty of the king were swept away, and when the people became sovereign they were encouraged to think that their sovereignty was, henceforth, absolute. And again, it was argued that the people's state is the instrument of the people's freedom because it belongs to them.

I think it is probably true that this kind of continental, rationalistic argument has never had much appeal for us Anglo-Saxon empiricists, because by the eighteenth century the English-speaking world had learned from its own experience that liberty was only to be secured on a basis of limited sovereignty, and that it was not only a matter of tying the hands of the king but of tying the hands of Parliament or any other institution which took the place of the kings. Now, I think the founders of the United States were not in love with the idea of a republic. They were in love with one idea, which was the idea, simply, of liberty. And liberty they conceived, much as the English themselves had done before them, as being substantially a matter of being left alone in doing what they wanted to do, so long as it was lawful. That's what liberty meant—not being interfered with, above all by the state.

It is a very nineteenth-century habit, inspired by the French revolutionaries and by Napoleon, and made more elegant by Georg Hegel and the like, to believe that freedom is to be found in the state and to believe that freedom could be enlarged by the magnification of the state; the result was that what came to be called "liberalism" in Germany was an extraordinary alliance of progressives, who thought that the people's state should become more powerful, and imperialists who wanted to absorb the minor kingdoms in one great empire.

This brings us to a parting of the ways between the idea of constitutional democracy—democratized constitutional state, where the powers of the state are very scrupulously limited—and the idea of the popular republic, where the powers of the state are enlarged almost indefinitely to give effect to what is said to be *the* people's will.

It would be idle to deny that the idea of the magnified

republic has not become enormously influential in modern times. Its popularity has coincided, not unnaturally, with that of nationalism. Nationalism is at once a very progressive and a profoundly reactionary ideology. This explains why liberals and imperialists combined in Germany to promote it. The first ideologists of Asian and African nationalism, Mr. Gandhi and the like, were high-minded intellectuals, but the rulers of the Third World states have turned out to be people who have forgotten Mr. Gandhi and shaped themselves on the model of Napoleon, when they are not something worse.

The ironic situation is that the disappearance of so-called imperialism has meant the proliferation of little emperors, in what remains of former empires. This, of course, has proved a breeding ground for ideologies which are logically opposed to democracy. And it is for this reason I think the prospects for democracy grow daily less substantial, rather than more substantial, in those parts of the world.

The impact of imperialism on the history of the world has been unfortunate from the perspective of democracy. Because it is certainly arguable that in the simple societies of, say, Africa, before the Europeans intruded, there were little tribal societies like those of the Swiss Alps, where certain groups acquired what we might well call democratic social habits and had formed their own rules and chose their own ministers, so to speak, to work for them. And this was all abolished when the emperors came, because the emperors necessarily modeled themselves on ancient Rome, and they introduced the rule of law, rather than self-government, which we think of as the central part of democracy. Unfortunately, when imperialism fell into disrepute, and the European rulers withdrew and left the states that they had created, these states had lost the social conditions of a primitive democracy without having acquired the social conditions for a sophisticated democracy. The impact of European imperialism put an end to one primitively democratic society without introducing the more modern, sophisticated kind of democratic society such as we see in England and America.

There is, of course, another vigorous alternative to democracy that flourishes in the modern world, and that is communism. Many people think that communism itself is getting more democratic. We read in the newspapers about Eurocommunism. We see the French, Italian, Spanish, and Portuguese Communist parties using a very democratic sort of language, and volunteering to become champions of democracy against the threat of fascism and so forth. But how real is all this, and how far is this not to be seen as part of the world communist strategy which requires for the moment that communism in Europe should keep quiet?

Europe is not a place in which world communism can now afford to have any trouble. Because, obviously, world communism now has got to conquer nationalism, capture nationalism I should say, in Asia and Africa; that is its immediate and necessary objective. The Third World has got to be converted to communism before the problem of Europe, of old and tired Europe, can be dealt with. Therefore, very naturally, the party line allows Eurocommunists to play any role, so long as it is the sort of role that placates people and discourages any kind of anxiety about communism. Where possible, Eurocommunists have been allowed to go farther to the right, not only to become champions of democracy, but to become champions, as the Italian Communist parties have become, of law and order; and Eurocommunists make speeches, as Enrico Berlinguer does nowadays in Italy, that might have been spoken by Ronald Reagan on American television, in defense of the police and of property. All this is not, I think, a sign of democracy winning the support of European Communist parties. Rather it is the case that the political situation in Europe is becoming more and more unstable; and I don't think democracy has ever flourished, or grown out of an unstable situation of this kind. Democracy has usually come about where some kind of liberal constitutionalism has got deep roots, when there is a free system of government that can democratize itself.

Democracy, I think, is not a revolutionary type of political

institution. It cannot develop in a critical situation; it cannot
be produced by war—a point, I think, that Mr. Adler made.
You cannot spread democracy by war. It was the absurd belief
of Woodrow Wilson that you could somehow make a war
for democracy and set up democracy in the fragments of the
old Austrian Empire. But then of course Wilson was not a
real politician, he was a professor of political science.

Finally, I would like to refer to a very important point,
perhaps *the* most important point, of Mr. Adler's presentation. He put great stress on Aristotle's principle that man is
a political animal. He suggested that you can't keep nature
down, that a natural, political man will come out, and that
this political man must be democratic, because if every man
is a political man, he can only achieve his politicalness in a
democratical sort of society. I disagree with Mr. Adler on this
point because I believe that modern man is very largely denaturized, is a product of culture much more than nature. And
culture has become oppressive nowadays, even intrusive. It
is not education that shapes us, because what deserves the
name of education is something that we receive less and less
of, as Mr. Adler points out. What we receive is a culturalization imposed upon us by modern media, and modern institutions, and so forth, so that modern man is no longer the
political man as he was intended by God, by nature, or by
Aristotle to be. Nor does modern man know what politics is.
Modern ideologies—nationalism, communism, and so forth
—provide a kind of imitation political experience for people.
They receive satisfaction only from an ideology which is a
perverted religion, combined with a perverted politics. Ideology gives an emotional satisfaction which prevents man
from realizing his own nature as a political man. To assert
that man is a political animal is to me not sufficient grounds
for believing that democracy will come to flourish in the near
or perhaps even the distant future. But I think, perhaps, that
democracy will, with difficulties, survive and improve itself
in places where it is well rooted, and where people understand

what democracy is, provided that people's understanding of it is enlarged.

That is why I am very deeply impressed by what Mr. Adler said about education. I think that unless we do have a real liberal education, people will begin to forget what democracy really is, because all the modern ideologies are trying to sell us a false concept of democracy. To be a democrat, man, the *zoon politikon*, has to be either simple or very sophisticated—or very educated, should I say—and modernity has prevented us from being very simple without enabling us to be properly educated. This I think is the terrible danger of the present situation. And because I see no prospect of an escape from the dilemma, I'm afraid I cannot share the hopes put forth by Mr. Adler in his brilliant and impressive presentation.

BILL MOYERS:

All right. Mr. Adler has now begun, and has defended very forcefully the proposition that democracy should prevail everywhere in the world, that it can prevail everywhere it now exists and be improved there, and that in time it will probably come to exist elsewhere as well. Mr. Cranston has responded to this proposition, agreeing that democracy should prevail everywhere, but being skeptical that it can be realized anywhere except the parts of the world in which it now exists, and being uncertain that it can survive even there. I thought of the story of a man who said to a friend of his on Wall Street: "How do you feel about the market?" And he said, "Well, I am optimistic"; and he said, "Why then do you look so worried?" And he said, "Because I am not sure my optimism is justified." As Mr. Cranston spoke this afternoon, I was not sure about his optimism nor about Mr. Adler's. This evening we begin this session with the second response to Mr. Adler's presentation, from Anthony Quinton.

ANTHONY QUINTON:

Taking part in a disputation was something I was not too worried about because I knew it would be a disputation in a modern style. That comforted me; it meant it wasn't going to be in Latin. Furthermore, from the moderator's remarks I have the impression that it is not to be a debate, and so there is not going to be any dirty work, abuse, or snide observations about the appearance, antecedents, background, and so forth of the other participants. And I shall try to adhere to the high moral level of discussion of my two predecessors. But of course a disputation must involve a dispute, and so originally, in a rather sporting spirit, I think, I took on the job of devil's advocate. I agreed to be the man who would reject the view that democracy is an ideal form of government. As I say, I did this in a sporting spirit, like an actor working up the part of a child molester. But in the course of reflecting on Mr. Adler's presentation of the case for democracy and developing my own thoughts on the subject, in a primarily disputatious spirit, I totally convinced myself. So what I shall say this evening comes from the heart.

Now as we have had a break in between the presentation of Mr. Adler's three theses and Mr. Cranston's reflections on them, it might be a help if I started by reminding you of what they were. The first of them was that democracy ought to prevail everywhere. The second was that it can do so or, to be a little more detailed, that it can survive where it currently exists and be perfected there, and that it can be introduced into places where it currently does not exist. And finally, rather tentatively, Mr. Adler admitted that he thinks it *will* do all these things.

His arguments for these propositions were roughly, and in very sketchy terms, the following. For the view that democracy ought to obtain everywhere, he advanced the consideration that democracy, of all forms or systems of government, is alone perfectly just. And that itself rests on the further consideration that the justice which democracy peculiarly possesses is attributable to the fact that it alone secures to men their natural right to participate in the making of laws and in the management of government. This right in turn is based for Mr. Adler on the fact, as he conceives it to be, that all human beings are by nature political.

For the other two sides of the system of theses he presented, Mr. Adler argued that there are certain obstacles or impediments to democracy, both to its survival and perfection where it exists and to its introduction where it does not, and he contended that these can be removed. The first obstacle is the ignorance of the ruling majority, which is to be removed by liberal education. The second obstacle is inequality of condition, the nonexistence of social democracy, which he regards as a desirable if not essential prerequisite for effective political democracy, and he contends that equality of condition can be assured by increasing men's economic independence. And finally there is the dire influence of international anarchy, and Mr. Adler's main proposal to cope with that is some form of world government.

Now, more of Mr. Adler's time was spent on thesis number one, that democracy ought to prevail whether or not it can or will, and on the whole, allowing for a few marginal adjustments here and there, Mr. Cranston broadly agrees with that thesis. So already we have the materials for a division of labor. I shall largely concentrate on the first thesis, the one about the desirability of democracy, and leave the further defense of his position about the actual future prospects of democracy to Mr. Cranston. (That will be when we get further involved in the intimate small-arms fire of the disputation, rather than the present stage of remote artillery bombardment from prepared positions.) I shall concentrate on it because I see Mr. Adler as approaching this topic very much in the manner of a philosopher. It is no surprise that, as such, he should devote more of his time to thesis number one than to thesis number two or thesis three. These latter are, after all, in the realm of crude, raw, concrete fact. They don't lend themselves to general reasoning very much. You cannot draw inferences from the sort of messy historical circumstances in which human beings find themselves. It is interesting that even when Mr. Adler does discuss the question, "Can democracy survive and be spread further?" he does it in a rather abstract way by talking about three very general obstacles or impediments: ignorance, inequality of condition, and international anarchy. But when Mr. Cranston talks about the same subject, he does so more in the style of a student of form, a man hanging around the world-historical stables, looking at the various runners to see what sort of shape their hoofs are in.

Let us principally concentrate on the question: is democracy the ideal form of government? Mr. Adler in his presentation took a firm line when he said, "This is what I intend to mean by the word 'democracy,' " and by and large he stuck to it in what followed. Nevertheless, I find a certain difficulty in his definition, and I propose to be troublesome right at the outset with regard to it. It is not a thing I wish to deprive him of in any way. In the liberal spirit that I hope will animate our discussion here, let a thousand definitions of democracy bloom. But there is a certain complexity which we have to recognize in Mr. Adler's definition of democracy. I would counter his definition by the observation that what I primarily regard as democracy is only a part of what he takes to be democracy. That is, a number of other systems are included under or deserve to be called democracy, according to my definition, which would not count as democracy under his. Now, I do not think I am peculiar in this. I think most people would say, yes, that is how I understand democracy. I don't understand it in quite such an exclusive, quite such a complex, quite such a conjunctive way as Mr. Adler does. He says that democracy is a political system where you have constitutional government in which people's natural rights are protected, together with universal suffrage. But what I mean by democracy, and I suspect what most people mean by it, is that it is government by universal suffrage or some reasonably close approximation to it.

We have to bring in the notion of orders of magnitude here. I thought the figures for ancient Athens, even Mr. Adler's figures, did not show Athens in too bad a light from a democratic point of view. A five-figure number of persons had votes out of a six-figure population. There is an enormous difference between that and five hundred—a three-figure voting group, an oligarchy proper—with the same six-figure population. This qualification is, I think, part of the most widely accepted notion of democracy, which is that it is a form of government in which government depends upon universal suffrage or some reasonable approximation thereto. Suffrage in a democracy need not be absolutely universal, as Mr. Adler wants to insist.

Of course, this is only a prima facie account of what democracy is, one that says nothing about the constitutional character of the government, or about that government's protecting natural rights. And if we reflect on a system of government in which universal suffrage is the prime moving part, as it were, it must occur to us that such a feature is not enough. For universal suffrage to be worth anybody's bothering about it seriously, there must at least be the protection of some associated rights. It is after all worth noticing that all up-to-date totalitarian systems have universal suffrage. Ninety-eight percent of the registered populations will go to vote in a people's democracy, as the Russian colonies are quaintly called, and of those 98 percent voting, 97.42 percent will vote in favor of the central committee or the presidium or whatever it may be; 1 percent will vote against it; and then there will be some spoiled papers, and so forth. Similarly, Hitler relied from time to time on public voting by vast numbers of persons. That, too, was a travesty.

What makes universal suffrage worth bothering about is that there should be something to choose between; that there should be a genuine, really competitive, alternative to the incumbent regime about whose continuation in office the vote is being taken. Voting without alternatives is like having a toilet which is always engaged. There are seven toilets, somebody says, in this plane, but if they all have "Engaged" on them all the time, then there are in effect no toilets on the plane, as far as the suffering passengers are concerned. Something similar is true with regard to universal suffrage. There are a number of different things that can make it a mere pretense. There can be falsification of returns. There can be no secret ballot. All sorts of things can ensure a result of the form which is standard in uses of universal suffrage in totalitarian states. But any serious belief in the institution of universal suffrage involves at least the protection of two directly connected political rights, one of which is freedom of political association, the other, freedom of political expression. Such rights ensure that organizations other than the group that supports the current regime are able to get themselves organized and can put themselves in a position to communicate their policy, their alternative offer, to the broad mass of the electorate.

But even with these additions to universal suffrage, we are still a long way short of a constitutional system of government in general when we have got this far. That is, we have got the central notion of democracy as I understand it, but we have only part of what Mr. Adler means by the term. And the point I wish to make is that the rest of what he means, what he puts in besides universal suffrage and these associated rights, is something that is really a value that could exist without the democratic attachment and so has no essential connection with democracy proper at all.

One may ask, it is true, why Mr. Adler should not be allowed to define the word as he chooses, particularly as there is nothing wild or idiosyncratic about his definition. It is the definition, indeed, as Mr. Cranston has suggested, that would naturally occur to anyone reflecting on the English-speaking experience of democracy. In the English-speaking countries, Mr. Cranston pointed out, democracy grew generally within a framework either of an established constitutional system or, in the United States, of a system which, because of the past experience by the founders of the republic of English liberal constitutionalism, could draw on that experience. The democratic systems of government that prevail in the English-speaking world *are* democracies in the sense of Mr. Adler's rather exclusive definition.

But there is also, as Mr. Cranston also pointed out, a quite different tradition, which seems to him and to me to have a very fair title to be called democracy, the tradition that primarily stems from the French Revolution. In the somewhat disturbed history of France since 1789, France has consistently reverted at intervals, although often for not very long, to what one might call "democracy à la française." This is not direct democracy, which is a Swiss invention, both in theory and practice, although Jean-Jacques Rousseau, a Frenchman, was its great theorist. The French specialty is, rather, populistic democracy in which the idea is that the people, or the people's will, has been expressed through the institutions of universal suffrage. This is the absolutely sovereign factor in the political life of the community. If it is there in a strong form nothing can be done to override it, and nothing can properly obstruct its being put into effect.

Although distinctively French, this style of government is rather intermittent in France. There was a distinct popular will element in the revolutionary governments up to the Thermidorian reaction at the end of the Reign of Terror. Then there was government by extortion, in the manner of the racketeers, under Thermidor itself. And then there was Napoleon, the Restoration, Louis-Philippe's kind of quasi-English eighteenth-century government. In 1848 there was a short period of genuine democracy. Then what happened? In the election of 1851 a vast majority of the French electorate voted in effect for the abolition of democracy, because they voted for Prince Louis-Napoleon, who very shortly became the Emperor Napoleon III. That kind of populistic democracy has a tendency to demolish itself. The history of France repeatedly shows the liability of populistic democracy to lapse into Bonapartist rule by a charismatic leader.

Now it is quite understandable that Mr. Adler should have chosen the definition he did of democracy, with its English-speaking origin. But I think it simply picks out one kind of democracy, the democracy that prevails in the English-speaking world. It does not include something that has just as strong a claim to be called democracy, namely, the European, rationalistic, primarily French, tradition of populistic democracy which was originated in the French Revolution.

I think it is worth emphasizing this purely historical fact, because there have been two great democratic waves in English history. The first of these waves was during the English Civil War period, say 1640 to 1660. At that time a lot of very extreme democratic doctrine was produced by loose adherents of the winning side who were situated on the left-hand end of its political spectrum. With the Restoration of 1660 they all disappeared from view (perhaps they fled to the American colonies). From that time onward there is dead silence in England on the subject of democracy, a silence that persists until the outbreak of the French Revolution. But very soon after a large number of highly sympathetic fellow-traveling individuals came to the fore in England, such as Richard Price, the person primarily attacked in Edmund Burke's *Reflections on the French Revolution*. And all through the ensuing period, up until the Battle of Waterloo, the official government was engaged in repressing sympathizers with the French Revolution. The primary message they got from the French Revolution was that of populistic democracy, seen as sweeping away all the old constitutional obstructions to the will of the people. This was the second wave of democratic sentiment in England, of which something lasted as late as the Chartist movement of the mid-nineteenth century.

I do not bring up these matters simply for the sake of producing more historical material for us to consider. My point is that Mr. Adler's definition of democracy is complex because it involves two things: universal suffrage and constitutional government. I am arguing that there is no essential connection between universal suffrage and constitutional government, except to the rather small extent I have admitted, that universal suffrage, to be real at all, must allow for freedom of association and expression. I am in strong agreement with Mr. Adler about the desirability of constitutional government. Constitutional government in the English-speaking world in the last hundred years or so has become increasingly democratic. But it preceded democracy by my definition, let alone Mr. Adler's very much more stringent requirement of strict universal suffrage plus constitutional government. Therefore it is historically evident that it can function perfectly well without universal suffrage.

What I want to assert here (this is where I get really disputatious) is that despite his ostensible commitment to the view that democracy is constitutional government plus universal suffrage. Mr. Adler really thinks of democracy in a different way. At certain essential points in the argument which I shall enumerate, Mr. Adler thinks much as I and, I suspect, as most people do of democracy as simply a system of universal suffrage. I have three pieces of evidence for this claim. At one point, you may remember, he was speaking with great respect of John Stuart Mill. Mill believed that universal suffrage was dangerous because it made possible tyranny by a unified majority against all sorts of minorities to which it was hostile. That is one reason why simple, universal-suffrage democracy does not work well in countries where there is a substantial minority, clearly or permanently divided from a unified majority. Canada would be an example. In divided countries of this sort we see the tyranny of the majority to some extent at work, or anyway we see a minority contending that the tyranny of the majority is at work, and the very ferocity of the response of the minorities in question is some indication that the contention is not altogether false.

Now, as Mr. Adler recalls, Mill feared that the introduction of universal suffrage would produce majority tyranny, so he proposed various devices for putting a brake on it, keeping it under control. Mr. Adler says that these proposals, these devices, would have nullified democracy in practice; he says a little later on that to be in favor of universal suffrage while at the same time seeking somehow to undercut the rule of the majority is self-contradictory, since it is to be for and against democracy at the same time. And what I am saying is that when he says this, he in effect acknowledges that being committed to universal suffrage is the absolute essence of being in favor of democracy. Mr. Adler's own definition of democracy as constitutional government with the protection of natural rights in effect puts restraints on government, whether it be democratic or not.

I applaud this. It is a thing that should be done. What it implies is eliminating certain things from the sphere of possible and legitimate government activity, such as—let us say—the imposition of a single type of religious belief on the entire population. Suppose you get a majority with some passionate religious commitment confronting a minority with other commitments or none and, in its enthusiasm, desiring to impose that religious system on the minority. In that case the theory of pure democracy says that such a system should be imposed as the will of the people. Anyone who believes in constitutional government, on the other hand, must want to set limits to the legitimate sphere of government activity. And clearly Mr. Adler approves of limits of this kind.

Let me just mention a second example of Mr. Adler's implicit commitment to what I see as the common concept of democracy. When he gets down to argue his main thesis, that democracy is uniquely just as a form of government, the argument is almost entirely based on the thesis that universal participation by voting in the making of laws and in governmental activity generally is required by justice. The thing he lays all the emphasis on here is the activity of participation. The conclusion that universal suffrage is the institutional realization of the special justice of democracy arises entirely from this particular feature of it. And that is, as I say, really the distinctive feature of democracy, whereas Mr. Adler in his official definition makes it only a partial feature.

Finally, just a very brief mention of a third case which comes when he is talking about the obstacles to democracy in the discussion of the second thesis that democracy can survive and spread. When Mr. Adler talks about that, the prime obstacle he cites is the ignorance of the ruling majority. What he is really concerned with are defects in the operation of universal suffrage. He is not really concerned with what in his defining mood he says is also necessary to democracy, namely, constitutional government.

Now my main disputatious development of this is simply the following. The constitution sets out the idea of a limited government. I think that is absolutely splendid. I don't think it has to be democratic at all. I can give an obvious example, one to which Mr. Cranston alluded—the government of eighteenth-century England—as a case of nondemocratic constitutionalism. At that time there was a minute proportion of voters. Yet it was a period of great political liberty. That is merely to say it is perfectly possible to have a constitutional or limited government without democracy.

I go on to repeat something I have already sketched. If a constitutional form of government is democratic, it has to be limitedly democratic, or, in Mr. Adler's phrase, the rule of the majority has to be undercut, its scope has to be limited. I am not saying that the suffrage has to be limited in the numbers to whom it is given, but that the field in which it is exercised, the topics on which it is decisive—this has to be limited. The legislative and executive power of the people or its elected representatives must be confined in a constitutional system. From its very nature a constitution has to be independent of current popular will. That is what a constitution essentially is.

I speak with some fervor about these matters. One of the most worrying things about England at the moment is that we barely have a constitution. That leads some people to think we need a bill of rights. People often complain about imitating things from the United States; here is something I wish we would imitate. We have a sort of vestigial constitution, but it has been a matter of convention, understanding, practice—not a matter of explicit documents. Even something as sacred as habeas corpus is only a piece of ordinary legislation. It would be much more bold, of course, for any parliamentary majority to repeal the habeas corpus act than to repeal a supplementary provision of the whitefish storage registration act of 1958. The latter is going to leave people very much at ease, on the whole, except for the people who register the storage of whitefish. But measures which would leave most people very much other than at ease are only prohibited in England by convention, not by law. Here, because of the wisdom of your Founding Fathers, you have constitutional limits on government all nicely written down in eighteenth-century prose. Our limits come merely from tradition and in a rather nebulous form. (May I just add that your Founding Fathers weren't voted for by the majority of the population. And that they certainly were not voted for by anyone who lives now.)

The crucial point about a constitutional system of government in which there are limits set is that the rules that set the limits cannot be changed simply by the will of the majority. That is what really defines a constitutional system of government. These limiting rules cannot be changed by the existing executive or rulers, whoever they may be. Like Mr. Adler, I strongly favor constitutionalism. And my reason for doing so is of a very antique character, going back, I have no doubt, well beyond the Fathers of the Church, who must be the furthermost point of appeal in any decent disputation.

My reason is that I think that government is a necessary evil, in direct opposition to the view of the etatist tradition of which Mr. Cranston spoke, for which the state is a proper object of worship. I see the state as existing primarily to protect men and communities from the bad conduct of other men and communities. Since the government itself is a man, or more usually a community—a small one—it is capable of bad conduct itself, and a constitution is a precaution against that. Mr. Adler is well known to be fonder of Aristotle than of anyone else. He will hear the notes of that great thinker in what I am saying here. Aristotle had the idea of law as a transpersonal wisdom, a wisdom that does not suffer from the ups and downs of an individual personality but is the accumulated product of a great many different individuals slowly proceeding to work an idea out. That is the virtue of these precautions against a kind of human failing which can occur in governments, though governments exist to control it.

A constitution can limit a government in various ways. The one I have been emphasizing most, so far, is by circumscribing the powers of government so as to limit the fundamental rights of the government itself, and this protects the fundamental rights of the citizens. It can also divide the powers of government as is explicitly done in the American Constitution. As an Englishman I always feel that some parts of your judiciary aren't quite as much divided off as they might be, but you can come back at me with the hopelessly inadequate separation between legislative and executive in the British system. This has now gone so far that the legislature is a sort of large, cumbersome, woolly tail wagged by the executive dog, and it occasionally manages to pull the dog over. The last time this happened was in 1940, as far as I can remember.

A third sort of constitutional limitation, again much more noticeable in this country than in my own smaller, more congested one, is the division of governmental power between the center and the regions. I think this highly desirable. People often refer to the sense of powerlessness that the individual feels in large societies. Even if there is effective choice and universal suffrage, the party choices may not be what he wants, especially if a lot of the collective matters in which he has an interest are decided remotely in Paris, as everything is decided in France, or in Whitehall, where nearly everything is decided in England. You have a similar emotion about the remoteness and impersonality of Washington in this country. But because of your federal Constitution, because of the fact that the federal government has only its enumerated powers and the reserved powers are still allotted to the states, your position in this country is different. There is still a genuine reality to the taxing power of the states. States do have a taxing power and dispose of their own tax revenues. And an American state is a much more intimate and local thing than the community at large.

I applaud all of this, and I also applaud what might be called a social parallel to Mr. Adler's notion of social democracy. That is, roughly speaking, pluralism, the fostering of nonpolitical kinds of power, in churches, businesses, trade unions—in things generally other than organized political parties. Of course there is always danger; here, too, just consider the three centers of nonpolitical power I mentioned. They can be far more tyrannous than political parties themselves. They can dominate political parties and exercise power through them. I prefer them to be genuinely independent of the political parties. That leaves a large mass of decision within a community beyond the direct reach of professional politicians and their servants in the bureaucracy.

In thus agreeing with Mr. Adler in favor of constitutionalism, I might at the same time be thought to disdain democracy. Am I self-contradictorily *for* government and *against* it? Well, yes, I am for government and against it, but, I think, quite consistently. I am for as little of it as I can get away with. I take much the same view of it as I do of surgery. In an ideal world, what necessitates surgery would not exist;

but the world is not as ideal as that. In the world as it is, surgery is necessary. People often seem inclined to have more surgery than is strictly necessary. On the other hand, they may get a great deal of direct benefit out of surgery whether the operation comes out perfectly or not. To say that (and one might say exactly the same of government) is not to say surgery is not vitally important. Like half of us in this room, I expect I would not be here now if modern surgery did not exist. But even so, I think there are limits to its use. I am even a little hostile to various forms of ornamental or cosmetic surgery, just as I am to various sorts of ornamental or cosmetic political action; by that I mean what is not necessitated by the removal of an evident evil but is carried on for the purpose of producing some supposed good. I think you look prettier with your old nose.

So far Mr. Adler and I largely agree. What we disagree about is this: democracy, as I see it, is among the dangerous types of absolute or unlimited government. Indeed, I suspect absolute democracy may be more dangerous than absolute government of any other kind because it will be self-righteous, while the others will be less morally self-confident. A dictator will say it's only me against them, but if it is all or most of us we shall be at ease in crushing the residual few we collectively feel disposed to crush. The mere number of us agreeing about this may lead us to feel we are wholly justified in doing so.

Let me turn then to my final observation on Mr. Adler's argument for democracy. It is an argument for universal suffrage without any explicit limitations of scope. Mr. Adler says that only a system of universal suffrage is perfectly just, because it is a natural right to participate in government. I quite agree that if there is a natural right to participate in government, any system in which that natural right isn't respected is not completely or perfectly just, because that one natural right is not respected in it. But I claim that if the powers of government are not constitutionally limited, then, even where this comes about because of universal suffrage, even though the right, if there is a right, of universal political participation is granted, nevertheless other natural rights may well be overridden. In other words, the cost of this right to participate in terms of other rights or other good things, socially good things generally, may be very expensive.

On the whole, the history of powerful and well-established majorities shows them to be hostile to freedom. To start with, the first great effective democratic majority of the modern period of history, which I have already mentioned, produced the French Reign of Terror. At various times in the history of this country there has been an absurd overreaction, with a great deal of popular support, to the external menaces of communism. You can be anticommunist without attacking somebody with a mild view about the redistribution of income. But when you cannot get at the Russians, the tendency is to visit your wrath on some harmless being who has been reading George Bernard Shaw. If the eye is sufficiently incarnadined with prejudice, even the faintest pink looks red. To take a slightly different example, in Great Britian in the postwar period there has been considerable migration of blacks—from excolonial nations in Africa, from the West Indies, and from the former Asian possessions of the British Crown. There is a great deal of mass hostility to this immigration. It is only the highly undemocratic, high-minded, paternalistic, upper-class, snobbish, oligarchical insistence of government that has allowed them to keep coming in and has kept Enoch Powell and other violently hostile individuals from making life even worse for the immigrants than it is already. What would have happened if this had been a matter of plebiscitary decision? Given a direct democratic participation by the whole populace, if Enoch Powell were to propose that every black person not born in the United Kingdom should be given a sum of money or a ticket and a period of three months in which to leave the country, I am strongly inclined to suspect that the proposal would receive majority support. I also think it highly beneficial that such a proposal was never put. That is a ground for saying that unrestricted, uncontrolled majorities are very dangerous things. It illustrates my thesis that justice in respect of the *form* of government, which is what Mr. Adler emphasizes, may lead to a much larger loss of justice or other virtuous qualities in the *acts* of government.

Consider it from a slightly different angle. Two men are offered a job. One has worked as the second in command for a very long time. The other is a new, bright upstart. Justice, you might say, requires that the first of them be appointed. But what if he had made life absolutely intolerable for everybody in the organization, whereas the second man, a very reasonable, pacific, and diplomatic individual, would treat everybody justly? There are simply two different justices in conflict here. One is the justice of making the appointment, the other the justice of the act or consequences of the appointment.

For the moment, I have assumed that universal suffrage is, as Mr. Adler says, just. I say that even if it is, that is not a complete argument for it. But is it just? Is the assumption correct? Mr. Adler's reason for saying so is that all men are by nature political. There may be an element of appeal to authority here, for there is a sentence much like this at the beginning of Aristotle's *Politics*, a work that I know Mr. Adler greatly admires. But Greek being what it is, it doesn't mean quite what Mr. Adler means by his very similar form of words. When Aristotle said that man is a political animal, he meant that men don't realize their potentialities unless they are members of a society larger than a minimal domestic unit. Get off the farm, is what was implied by Aristotle's remark about the political nature of man. But Mr. Adler has something quite different in mind, and I am not entirely clear what it is. Is it that all men want to vote? It seems clear that they do not. Is it that they would all be better for doing so? John Stuart Mill thought something like that. It is his reason for putting up with the dangers he saw in universal suffrage. He thought it would make people better, more public-spirited, more responsible.

Mr. Adler simply affirms the thesis that men are by nature political, but he does not argue for it. He offers what is in fact a rhetorical appeal. He says the alternative is to treat men as children or slaves or foreigners. I do not think that is quite correct. In restricting the vote, you give a right to some men who may be more qualified to exercise it which you do not give to others. It is a very loose analogy to say that that is immediately to divide human beings into two groups: parents and children, or slave owners and slaves. Let me consider myself as a political being. I have voted from time to time. I have never been a member of a political party. I am interested in politics in the way many of us may be interested in football. That interest does not depend on participation. I was going to say that politics for me is a spectator sport, and then I realized that I am more like a sports columnist since I do earn some of my living by talking in an abstract and generalized fashion about politics. But that is consistent with not being involved directly in politics. In fact I vote out of a sense of shame; the opportunity exists and I feel I should go and do it. I talk with people about politics, and I may be mildly persuasive in one direction (the one I intend) or the other, as the case may be. But I do not feel any very pronounced need for it. I am much more interested in being able to express my views about it and also to complain if the occasion warrants it, than in actually organizing political activity. Nevertheless I can see a reason why despite that cool attitude, I should have some interest in such activity. It is the interest the traveler on a reliable ferry has in a life belt. I want the right to be available in case dire circumstances arise in which I need to use it.

To generalize this rather autobiographical excursion a little, I think there is a better case for the justice of universal suffrage than the one that Mr. Adler mentioned. It is that everyone has a vital interest in the actions of government. I do not think that this, while it is a better case, is a terribly strong one. We all have a vital interest in the actions of doctors, but we do not claim a right to be present and vote at meetings of the medical association. And there is a counterargument which I have mentioned: the measure of power that goes with the vote should be given only to those qualified to exercise it. And there is a further counterargument to that. The qualifications for voting are very hard to agree on and, even if they are agreed on, they are not very easy to identify. In that situation the simplest thing is to give the vote to all.

As a practical matter, I take the following view. Where universal suffrage already exists, I am strongly in favor of letting it alone. It would be highly offensive to propose that any particular class of persons should be called upon to give up a right they have long exercised. And apart from being offensive to them, the frustration of habitual or settled expectations is objectionable. Of course it is sometimes necessary that habitual and settled expectations should be frustrated. But where there is no particular clear and evident necessity for interfering, leave things alone.

There is a well-known argument for democracy which I often favored in the past. But Mr. Adler has caused me to reflect about this in seeking to do my duty as a disputant. And I have come to see that it is not really an argument for democracy. It is an argument for the peaceful removal of bad governments. If you live under a nondemocratic system, and there is a bad government, then to get rid of it there has to be a certain amount of fighting in the street. In a democracy, all that is required is making pencil marks on pieces of paper, or pulling of levers, or pressing of buttons, or whatever the local technique is. But even that does not require *universal* suffrage. All it requires is some class of persons considerably larger than those directly involved in ruling to whom the ruler should be made accountable.

I go back to good old eighteenth-century England again. As long as officeholders are periodically accountable to some set of critics, there will be a device for getting rid of them if they get badly out of hand. Mr. Adler very properly calls upon his opponents to supply an alternative. Mine is essentially constitutionalism. There should be representatives for the sake of accountability, but just to endorse that is not to endorse anything like universal suffrage. Constitutionalism is part of what Mr. Adler explicitly says he favors. I maintain that it is quite independent of the thing he associates it with, that which I think is the essence of democracy, namely universal suffrage. It is compatible with universal suffrage, but it is not required by universal suffrage, and it does not require it. What it is opposed to, and quite incompatible with, is constitutionally unlimited government by the people—wholly unfettered majoritarianism in the French Revolution style. As I said a little while ago, I favor universal suffrage where it is already established, but only where the universal according of the right to vote is combined with firm constitutional checks on the scope of its exercise.

BILL MOYERS:

Thank you, Mr. Quinton. We will now give Mr. Adler an opportunity to reply to the criticism that you and Mr. Cranston have offered of his original presentation. Then I will let the three of you continue the discussion by yourselves. Mr. Adler?

ADLER:

I am surprised, Mr. Quinton, that you did not catch the reason why I proposed a complex definition of democracy—as constitutional government with universal suffrage. The reason is that a good definition should be constructed by combining a genus with a difference. When I use the term "constitutional democracy," constitutional government is the genus; the only differentiating trait is the set of qualifications for citizenship and public office. In constitutional government the two kinds of offices are those of the citizen and those of the public officials. The primary office is citizenship. Constitutional government is a government in which the citizens rule and are ruled in turn. This means that citizens out of office are the permanent principal rulers. Citizens who are for a time and only for a time in office are the transient instrumental rulers. Citizenship is the common status of both citizens in office and citizens not in office.

When any of the disqualifications for citizenship or public office are unjust, whether they are based on sex, race, property, or color, you have an unjust constitution. I use the word "oligarchy" for any unjust constitution and the word "democracy" for a just constitution in which the qualifications for citizenship and public office satisfy the criteria of justice.

Let me comment on the Constitution of the United States. I think Mr. Quinton is wrong about that. The persons who took part in the constitutional convention *were* picked by the people to represent them, so far as the franchise extended in that day and age. The Constitution was drafted by representatives of the people. It was then submitted to the people for ratification. It was adopted by their consent. I am consenting right now to the Constitution of the United States by living in this country, by participating in its government, by voting, by taking part in its political life. That is what John Locke meant by "tacit" consent.

I am sure Mr. Quinton is glad to have me agree with him that the unlimited power of a majority produces the worst form of government possible. But I wish to defend what I said about John Stuart Mill. Mr. Quinton charges me with having done what I said Mill should not have done—nullifying majority rule. Mill's proposals for proportional representation and for plural voting would have given weight to a minority over the majority. That would have nullified majority rule. I am not nullifying majority rule when I say that the majority should not be allowed to enact unjust legislation. That merely limits the majority from transgressing the rights enshrined in the Constitution. It is not a nullification of majority rule but a proper limitation of it. When the Supreme Court declares legislation unconstitutional because it violates rights, it does not nullify, it merely limits, majority rule.

Let me turn now to the question about man as a political animal. Man is a social and political animal in the sense that he cannot live well, he cannot realize his potentialities, except in a political community. That is true, but it is not the whole truth. When Aristotle describes constitutional government, he says two things about it: (1) it is a government of free men and equals; and (2) it is a government in which the citizens rule and are ruled in turn. To say that man is a political animal is to say that he should be governed as a free man and as an equal, not as a slave or a subject. He should have political liberty, which is to say he should live under laws in the making of which he has a voice.

I would like Mr. Quinton to consider the enfranchisement of women. I am not satisfied with Mr. Quinton's concession that he would not seek to abolish universal suffrage *now that it exists*. I want him to consider the position he would have taken at the beginning of this century.

Were the suffragettes right or wrong? Was their demand for citizenship purely emotional? Were they not asking for a human right? Did they not wish to have equal participation in political life? Was this not a rightful claim on their part?

Mr. Quinton and I agree about the desirability of constitutional government. That much is clear. But I would like to have him go farther. I would like to persuade him that universal suffrage is also desirable. You cannot have universal suffrage without constitutional government, but you can have constitutional government without universal suffrage. That, in my judgment, is less desirable than constitutional democracy.

Mr. Quinton, Mr. Cranston, and I all abominate absolute or unlimited power in the hands of the people. That is the kind of unconstitutional democracy which Plato regarded as the worst form of government. We all agree that it is the worst form of government. There is no merit in popular power *by itself*; the merit lies only in universal suffrage under the limitations of constitutional government.

Now let me address myself to Mr. Cranston's main points for a moment. Here the verbal differences are slight. He prefers the phrase "constitutional democracy" to "political democracy." I am quite happy to accept that change in language. But I would like to make one correction in the history of the subject that is of some importance. "Direct democracy" and "representative democracy" do not differ essentially if both are constitutional governments. Constitutional governments can be divided in two ways: according to limited or extended suffrage; and according to whether the citizens act directly or through elected representatives.

I would like to agree with Mr. Cranston that the theory of representation is very difficult to state in a satisfactory manner. The most difficult chapter in Mill's essay on representative government is his chapter on representation. Should representatives exercise independent judgment? Or should they comply with the wishes of their constituents? That is a very difficult question. Upon a sound solution of this problem the soundness of democratic rule depends.

Leaving that aside for a moment, I would like to deal with Mr. Cranston's further point. He agrees with my interpretation of the proposition that man is a political animal, but he then goes on to say something which frightens me, namely, that human nature has now been so denaturized, or so badly nurtured, so perversely nurtured, contrary to its natural tendencies, that, far from being fit to rule and be ruled as free men, man in the modern national state is not fit to be the citizen of a constitutional democracy.

That is a very challenging statement. It may mean that the future of democracy is very dim, indeed. My response to Mr. Cranston's challenge is the kind of response that Rousseau made to Aristotle in criticizing Aristotle's doctrine of natural slavery. He said that Aristotle was right about slavery, but that he mistook the effect for the cause. If a man is born into slavery, and brought up as a slave, he will appear to have a slavish nature when he is mature. We will be deceived about his nature. His nurturing cannot obliterate his nature but can overlay and conceal it.

We are by nature political and should be ruled as free men and equal, but if we are nurtured as slaves, we will not be able to act according to our nature. To prevent this from happening, we must see that men are nurtured in a way that befits their nature. Upon this, the future of democracy depends.

Moyers: Thank you, Mortimer. We will take that as your reply to the replies you have had. Let's see if Mr. Cranston and Mr. Quinton think it satisfactory. Mr. Quinton, you go first.

Quinton: I am not going to give a long address here, but I just want to take up Mr. Adler on one or two points. It often seems to me that the study of the Greek world leads one to find more and more things that the Greeks didn't have. For example, I can remember the day I was taught that they didn't have the notion of duty. And I don't think they had the notion of constitution in the sense in which I and, I suspect, Mr. Adler both take the term. Neither of us takes it as Aristotle does when he says that *every* state has a constitution. What he means is simply that every state has some formula whereby the choice of who is to rule is specified. And of course it is true, there isn't any government unless there is some kind of formula for this. But that is quite different from what we are talking about. At least it is quite different from what *I* mean by constitutional government, which is at least minimally a system of government where a whole lot of limitations are set on the activities the government may engage in.

Adler: Aristotle does use the word "constitution" loosely sometimes to mean any form of government. But the clear passages in his writings are those in which he draws a distinction between constitutional government, or political rule, and royal rule—rule by a man without a constitution.

Quinton: But when a man rules without what you and I would call a constitution, and without what Aristotle calls a constitution when he is being clear, as you say, such a man still *rules*; no one else does. Even there, I mean, you have a sort of minimal formula, a rule by rule, if you like. In every state there is some general principle that applies at all times which determines who of this collection of people does the ruling and who doesn't. And that is enough for Aristotle to say that such a state has a constitution, though he means more by the term at other times. My point is, we don't find him using the term consistently in our sense. Though, by the way, there is, even among us, an accepted use of the term "constitution" as meaning nothing more than the arrangement of offices.

Adler: In the case of the United States, offices with limited powers assigned to them.

Quinton: You are beginning to get to something else when you talk about that—about legitimate activity. You are talking about something like the Bill of Rights. That is what makes the American Constitution constitutional in our sense.

Adler: I don't think it does. It wasn't part of the Constitution originally—

Quinton: I think it does in the sense in which I want to defend it and in the light of what you say justice is—having a government duly constituted, giving general protection to natural rights, pursuing the common good or general welfare, and assuring universal suffrage.

Adler: I would agree that constitutionalism in the Western tradition sometimes has had different aspects. Charles McIlwain, in his book *Constitutionalism, Ancient and Modern*, sharply distinguishes the constitutionalism of the Greeks, of the Middle Ages, and of modern times. But there is a common strain in these three kinds of constitutionalism. You have constitutionalism all the way through. I agree, though, that it is not until the eighteenth century that you get explicit declarations of rights. In that sense, Greek constitutionalism is weak.

Moyers: Mr. Cranston, do you have anything to add?

Cranston: I am not well qualified for the exegesis of Aristotle, but he did indicate that he thought some mixed form of government or constitution, which would have elements of aristocracy, monarchy, and democracy, was probably the most preferable. And I really think that that should not be forgotten. We should not become too enthusiastic about democracy and lose sight of the merits of monarchy and aristocracy. I think one of the reasons everyone feels uneasy nowadays about developments in England, for example, is that the House of Lords is progressively moving from being a hereditary institution toward one of appointed peers, and there is thus being lost an element of representativeness such as you have in a hereditary house where the members are in effect chosen by God or, if you please, by chance: it is a providential aristocracy. Nowadays the members are chosen by the chief of state and are therefore party hacks—of varying degrees of intellectual distinction, to be sure. It is instructive to compare the debates of the House of Lords in, say, 1926 with those of 1976. The first were perhaps lacking in intellectual brilliance, but they contained strong elements of character and I think are very important to the continued existence of constitutional government. And on the whole I think it very important that democracy in England should not lose this aristocratic element, as I think it desirable that democracy in America not lose its monarchical element, such as an independent executive provides. There seems to have been some doubt about the wisdom of this during the Nixon era, but I gather it is now overcome.

Moyers: May I ask a question? What makes universal suffrage just?

Adler: The securing of a natural right. The right to be ruled as free men and equal. To be ruled as a free man is to be ruled by a government which is based on voluntary consent. I say every man has a right to that kind of liberty. That right of liberty is inseparable from the right of political suffrage.

Moyers: Is any right more important than this right of participation?

Quinton: I should say that habeas corpus and protection against arbitrary rule or the invasion of property are more important.

Adler: Mr. Quinton has implied that the right of suffrage will militate against the protection afforded by these other rights. I think that is wrong. In a truly constitutional government the right to suffrage won't do that because the majority with the suffrage will not be able to violate those rights constitutionally.

Quinton: I am reflecting on recent English experience. We have a situation at the moment where the ostensible government exercises its authority as directed by organized labor. The demand of organized labor is that the freedom of the press should be abolished. Legislation has been pushed through to bring this about. It hasn't been applied yet, but the material is there. Now there ought to be a constitutional provision to prevent that.

Adler: That is a defect of the British constitution.

Quinton: It is.

Adler: Unfortunately, you have in Great Britain unlimited majority rule in the sense that an act of Parliament can't be declared unconstitutional. One of the great inventions of the United States is the judicial review of legislation with the ability to declare both executive acts and legislative acts unconstitutional. The only way an act of Parliament can be undone is by another act of Parliament.

Moyers: Mr. Cranston said that the constitution is there to ensure that the state does that which it has to do and no more. I thought I saw you shaking your head negatively when he said that.

Adler: There are two often-repeated little maxims, one of which Mr. Quinton has used himself, with which I disagree. The first says that that government is best which governs least. It is often attributed to Thomas Jefferson, but I don't believe he ever said or meant it. The second one is just as bad—the one which says that that government is best which governs most. I say that that government is best which governs most justly—which secures justice, protects all rights, sees that no one is injured, and pursues the common good. The *amount* of government is indifferent. It is indifferent because there can be no loss of liberty under a just government. Under a just government every man has as much liberty as he has any right to. More than that would not be liberty, it would be license.

Cranston: What about a government which has a different idea of justice from yours? I am thinking of the matter of affirmative action in the United States, but it might be other forms of social justice that were being sought. Well, they certainly infringe upon liberty. Equal opportunity legislation cannot but infringe upon liberty.

Adler: You are quite right, and therefore my claim depends on the view of justice that I take. In my view, justice consists of three things. It consists in acting for the common good, in treating equals equally and unequals unequally in proportion to their inequality, and in securing natural rights. The policies you mentioned are difficult to reconcile with these principles. It can certainly be argued that when the government adopts such policies, injustice will result. I think I can defend my three-part statement of what justice is. And by that criterion, I can say that a government that governs justly infringes upon no one's liberty. Anyone who denies this is asking for more liberty than he has a right to.

Moyers: But you are saying, are you not, that in a constitutional democracy men will govern justly?

Adler: I am not saying that at all. Like most governments, the government of the United States is unjust in many ways, and was at one time even more unjust than it is now. Just think how recently we have done justice to one-half of the whole population—if, indeed, we have done it yet. Apart from that, think of our recognition of economic rights and remember that it goes back only as far as 1944, with FDR's State of the Union Message. The right to earn a living, to have a decent amount of free time, to have a variety of economic goods—these rights were not recognized in this country as among the natural rights that government ought to protect until that time. And of course there were many ways in which the government of the United States operated unjustly between 1865 and 1900, though in accordance with its Constitution as then interpreted.

Moyers: Then why is it not good to accept Mr. Cranston's definition of the constitution as something to ensure that the state does what it has to do and no more?

Adler: Well, but what *does* it have to do and no more? I say it has to do justice and no more.

Moyers: Mr. Cranston, do you agree?

Cranston: I agree if I am allowed to specify the justice I believe in, but not if Mr. Adler is allowed to define it.

Moyers: Well, what would be your definition?

Cranston: I believe justice must firmly maintain all civil and political rights. Whereas I am afraid (I am very sorry to say) that Mr. Adler believes we ought to incorporate the so-called social and economic rights into the sphere of government activity. And this seems to me really to open the floodgates to the death of liberty. Socialism does that, in my view.

Quinton: The weak element in Mr. Adler's account of justice from some points of view is his first clause, about justice being the pursuit of the common good. Because on the whole I take it we old Whigs here want the common good to be pursued largely by individual energies. And if the common good is going to be pursued by government, it is not going to be pursued by individual energies. I do, however, think, unlike Maurice, that government does have economic responsibilities.

Adler: I think I *am* a socialist, though you will perhaps not agree. I don't mean a communist. I mean that I think everyone should participate equally, up to a certain minimum, in the general economic welfare. No one should be deprived of the economic goods that all men need to live decent human lives. I agree with Abraham Lincoln that, apart from this, government should do for the people only what they cannot do for themselves. The people, individually or in their corporations and associations, should do what they can and should leave to government only those things that they individually or collectively cannot do.

Moyers: Can we have, at least, from each of you, a concise statement in which you sum up your position with respect to the argument that Mr. Adler has made?

Quinton: Well, I thought it was a noble proclamation of faith, but if we look around at the total history of man, we can see what men have settled for. All over the world they have settled for systems that require only their obedience. And I acknowledge my brotherhood in the species that accepts this state of affairs. Happily? Not happily; I am not entirely happy; who's entirely happy? But I have no doubt most of them are reasonably content, as I am. They don't expect anything much better, as I don't.

Cranston: I think probably in everybody there is some spark of desire for liberty which sometimes expresses itself as a desire to participate in politics. I don't think there is a natural right, a universal right, to participate in politics, even though there is a natural right to liberty. I think there is a civil right in societies which are so organized as to have civil rights—where they have parliaments, tax rolls, and that sort of thing. In such societies, people can reasonably claim a right to vote because of their participation in paying taxes and doing duties imposed by the society. And as more and more people are incorporated into civil society as taxpayers, the right to vote is progressively enlarged. But I think it absurd to say there is a universal right to participate in politics, irrespective of any duties done. Up to the late nineteenth century, women as a class very rarely even thought about a vote; they felt that their husbands or fathers represented them. Now, of course, the place of women has changed. They have *earned* the right to vote. Foreigners still don't claim the right to participate, however; they would think it inappropriate to do so. For a vote is *not* a universal right. It is an earned right.

Adler: Could I ask my colleagues here whether I am misreading history when I say, looking at the last 6,000 years of civilization, the period since the emergence of cities (a very short period, indeed, in the total life on earth), that during this period political liberty has been achieved by an extraordinarily vigorous fight? This seems to me to indicate the high esteem in which it is held by men. The Greeks, who were a very small group, stood up against the Persian hordes because they thought that, with constitutional government, they had, as citizens, rights of a kind that under the Great King of Persia they would not have. The Roman republic threw off a monarchy because men wanted political liberty badly enough to demand a different form of government, and again it was political liberty of the sort I connect with citizenship and suffrage. And the fight has continued. In fact, if you look at human society in the twentieth century, I would say that we have made great advances beyond the Greeks, the Romans, and the Middle Ages in the realization of the right to political freedom. Don't you think that is a sign of progress?

Quinton: Yes, but I think there is another lesson to be drawn, which is the cyclic lesson. Most of human history—recorded history—is a kind of dark corridor, like a badly lit tunnel. Every now and then there is a bit of light somewhere, where the individual human being emerges from the sort of awful anonymity in which most human beings have always lived. One freedom is political freedom; I don't wish to deny that. But it doesn't necessarily have to be universal suffrage. It seldom has been that, even in these lighted places. In any case they come and go, these lighted places, and there doesn't seem to be an increase in their frequency over time. Someone like Oswald Spengler might look and see a sort of fitful groping toward freedom and from this draw the conclusion that the desire for freedom is very strong. But that doesn't mean you can't reasonably entertain the opposite notion—that such an idea is by no means certain of historical fulfillment, that on the contrary, it is only now and then, with great difficulty, actually realized.

Moyers: Mr. Cranston, would you like to ask a last question of Mr. Adler?

Cranston: No.

Moyers: All right. I guess that's a constitutional form of restraint. Thank you, gentlemen. Our thanks also to all of you who have listened to this discussion.

ENDNOTES

1. See *Great Books of the Western World,* first edition, vol. 43, pp. 325–442.
2. See *The Great Ideas Today, 1966,* pp. 454–528.

THREE

Robert Bork: The Lessons
to Be Learned

1

Robert Bork in his book entitled *The Tempting of America: The Political Seduction of the Law* reflects the lessons he learned from the Senate hearings on his nomination for a seat on the United States Supreme Court, culminating in a majority vote against him. The book attempts to teach the American public about the basic political opposition in this country between those on the conservative side of the conflict who understand and respect the principles of our constitutional democracy and Bork's opponents on the liberal side who, in his judgment, have little understanding or respect for those principles.

Judge Bork's book is testimony to the dismal failure of the Senate hearings to focus on the heart of the problem concerning his nomination. Though the negative decision reached was, in my judgment, a correct one, most of the questioning of the candidate that occurred and most of the overheated oratory directed against him could not help but give him the impression that the attack on him was entirely a political machination. It seemed to him all fire and fury, with little or no light thrown on the basic jurisprudential and philosophical issues with respect to which a candidate for the Supreme Court should be expected to take a stand and defend his position.

The miscarriage of the Senate hearings as conducted is all the more difficult to comprehend and condone in view of the ample paper trail that the Senate was afforded, drawn from Robert Bork's many published articles written when he was a professor of law at Yale University. Readily available were his explicitly expressed views on how the Constitution should be interpreted, on specific constitutional questions, on the proper role of the Supreme Court in the judicial review of legislation enacted by the state governments, as well as on broader questions about natural rights and about the justice of laws enacted by legislative majorities.

On all these subjects, so relevant to the consideration of his fitness, there was not the slightest unclarity or doubt about where Professor Bork stood. He was not asked whether, in his subsequent career as a federal judge, he had changed his mind on any of these crucial points. He was not asked whether, as an appointed justice of the Supreme Court, he would decide cases before him in the light of his basic philosophy of law and government and his well-known views about human rights and liberties.

The crucial issue was not whether judicial restraint should be exercised in the Supreme Court's review of legislation by Congress and by state legislatures. Of course, it should be.

It was not whether trying to discover the original intent of the writers of the Constitution and of its amendments can always be followed by adhering strictly to the letter of the law. Reasonable men can disagree and have disagreed on this point.

It was not whether Bork would turn out to be a conservative or a liberal member of the Court or, perhaps, a moderate centrist, as these terms are currently understood.

It was not whether Judge Bork's prior judicial decisions indicated that he might be against legalized abortion under any conditions, against the equal protection of women by our laws, against the civil rights of blacks, against affirmative action, against antitrust legislation, and so on.

Reasonable citizens—and reasonable justices of the Supreme Court—may disagree about where the Constitution stands on these substantive legal issues, and also about the reasonableness of dissent from judicial precedents on all these matters.

The lessons that should have been learned by the general public, and even by Robert Bork, were not learned because the right questions were not asked—questions about human rights and liberties; about the tyranny of the majority and whether an unjustly treated minority can appeal to the Supreme Court for the nullification of legislation because it is *unjust* even though it is not *unconstitutional*; about the objective validity of prescriptive judgments of what ought to be sought and what ought to be done; about what is good and evil, right and wrong.

The nominee might even have been asked whether he thought the eighteenth-century Constitution, allowing as it did for the disenfranchisement of women, blacks, and the poor who could not pay poll taxes, was or was not unjust; and if he said that no objectively valid principles of justice enabled him to answer that question, he might still have been asked on what grounds the Thirteenth, Fourteenth, Fifteenth, Nineteenth, and Twenty-fourth amendments were adopted in subsequent years and whether they represented progress in the direction of social justice, regress, or neither. [1]*

These are, of course, philosophical questions, but it is precisely Robert Bork's fundamental philosophical errors, manifest in the answers he would have given to these questions, that would have provided a sound basis for denying him a seat on the Supreme Court. In saying this, I must add at once that, in committing these philosophical mistakes, Bork

* Endnotes for this chapter begin on page 212.

is in good company. He is no worse than Mr. Justice Holmes, Mr. Justice Frankfurter, and Judge Learned Hand. [2]

The writings and opinions of Mr. Justice Holmes clearly reveal the same brand of legal and philosophical positivism that Robert Bork's writings betray. Holding in reserve a fuller statement of what legal positivism entails, it is enough for the moment to say that legal positivism places law on a plane apart from any moral norms. It regards all such norms as being subjective in nature; thus they cannot be treated as having objective validity. Positive law, however, in the sense that it is the law of the state, can be ascertained without regard to moral considerations.

I have no hesitation in placing Mr. Justice Frankfurter and Judge Learned Hand in the same group in the light of arguments with them that Robert Hutchins and I had when he was president of the University of Chicago and I was professor of the philosophy of law in its law school.

Regarding the jurists just named, there is no question about their high degree of competence in dealing with cases arising in terms of the Anglo-American common law; nor is there any question about their judicial competence in dealing with many cases in which the strict constitutionality of a law is at issue. But there are still other cases that come before the Supreme Court in which it is not *unconstitutionality*, but *injustice*—the violation of human rights and liberties—that calls for rectification and redress.

It is with respect to such cases that the Supreme Court's power of judicial review is the only remedy for the tyranny of the majority. The great nineteenth-century proponents of democracy, John Stuart Mill and Alexis de Tocqueville, declare that democracy's chief defect is the oppression of minorities by tyrannical majorities acting in self-interest. [3]

The United States is the only constitutional government in the world that has a remedy, in its power of judicial review, that can nullify majority legislation that is unjust. Constitutional democracy can strive to sustain in practice the two-sided demands recognized by Thomas Jefferson in his First Inaugural Address when he said:

> All . . . will bear in mind this sacred principle, that though the will of the majority is in all cases to prevail, that will to be rightful must be reasonable; that the minority possess their equal rights, which equal law must protect, and to violate would be oppression.

Holmes, Frankfurter, Hand, and Bork confess that they find no grounds for doing what must be done in these crucial cases in which the majority legislation is unjust without being unconstitutional. [4] That, in my judgment, is sufficient reason for being opposed to them, either as justices of the Supreme Court, or as candidates for that position.

2

If the senators conducting the inquiry concerning Bork's fitness for a seat on the Supreme Court had asked their staffs to do just a little research into the legal philosophy expressed in his professional writings, they would have readily discovered Bork's explicit answers to the questions they should have asked but did not.

Professor Bork declared that no "system of moral or ethical values . . . has [any] objective or intrinsic validity of its own." [5] He was indoctrinated with this skepticism about the objective validity of all value judgments when he was a young student at the University of Chicago, inculcated by a philosophy department committed to the twentieth-century doctrine of noncognitive ethics, which holds that value judgments are subjective prejudices, expressing wishes or commands.

This doctrine had its roots in early modern thought. The sixteenth-century French essayist Montaigne, echoing Shakespeare, wrote that "there is nothing good or evil, but thinking makes it so." The seventeenth-century Dutch philosopher Spinoza maintained that the word "good" applies to whatever we actually desire, and that what *appears* to us to be good changes with changes in our actual desires. For Spinoza there is nothing *really* good that we *ought* to desire, whether we actually do or not.

It follows that prescriptive judgments using the words "ought" and "ought not" are neither true nor false, and that statements about what is just and unjust, about what is right and wrong, are merely subjectively held opinions, changing with the changing circumstances of time and place.

Professor Bork declared that "if a right is not specifically listed in the Constitution, then it is just a preference or a 'gratification.' " [6] If an individual claims that something is a right that the state should secure, that claim is nothing but a wish for a certain kind of treatment, a desire that he and other individuals may strive to get the state to gratify.

In other words, the only rights that a constitutional government is called upon to secure are those that are in the provisions of its constitution or are enacted by legislators. What Bork calls "preferences" or "gratifications" may become legal rights by constitutional amendment or by legislative enactment, but until that happens all claims concerning rights not specifically covered by positive laws indicate political objectives on the part of one or another group in society, but their claims cannot be jeopardized by judicial decisions until they have gained the status of legal rights. What in contradistinction to legal rights are called "natural" or "inalienable" rights should not be acknowledged by any court that exercises judicial restraint in abiding by the letter of the law.

Professor Bork declared that "courts must accept any value choice the legislature makes unless it clearly runs contrary to the choice made in the framing of the Constitution." [7] The value choices made by any legislature, federal or state, are those adopted by the reigning majority in that legislature and, supposedly, represent a majority in that legislature's body of constituents. The value choices made in the Constitution similarly represent the will of the reigning majority at the time that the Constitution was ratified or at the time its amendments were adopted.

Since the Constitution is the fundamental law of the land, the choices expressed in its provisions overrule contrary choices made subsequently by Congress or by the legislatures of the several states. In other words, the Supreme Court, in its judicial review of state legislation, should reject as unconstitutional (that is, as contrary to the specifically declared intent of the constitution) those contrary legislative choices.

Professor Bork declared that "every clash between a minority claiming freedom from regulation and a majority asserting its freedom to regulate [i.e., legislate] requires a choice between ... gratifications." [8] In other words, in a constitutional democracy, the preferences and gratifications of the majority, popular or legislative, must prevail. Accordingly, those who speak of the "tyranny of the majority" and who think that an oppressed minority should be able to get redress for its grievances in any other way than by itself becoming a reigning majority are using words without meaning.

Why? Because, as Professor Bork declared, "there is no principled way to decide that one man's [or one group's] gratifications are more deserving of respect than another's or that one form of gratification is more worthy than another." [9] The clash between minorities and majorities can be resolved by minorities becoming majorities and by majorities becoming minorities, not by unrestrained Supreme Court decisions that appeal to principles of natural law, justice, and natural rights as the basis for rejecting majority legislation that is tyrannical, that is, unjust because it violates the natural rights of the minority.

If a minority brings its appeal to the Supreme Court for redress from the tyranny of the reigning majority, its appeal must be rejected if the Constitution, in its framers' intent and according to the letter of its provisions, does not specifically define the liberty that the minority claims has been encroached or the equal treatment that the minority claims has been denied.

As Professor Bork declared, "There is no principled way in which anyone can define the spheres in which liberty is required and the spheres in which equality is desired." [10] Bork's repeated stress on the phrase "no principled way" expresses his denial of any principles for deciding cases before the Court that lie outside the intent and language of the Constitution. Philosophers may talk about the principles of law as opposed to positive or man-made law; they may talk about the principles of justice; but philosophers are not judges who, if they exercise judicial restraint, are bound to decide the cases before them by the letter of the law, not by what, for Bork, are questionable philosophical principles.

In other words, if the law in question is clearly constitutional, it cannot be rejected as unjust because at that time the Constitution was itself unjust and in need of further amendment. For example, the time of Mr. Justice Taney's *Dred Scott* decision, the Constitution had not been amended to rectify the injustice of chattel slavery. [11] Hence Chief Justice Roger Taney's decision that runaway slaves were property that had to be returned to their owners was constitutionally correct, but it also was unjust. [12]

Chattel slavery did not become unjust until the adoption, after the Civil War, of the Thirteenth, Fourteenth, and Fifteenth amendments. In terms of the natural right to liberty, it was always unjust, but on Professor Bork's positivistic jurisprudence, it only became unjust when, by the enactment of positive laws, it became unconstitutional.

In other words, it is positive or man-made law that, at any time and place, determine what is just and unjust at that time and place. Since positive laws—constitutional provisions or legislative enactments—are the *only* basis for declaring what is just or unjust at a given time and place, there cannot be any possible way to declare that constitutions themselves are unjust and in need of amendment, or to declare that legislative enactments are unjust when they are clearly not unconstitutional.

3

The issue on which Robert Bork definitely takes one side runs throughout the history of Western jurisprudence. It is the most fundamental issue in the philosophy of law and justice. It is the issue between the positivists and the naturalists—between

a. those who hold that positive or man-made laws are prior to and determine what is deemed to be just and unjust in any community at any time and place and who, accordingly, also hold that what is deemed just and unjust changes with changes in the positive laws and government of a given community; and
b. those who hold that there are principles of natural law, criteria of justice, and natural rights that enable us to determine whether laws and constitutions are just or unjust and, if unjust, in need of rectification and amendment.

Participants in any well-conducted Aspen Executive Seminar become acquainted with this age-old issue when they read and discuss the first two books of Plato's *Republic*. There they find the sophist, Thrasymachus, arguing against Socrates, saying that "justice is nothing but the interest of the stronger" and Socrates trying to refute Thrasymachus by defining justice without any regard to the edicts or laws of those with the might to enforce them. [13]

According to Thrasymachus, those with the power to ordain and enforce the laws of the land call those who by obey their laws just subjects, and those who disobey them unjust. The words "just" and "unjust" have no other meaning, certainly no meaning whereby a despotic tyrant or a tyrannical majority, ruling in self-interest, not for the good of the ruled, can be called unjust.

With the statement that justice is nothing but the interest of the stronger, we have the origin of the doctrine that might is right, for those with the might to govern are the only ones who can determine what is right and wrong. [14]

The position taken by Thrasymachus is taken later by the Roman jurisconsult Ulpian for whom "whatever pleases the prince has the force of the law," and still later by Thomas Hobbes in his *Leviathan* where he declares that, in any community, what is just and unjust is wholly determined by the positive or man-made laws enacted by those with the power to ordain and enforce them. In the nineteenth century, the positivist view is advanced by Jeremy Bentham in his *Principles of Morals and Legislation*, and by John Austin in his *Province of Jurisprudence Determined*, and in the twentieth century it is advanced by professors in American law schools who call themselves legal realists.

On the other side, the naturalist view initiated by Socrates in his dispute with Thrasymachus finds amplification in Aristotle's distinction between natural and legal justice; in Cicero's discussion of natural [15]; in Augustine's statement that "an unjust law is a law in name only" (representing might without right, power without authority); in Aquinas's philosophy of law wherein principles of justice are antecedent to, independent of, and applicable to positive or man-made laws; and in the doctrine of modern philosophers, such as John Locke and Immanuel Kant, for whom natural rights preexist positive, man-made laws and become the basis for assessing their justice and injustice.

4

In our own century, representatives of the positivist and the naturalist sides of this basic issue in jurisprudence have occupied positions in our federal judiciary—on the positivist side, Oliver Wendell Holmes, his disciple Felix Frankfurter, Learned Hand, and Robert Bork; and on the naturalist side Louis Brandeis, Benjamin Cardozo, William Brennan, and Harry Blackmun.

This recitation of the names of eminent philosophers and jurists who, over the centuries, have engaged in disputing this issue does not by itself give the slightest indication on which side the truth lies. Readers must decide that for themselves. However, I think I can be of some help by presenting a clear statement of the consequences that follow from embracing the positivist or the naturalist side of the issue.

If the positivist view of the relation between law and justice is correct, it follows:

1. that might is right;
2. that there can be no such thing as the tyranny of the majority;
3. that there are no criteria for judging laws or constitutions as unjust and in need of rectification or amendment;
4. that justice is local and transient, not universal and immutable, but different in different places and at different times;
5. that positive laws have force only, and no authority, eliciting obedience only through the fear of the punishment that accompanies getting caught in disobeying them; and
6. that there is no distinction between *mala prohibita* and *mala in se*, namely, between
   a. acts that are wrong simply because they are legally prohibited (such as breaches of traffic ordinances) and
   b. acts that are wrong in themselves, whether or not they are prohibited by positive law (such as murdering human beings or enslaving them).

If the naturalist view of the relation between law and justice is correct, it follows:

1. that might is not right;
2. that majorities can be tyrannical and unjust;
3. that principles of justice and of natural right enable us to assess the justice or injustice of man-made laws and constitutions and to direct us in their rectification and amendment;
4. that justice is universal and immutable, always the same everywhere and at all times, whether or not recognized at a given time and place;
5. that positive laws have authority as well as force, obeyed only by criminals because of fear of punishment if caught disobeying them, but obeyed by just individuals by virtue of the authority they exercise when they prescribe just conduct;
6. that there are *mala in se* as well as *mala prohibita*, that is, acts that are wrong in themselves whether or not they are prohibited by positive, man-made laws.

One point more should be added. Only on the naturalist view does the great second paragraph of the Declaration of Independence proclaim self-evident truths. On the positivist view, it is, as Jeremy Bentham claimed at the time, a piece of flamboyant rhetoric, aimed at winning converts to the cause of the rebellion, but without an ounce of truth in its pious proclamations about unalienable rights and how governments, which derive their just powers from the consent of the governed, are formed to make preexisting natural rights more secure.

5

There are other considerations that have a bearing on the issue and may help readers to decide which side they should favor. Let me call attention to some of them.

In this century, the government of the United States, under both Democratic and Republican administrations, with the approval of a majority of its citizens, has introduced a new note in its conduct of international affairs and in its diplomatic relations with other countries. It has been, almost alone among the great nations, a stalwart proponent of human rights. Its stance has been the same everywhere in the world—in Eastern Europe, in South America, in Central America, and in the Far East—because human rights, not being legal or civil rights, are the same everywhere in the world. The United States government has hinged its relations with and action toward other countries on their eliminating their abuse and violation of human rights.

Let me dwell a moment more on the sharp distinction between human and civil or legal rights, rights that are explicitly proclaimed in constitutions (as in the first eight amendments to our Constitution), and in the positive laws enacted by legislatures. Such rights differ from century to century and they change from time to time, as they have changed in this country with the nineteenth- and twentieth-century amendments to our Constitution. But human rights are not local and mutable. If they are everywhere the same, and at all times the same, it must be because they have their foundation in human nature, which is also everywhere the same and at all times the same. [16]

If one understands what it means to speak of human rights, one understands that "natural rights" and "human rights" are two ways of referring to the same set of rights, identical also with the "inalienable rights" proclaimed in our Declaration of Independence.

What does the word "inalienable" add to the adjectives "human" and "natural" as applied to rights? Since the rights in question are rooted in the nature of man and not established by the positive enactments of governments, they are inalienable in the sense that governments cannot take away what they do not bestow. These rights can be violated and transgressed by governments, as they have been over the course of centuries, but governments cannot abrogate or rescind them. Their unalienable existence is an irremovable basis for dissent from governments that transgress them.

It is paradoxical, to say the least, that in the politics of the United States, the leading proponent in the world of human rights, there should be strict constructionists, represented by the positivists in jurisprudence, who deny the validity of appeals to human, natural, and unalienable rights in the making of judicial decisions on constitutional questions. Admittedly, the words of our eighteenth-century Constitution did not explicitly name such rights in the listing of the rights to be safeguarded and implemented in the amendments regarded as our Bill of Rights. However, though not explicitly named, human or natural rights *are* presupposed in our Bill of Rights. I will return to this point in the section to follow.

I wish to call attention here to another twentieth-century phenomenon that manifests the prevalent belief in this country that rights exist, rights that are nowhere legally enacted, but the transgression of which deserves judicial trial, sentencing, and punishment. Consider the Nuremberg Trials of the so-called Nazi war criminals. The trials were held in a court that had no jurisdiction under any body of positive law. The charge against the defendants was that they had committed "crimes against humanity," which obviously is still another phrase that refers to the violation of human rights. Consider also the trial, sentencing, and execution of the Japanese military leaders who were similarly charged and similarly tried.

If there are no natural rights, there are no human rights; if there are no human rights, there cannot be any crimes against humanity. The Nuremberg trials and the trial of the Japanese military should never have occurred, for the judges in these trials could not exercise the judicial restraint advocated by Robert Bork and his fellow strict constructionists, by not going beyond the letter of positive laws that could give them legitimate jurisdiction.

6

I said in the preceding section that there are clear grounds for holding that the eighteenth-century drafters of the first ten amendments had the natural, inalienable, and human right to liberty in mind when they listed, in what they regarded as a Bill of Rights, the specific rights they sought to protect. Rights, civil or natural, were not mentioned in the main body of the Constitution's seven articles. That defect deeply concerned those who had drafted those articles in the long summer of 1787. The adoption of a Bill of Rights in 1791 was intended to remedy that defect. In formulating its provisions, those who drafted it had in mind the excesses of government that had encroached upon individual liberty in the Great Britain with which they were acquainted. Look, for example, at the wording of the First Amendment:

> Congress shall make no law respecting an establishment of religion, or prohibiting the free exercise thereof; or abridging the freedom of speech, or of the press, or the right of the people peaceably to assemble, and to petition the Government for a redress of grievances.

The intention of the First Amendment is obviously to restrain Congress from making laws about those aspects of human conduct in which human beings have a right to be free in the choices they make and in the actions they perform: freedom of religious worship, freedom of speech, freedom of the press, freedom of peaceable assembly, freedom to petition the government for the redress of grievances. All these specific liberties to be enjoyed by citizens living under a government thus constitutionally restrained are enumerated aspects of the inalienable rights named in the Declaration of Independence.

It should be remembered that the Declaration said that the three inalienable rights it named—life, liberty, and the pursuit of happiness—did not exhaust the number of such rights. It should now be noted that the Ninth Amendment similarly calls our attention to the fact that the rights enumerated in the first eight amendments must not be understood as exhausting all the rights that deserve protection. The Ninth Amendment provides:

> The enumeration in the Constitution of certain rights shall not be construed to deny or disparage others retained by the people.

What can the words "others retained by the people" refer to except (a) the rights that are inherent in human nature and so are human natural rights, or (b) rights previously possessed under the charters of the several states that had just ratified the federal constitution, or (c) both? Is not (c) the most reasonable answer in view of the fact that the men who drafted the Bill of Rights in 1791 could hardly have forgotten the words of the Declaration of Independence in its proclamation of the the inalienable rights with which all human beings are equally endowed?

It is, in my judgment, damningly significant that Robert Bork regards the Ninth Amendment as a serious blemish on the Constitution, and wishes that it had never been included in the Bills of Rights. He would certainly not condone any appeal to it by Supreme Court justice in deciding whether certain aspects of the the right to liberty, itself not specifically mentioned in the first eight amendments, should be made the basis for deciding cases that could not have arisen in the eighteenth or nineteenth century. [17]

Robert Bork repeatedly raises questions about principles. Let us, therefore, consider the principle underlying all the specific aspects of the right to liberty, not only those aspects explicitly mentioned in the eighteenth-century amendments, but also other aspects of the right to liberty that have emerged under the quite different conditions of the twentieth century.

That principle has been stated by two great philosophers of liberty, John Locke and John Stuart Mill. In Locke's phrasing, liberty is the freedom of the individual to follow his own will in all matters where the law of the land prescribes not. In Mill's formulation, the individual should be free to do as he wills or wishes unless he is restrained from doing as he pleases by laws that protect other individuals from being injured by his actions and that also protect the common good of the political community from being disserved. Mill goes on to say that as the realm of conduct regulated by positive law enlarges, the sphere of conduct left to liberty diminishes. [18]

The line that divides the sphere of liberty from the sphere of law is the same line that divides conduct that is private from conduct that is affected with the public interest. Robert Bork has made much of the fact that the right of privacy, to which recent Supreme Court decisions have appealed, is not specifically mentioned in any amendment to the Constitution. Of course it is not there mentioned, nor need it be named there, because the "right of privacy," properly understood, applies to any act within the sphere of liberty itself, *any act that should not be regulated by law because it is in no way affected with the public interest*, in other words, does not result in injury to other individuals or detract from the public good. [19]

The principle that separates the sphere of liberty from the sphere of law, in terms of (a) conduct that is private because it does not affect anyone not engaged in that conduct, and (b) conduct that affects other individuals or the organized community, has a corollary. The corollary is that governments should not make laws aimed to prohibit actions that are thought by some, or even by all, to be immoral, if they are not affected with the public interest. Private morality should not be prescribed; nor should private actions be subject to prohibition as crimes when the crimes prohibited have no victims.

The Fourth Amendment stands on the same ground. It also protects matters that are essentially private from the intrusive and arbitrary action of government.

The right of the people to be secure in their persons, houses, papers, and effects, against unreasonable searches and seizures, shall not be violated, and no warrants shall issue, but upon probable cause, supported by oath or affirmation, and particularly describing the place to be searched, and the persons or things to be seized.

Despotic governments abridge and abrogate the liberty of their subjects by the power of their secret police to invade and ransack private homes, remove private papers, and seize their inhabitants, without warrants issued upon probable cause and supported by oath or affirmation.

The natural, human, and inalienable right to liberty does not lie solely in individual choice and conduct in all matters that are private. [20] The freedom to choose and act as one pleases is only one of the two forms of circumstantial freedom, a liberty that can be affected by what governments do, what constitutions proclaim, and what positive laws prescribe or prohibit.

There are also two forms of freedom that cannot in any way be so affected. One is the natural freedom of self-determination, the freedom of the will itself. That human beings either have or do not have as an inherent property of their specific nature. The other, the acquired freedom of self-perfection, is the moral liberty of those in whom reason dominates the passions, enabling them to will as they ought. Finally, there is a fourth form, a circumstantial freedom, that, like the freedom to choose and act as one pleases in the sphere of private conduct, can be bestowed upon individuals or withheld from them by constitutions or by legislative enactments. This fourth form is often called "political liberty."

Political liberty is the freedom of enfranchised citizens who are governed with their own consent and with a voice in their own government. The right to citizenship with suffrage is another aspect of the natural, human, inalienable right to liberty. In the eighteenth and nineteenth centuries, the United States would not have dared to adopt the protection of human rights as part of its foreign policy. In the centuries in which this country's blacks, its women, and its poor were disenfranchised, it could not, without serious embarrassment, have embraced a foreign policy so divergent from its policy in domestic affairs.

7

When we consider the changes brought about with respect to political liberty by the Thirteenth, Fourteenth, Fifteenth, Nineteenth, and Twenty-fourth amendments (the last as recent as 1964), we cannot avoid returning to the question asked earlier. Does this series of amendments, which constitute a slow march toward universal suffrage (universal except for infants, the hospitalized mentally incompetent, and imprisoned felonious criminals), also constitute progress toward the justice that recognizes the political liberty of enfranchised citizenship as an aspect of the natural, human right to liberty?

To answer this question affirmatively, as most Americans would answer it today, is to affirm the existence of principles of justice not embodied in the positive law of the land, either in its Constitution or in its legislative enactments. Otherwise it would be impossible to say that our Constitution has become progressively more and more just and that it may still have further to go to become completely just.

To answer this question negatively is, of course, to deny, as Robert Bork denies, that there are any principles of justice by reference to which it can be said that our eighteenth-century Constitution was unjust and that it has slowly become more just with the aforementioned amendments in the nineteenth and twentieth centuries. In addition, the burden of explaining the constitutional changes effected by the aforementioned amendments falls heavily upon Robert Bork's shoulders, a burden difficult, if not impossible, to discharge.

If in terms of justice the changes are neither from worse to better, nor from better to worse, what do they reflect? The only possible answer is that what was thought inexpedient by the reigning majority in the eighteenth century was thought expedient in the nineteenth or in the twentieth century. But it must be observed that the changes in question, thought inexpedient at an earlier time and expedient at a later time, were so assessed by reigning majorities at these different times. The oppressed minorities or portions of the population that the changes favored did not have the political power to bring about these changes.

In other words, the emancipated black slaves after the Civil War, the militant suffragettes in the first decades of the twentieth century, and the poor who were disenfranchised by poll taxes did not have the political clout needed to get the Constitution amended in their favor. If no principles of justice and of natural right were involved in the adoption of these amendments, it is extremely difficult, if not impossible, to set forth the considerations of expediency that led to their formulation and adoption by the reigning majorities of their day.

8

Law in relation to liberty and liberty in relation to law—each setting limits to the other—appear in the First and Fourth amendments. Liberty is not the freedom to do anything one pleases, but only freedom to perform actions that do not injure others and are not affected with the public interest. Legal regulation is limited to that sphere of conduct which eventuates in injury to others and is affected with the public interest.

Accordingly, the Supreme Court's annulment of laws that go beyond this limitation to encroach upon the sphere of conduct that is private, or judicial decisions that safeguard the right to liberty in that sphere, are in line with the spirit of these two amendments even if they do not conform to the letter of the law because there is no explicit mention of a right to privacy.

Section 1 of the Fourteenth Amendment generalizes what the First and Fourth amendments imply but do not explicitly state, when it declares,

> No State shall make or enforce any law which shall abridge the privileges or immunities of the United States; nor shall any State deprive any person of life, liberty, or property, without due process of law. . . .

Here for the first time the unqualified word "liberty" appears in the Constitution (except, of course, in its Preamble). Immunities involve rights not to have one's conduct encroached upon by improper legislation; privileges involve rights to freedom of conduct in all matters that are private.

The principle of justice that obliges a just government to treat equals equally appears for the first time in the Fourteenth Amendment as late as 1868. The closing words of Section 1 declare that no government shall "deny to any persons within its jurisdiction the equal protection of the laws."

Robert Bork has enthusiastically endorsed the 1954 decision of the Warren Court, in *Brown v. Board of Education of Topeka* [Kansas], to integrate the schools of the country. That decision held that segregated schools violated the "equal protection of the laws" called for in Section 1 of the Fourteenth Amendment. It can be presumed that Bork also approves, on the same grounds, the Supreme Court's more recent decisions annulling Jim Crow laws in Southern states and laws that prohibited blacks from taking seats at lunch counters.

The question to be asked here is whether this endorsement and approval by Robert Bork of the unconstitutionality of laws that segregated blacks from whites is consistent with his insistence that Supreme Court decisions should not depart from the letter of the law as originally intended by those who drafted it. In 1896, before the conscience of the nation had become sensitized to the injustices suffered by blacks under laws enforced by the Southern states, the Supreme Court, in

Plessy v. Ferguson, decided in favor of those laws. The opinion accompanying that decision held that equal but separate facilities—segregated black and white restrooms in the railroad stations—conformed perfectly to the Fourteenth Amendment's mandate that all citizens of the United States be accorded the equal protection of the laws.

The diametrically opposite decisions rested on the same words in the Sixteenth Amendment. How did those words come to mean "equal but separate" facilities in the earlier case and "equal and not separate" facilities in the later cases? How can the Constitution be read, in the manner of a strict constructionalist, to intend that the words "equal protection of the laws" gave approval at one time to laws that called for segregated facilities and at a later time called for annulling such laws to establish integrated facilities?

The answer is that one must go beyond the letter of the law to understand this change in the interpretation of its words. Equal protection of the laws means that the law must apply to all citizens without discrimination based on considerations irrelevant to their equality as citizens; as, for example, their being racially different, or different in gender. The earlier Supreme Court decision in *Plessy v. Ferguson* had an understanding of the injustice of racial discrimination radically different from the understanding underlying the later decisions of the Warren Court.

Which was the correct decision? That question cannot be answered by an appeal to the letter of the law or to the original intent of its framers. It can be answered only by determining which is the better understanding of the principle of justice that demands equal treatment for equals.

That there is no discrimination in laws requiring integrated facilities for blacks and whites is undeniable; nor can it be denied that laws requiring segregated facilities, however equal the separate facilities may be, do involve a significant discrimination between blacks and whites.

Hence, if any significant discrimination in the application

of the laws to persons who are equal as citizens is unjust, then it is a principle of justice, not the letter of the law, that determines which is the correct decision. The decisions of the Warren Court annulling laws requiring segregated facilities were not based on the unconstitutionality of such laws, but upon their injustice.

9

Let us return briefly once more to recent cases before the Supreme Court, one of which involved a majority decision in which the opinion cited the right to privacy and another in which the dissenting opinion cited that right. [21]

Robert Bork maintains that the majority decision in *Griswold v. Connecticut* and the dissenting opinion in *Bowers v. Hardwick* were illegitimate extensions of the rights specifically mentioned in the First and Fourth amendments. He thinks that the Constitution does not protect rights not specifically enumerated in its language. The right to privacy is such an unenumerated right. [22]

In my judgment, this contention by Bork is completely wrong. There is no way of reading the Constitution without understanding that it aims to limit the sphere of conduct subject to legal regulation to actions that involve injury to others and action affected with the public interest. The correlative understanding is that the Constitution, in the First and Fourth amendments, enumerates *some* examples of liberties that should not be encroached or fettered by government regulation and interference because they are entirely within the sphere of private conduct, involving no injury to other individuals or to the common good.

It is impossible to demarcate the proper spheres of liberty and of law without drawing a line between private and public. The so-called right to privacy expresses this understanding of the sphere reserved for the freedom to do as one pleases, whether what one wishes to do is regarded as immoral or moral and whether or not it has the approbation of some segment of the community, large or small.

To make laws that prohibit the purchase and use of contraceptive devices by married couples or that prohibit homosexual relations between consenting adults is to create crimes that have no victims. The fact that such actions may give offense to some segment of the community does not turn them into victims of truly criminal behavior.

When Robert Bork castigates the "right to privacy" as an unenumerated right and when he maintains that the rights enumerated in the First and Fourth amendments are not just *examples* of the right to privacy, but an *exhaustive* enumeration of the rights that the Constitution aims to secure, he espouses the view that a Constitution written and amended in the eighteenth century should be read as applicable without extension to types of action that did not occur at that time and could not even be imagined then. Nothing, in my judgment, could be more preposterous. To hold this view is to confine oneself to eighteenth-century thinking for the solution of twentieth-century problems.

The issue about the legality of abortion is a twentieth-century issue that was not and could not have been in the minds of the framers of the eighteenth century. Mr. Justice Blackmun's decision in the case of *Roe v. Wade* invokes the right to privacy, which is nothing but the freedom of an adult woman to do as she pleases with her own body in the first trimester of the pregnancy.

The crucial question here is a factual one: Is the fetus a viable organism outside the mother's body during that time? If it cannot live by itself as an independent organism, it does not have a life of its own. The life it has is as a part of the mother's body, in the same sense that an individual's arm or leg is a part of a living organism.

An individual's decision to have an arm or a leg amputated falls within the sphere of privacy—the freedom to do as one pleases in all matters that do not injure others or the public welfare. Accordingly, an adult female's decision to abort the fetus during the first trimester should not be subject to legal regulation by the federal government or by state legislatures.

10

Finally, a brief word about the Supreme Court's power of judicial review in connection with the system of checks and balances that Robert Bork thinks calls for severe judicial restraint on the part of the Court. If the Supreme Court did not have the power and did not exercise it to nullify laws that are either unconstitutional or unjust, the only check on legislation by Congress would be a presidential veto. But Congress can, by a two-thirds vote, override a Presidential veto, from which checkmate on his power the chief executive has no recourse.

In politics, as in chess, the process of checking must end in a checkmate. A constitution that sets up a system of checks does not eliminate all checkmates and imbalances. Just as the executive branch is checkmated by the congressional override of a presidential veto, so Congress is checkmated by the Supreme Court's nullification of its legislation. It has no recourse from such action by the Court. The imbalance at this point can be remedied and balance restored by the presidential power of appointment to the Court and by Congress's power of approval or disapproval of such nominations.

To wish to give Congress an unchecked power to make laws, because the laws it enacts represent the views of a reigning majority, is to forget that majorities can act in their own self-interest and thus be tyrannical and unjust in their oppression of minorities. There is no safeguard against such tyranny in a constitutional democracy where majorities prevail in the making of laws except through the institution of judicial review, which, though not established by the Constitution, has become through tradition an integral and unique feature of the government of the United States.

ENDNOTES

1. See Robert H. Bork: *The Tempting of America* (New York, 1990), pp. 1–11. His book appears to imply that the United States was established on democratic principles that we should be vigorous in upholding. But if he thinks our Founding Fathers were democrats or that the eighteenth-century Constitution was the charter of a truly democratic society, his conception of democracy deprives the post–Civil War amendments—the Thirteenth, Fourteenth, Fifteenth, Nineteenth, and Twenty-fourth—of any rational foundation or justification.

2. Justice Oliver Wendell Holmes, as the founding father of the school of legal realists, defined law itself in the following way:

> What constitutes the law? You will find some text writers telling you that . . . it is a system of reason, that it is a deduction from principles of ethics or admitted axioms, or what not, which may or may not coincide with the decisions. But if we take the view of our friend the bad man we shall find that he does not care two straws for the axioms or the deductions, but that he does want to know what the Massachusetts or English courts are likely to do in fact. I am much of his mind. The prophecies of what the courts will do in fact, and nothing more pretentious, are what I mean by the law (O. W. Holmes, "The Path of the Law," *Collected Legal Papers* [1920], pp. 167, 172–73).

For Justice Holmes's direct attack on the conception of natural law, see Holmes, "Natural Law," *Harvard University Law Review* (1918), p. 40.

3. Tocqueville noted the unlimited power of the majority in the United States and its consequences:

> I regard it as an impious and detestable maxim that in matters of government the majority of a people has the right to do everything, and nevertheless I place the origin of all powers in the will of the majority. Am I in contradiction with myself? . . .

... When I refuse to obey an unjust law, I by no means deny the majority's right to give orders; I only appeal from the sovereignty of the people to the sovereignty of the human race.

There are those not afraid to say that in matters which only concern itself a nation cannot go completely beyond the bounds of justice and reason and that there is therefore no need to fear giving total power to the majority representing it. But that is the language of a slave.

What is a majority, in its collective capacity, if not an individual with opinions, and usually with interests, contrary to those of another individual, called the minority? Now, if you admit that a man vested with omnipotence can abuse it against his adversaries, why not admit the same concerning a majority? Have men, by joining together, changed their character? By becoming stronger, have they become more patient of obstacles? For my part, I cannot believe that, and I will never grant to several that power to do everything which I refuse to a single man (Alexis de Tocqueville, *Democracy in America*, trans., G. Lawrence; ed., J. P. Mayer [New York, 1969], pp. 250–51).

4. For example, while on the D.C. circuit, Judge Bork wrote that judges "administer justice according to law. Justice in a larger sense, justice according to morality, is for Congress and the President to administer, if they see fit, through the creation of new law" (*Hohri v. United States*).

5. Bork, "Neutral Principles and Some First Amendment Problems," *Indiana Law Journal*, 47 (1970), p. 10.

6. Ibid., p. 8.

7. Ibid., pp. 10–11. Also cited by Ronald Dworkin in *The New York Review of Books*, November 8, 1984. The statement corresponds to the sense if not the precise language of Justice Felix Frankfurter's dissent in *West Virginia State Board of Education et al. v. Barnette et al.* (1943), known as the "second flag salute case." In this case the Court overruled its prior decision in *Minersville School District v. Gobitis* (1940), which held that a state could not require children of the Jehovah's Witness faith, contrary to their belief, to

salute the American flag. Frankfurter, author of the *Gobitis* opinion, now found himself in dissent:

> As a member of this Court I am not justified in writing my private notions of policy into the Constitution, no matter how deeply I may cherish them or how mischievous I may deem their disregard. The duty of a judge who must decide which of two claims before the Court shall prevail, that of a state to enact and enforce laws within its general competence of that of an individual to refuse obedience because of the demands of conscience, is not that of the ordinary person. It can never be emphasized too much that one's own opinion about the wisdom or evil of a law should be excluded altogether when one is doing one's duty on the bench. The only opinion of our own even looking in that direction that is material is our opinion whether legislators could in reason have enacted such a law. In the light of all the circumstances, including the history of this question in this Court, it would require more daring than I possess to deny that reasonable legislators could have taken the action which is before us for review (*Barnette*).

8. Bork, *Tempting of America*, p. 257.

9. Dworkin, op. cit.

10. Ibid.

11. See *Dred Scott v. Sandford* (1857).

12. In saying this, I am referring only to the *Dred Scott* decision as applicable to the "underground railway" in the Atlantic states by which runaway slaves were aided in getting to the abolitionist North, not as applicable to the Western territories that had become free states.

13. The full text reads:

> The different forms of government make laws democratical, aristocratical, tyrannical, with a view to their several interests . . . [which] are the justice [that] they deliver to their subjects, and him who transgresses them they punish as a breaker of the law, and unjust. And that is what I mean when I say that in all states there is the same principle of justice which is the interest of the government; and as the government must be supposed

to have power, the only reasonable conclusion is that everywhere there is one principle of justice which is the interest of the stronger (Plato, *Republic*, Book I).

14. The thesis has two implications. It means the stronger have the right, so far as they have the might, to exact from the weaker whatever serves their interest. Their laws or demands cannot be unjust, nor can they do injustice, because the laws they enact by virtue of their superior force are what defines justice. The thesis also means, for the weaker, that injustice on their part consists in disobeying the law of their rulers. Further, they are likely to suffer if they try to follow their own interests rather than those of the stronger. This thesis is the same as the one which sounded more than two millennia later in the Nazi chamber of legal horrors, and then from the lips of the Nazi defendants in the war crimes trials. Nazi law, they said, defined what was just. As good citizens, they obeyed the law and applied it as prescribed. They could not, therefore, be accused of being a party to any crime.

15. According to Cicero,

True law is right reason in agreement with nature; it is of universal application, unchanging and everlasting; it summons to duty by its commands, and averts from wrongdoing by its prohibitions. And it does not lay its commands or prohibitions upon good men in vain, though neither have any effect on the wicked. It is a sin to try to alter this law, nor is it allowable to attempt to repeal any part of it, and it is impossible to abolish it entirely. We cannot be freed from its obligations by senate or people, and we need not look outside ourselves for an expounder or interpreter of it. And there will not be different laws at Rome and at Athens, or different laws now and in the future, but one eternal and unchangeable law will be valid for all nations and all times, and there will be one master and ruler, that is, God, over us all, for he is the author of this law, its promulgator, and its enforcing judge. Whoever is disobedient is fleeing from himself and denying his human nature, and by reason of this very fact he will suffer the worst penalties, even if he escapes what is commonly considered punishment (Cicero, *De Re Publica*, trans., C. W. Keyes, Book III, p. 211).

16. See the criticism of the contemporary error on this point in my essay "Human Nature, Nurture, and Culture" in *The Aspen Institute Quarterly* 1:1 (Autumn 1989). That essay is reprinted here as Chapter Five.

17. I have in mind here the Connecticut law prohibiting the use of contraceptives by married couples and the Georgia law prohibiting certain sexual relations between consenting adults in a residence they occupy.

18. As Mill states it,

> The object of this Essay is to assert one simple principle, as entitled to govern absolutely the dealings of society with the individual in the way of compulsion and control, whether the means used be physical force in the form of legal penalties, or the moral coercion of public opinion. That principle is, that . . . the only purpose for which power can be rightfully exercised over any member of a civilised community, against his will, is to prevent harm to others. His own good, either physical or moral, is not a sufficient warrant" (J.S. Mill, *On Liberty*, Chapter 1).

19. In a column in *Newsweek* magazine in which he lavished unstinted praise on Robert Bork's recent book, George Will inadvertently gave the case away. He wrote: "The Constitution's fundamental distinction is between what is public and what is private—between the spheres where majorities may or may not rule" ("The Tempting of America," December 4, 1989). Will is quite correct. The First Amendment's restraint of government from making laws about matters that should be left to freedom of individual choice and individual action draws a line between the sphere of private liberty and the sphere of conduct that governments should regulate because the conduct affects the public interest.

20. In *The Idea of Freedom* (vol. I, 1958; vol. II, 1961) I distinguished four main types of liberty: (1) the natural

freedom of self-determination, or freedom of the will; (2) the acquired freedom of self-perfection, or moral liberty; (3) the circumstantial freedom of self-realization, or doing as one pleases; and (4) the circumstantial freedom of citizenship with suffrage, or political liberty.

21. The first case was *Griswold v. Connecticut* (1965), in which the Court annulled a Connecticut law prohibiting the purchase and use of contraceptive devices by married couples. The second case was *Bowers v. Hardwick* (1986), the Georgia case in which the dissenting opinion argued that homosexual relations between consenting adults in the privacy of their own residence should not be prohibited by a law of that state.

22. See Bork, *Tempting of America*, p. 120. ". . . The *Bowers* dissent, the natural outcome of *Griswold v. Connecticut* and *Roe v. Wade*, is a constitutional debacle."

FOUR

Lincoln's Declaration

Of the three great documents in the history of the United States—the Declaration of Independence, the Constitution, and the Gettysburg Address—there is a closer affinity between the Declaration and the Gettysburg Address than there is between those two documents and the Constitution. I wish not only to call attention to this fact, but in the light of it to say why I think Abraham Lincoln is unique among the presidents of the United States.

In taking the oath of office, presidents, Lincoln among them, swear to uphold the Constitution of the United States. All the others do that willingly and without reservation, but not Lincoln. In my judgment, Lincoln is the only president who did that with some unspoken reservations, for he would have much preferred to pledge himself to uphold the principles of American government stated in the magnificent second paragraph of the Declaration of Independence. (He is also the only true genius, like Shakespeare and Mozart, among our presidents.)

Why do I make this claim for Lincoln's uniqueness? It partly rests upon the words of the Gettysburg Address: "this nation conceived in liberty"; and "dedicated to the proposition that all men are created equal." It partly rests on the extraordinary statement in the Gettysburg Address that this nation came into being four score and seven years ago—in

1776—when it is so obvious that the colonies which rebelled in 1776 and sought to dissolve the bonds that tied them to Great Britain finally became the United States after the Constitution was drafted in 1787, after it was ratified in 1788, and only when George Washington took the oath of office as its first president in 1789.

Lincoln knew all these historical facts. Why then did he date the birth of this nation—its sovereign statehood—in 1776? That birth date was not something taken for granted by Lincoln, nor perfunctory for him. In his years of argument against the extension of slavery to new territories, Lincoln repeatedly appealed to the Declaration of Independence. His opponents resorted to the Constitution, with its covert references to the institution of slavery, as decisive for issues of policy regarding the extension of slavery. In effect, they took the adoption of the Constitution as the juridical birth date of the nation. Even that is incorrect, for it was not merely with the adoption of the Constitution that this nation came into being, but rather with its beginning to function in 1789 when Washington occupied the presidency and Congress assembled.

What precedes is only part of the evidence for Lincoln's unique relation to the Declaration of Independence. There is much more evidence to cite. Consider his impromptu remarks in Independence Hall in Philadelphia on February 22, 1861, shortly before his inauguration.

I have never had a feeling politically that did not spring from the sentiments embodied in the Declaration of Independence. I have often pondered over the dangers which were incurred by the men who assembled here and adopted that Declaration of Independence—I have pondered over the toils that were endured by the officers and soldiers of the army, who achieved that Independence. I have often inquired of myself, what great principle or idea it was that kept this Confederacy so long together. It was not the mere matter of the separation of the colonies from the mother land; but something in that Declaration giving liberty, not alone to the people of this country, but hope to the world for all future time. It was that which gave promise that in due time the weights should be lifted from the shoulders of all men, and that *all* should have an equal chance. This is the sentiment embodied in that Declaration of Independence.

Lincoln alone explicitly regarded the Declaration as the last great hope for all mankind and as a pledge to the future of all human beings. Consider his speech on the Dred Scott decision in 1857.

In those [early] days, our Declaration of Independence was held sacred by all and thought to include all; but now, to aid in making the bondage of the Negro universal and eternal, it is assailed and sneered at, and construed, and hawked at and torn, till, if its framers could rise from their graves, they could not at all recognize it.

Shortly after the Dred Scott decision, Lincoln learned from a speech by Stephen A. Douglas what Douglas thought the signers meant. Douglas said:

No man can vindicate the character, motives, and conduct of the signers of the Declaration of Independence except upon the hypothesis that they referred to the white race alone, and not to the African, when they declared all men to have been created equal; that they were speaking of British subjects on this continent being equal to British subjects born and residing in Great Britain.

I will quote here only a few paragraphs from Lincoln's response. He found Douglas's remarks ludicrous. He ridiculed them at length.

My good friends, read that carefully over some leisure hour, and ponder well upon it—see what a mere wreck—mangled ruin—it makes of our once glorious Declaration. . . . I had thought the Declaration promised something better than the condition of British subjects; but no, it only meant that we should be *equal* to them in their own oppressed and *unequal* condition. . . . I had thought the Declaration contemplated the progressive improvement in the condition of all men everywhere; but no, it merely "was adopted for the purpose of justifying the colonists in the eyes of the civilized world in withdrawing their allegiance from the British Crown, and dissolving their connection with the mother country." Why, that object having been effected some eighty years ago, the Declaration is of no practical use now—mere rubbish—old wadding left to rot on the battlefield after the victory is won.

Finally, let me add a long paragraph from Lincoln's speech in Springfield, Illinois, in 1857, after the Dred Scott decision.

Chief Justice Taney, in his opinion in the Dred Scott case, admits that the language of the Declaration is broad enough to include the whole human family, but he and Judge Douglas argue that the authors of that instrument did not intend to include Negroes by the fact that they did not at once actually place them on an equality with the whites. Now this grave argument comes to just nothing at all, by the other fact, that they did at once, *or ever afterwards,* actually place all white people on an equality with one or another. And this is the staple argument of both the Chief Justice and the Senator for doing this obvious violence to the plain, unmistakable language of the Declaration.

There are two great movements in the history of the United States. The first started with the War of Independence—the freedom of the American colonists from the despotic rule of the British Parliament. It is their achievement of political liberty that Lincoln had in mind when he spoke of this nation as being "conceived in liberty." But, unlike the French Revolution, equality and fraternity were not part of the social ideal at which our Founding Fathers aimed. Lincoln could not have said "conceived in liberty and equality," because he knew full well that the Constitution did not aim at nor provide for equality.

The phrase "we the people" with which the Preamble begins means only the few, not the many—not the blacks, not women, not the poor, all of whom were left without suffrage by the Constitution. If by liberty we understand the liberty of citizens with suffrage, citizens who are governed with their own consent and with a voice in their own government, then in all the decades before the Civil War and until the post–Civil War amendments, political liberty belonged only to the few, not the many, certainly not to all who were entitled to claim their right to it.

It is Lincoln in his devotion to the Declaration of Independence, not the Constitution of the United States, who ushers in the second movement in American history—the long, slow and as yet uncompleted march toward democracy.

Depending on the meaning we attach to the word "people," referring either to some small part of the population or to all, Lincoln's extraordinary formulation—government "of" the people, "by" the people, and "for" the people—defined constitutional government, which is either just or unjust, either a constitutional oligarchy (as ours was in the pre–Civil War decades) or a constitutional democracy (as ours has become with the Thirteenth, Fourteenth, Fifteenth, Nineteenth, and Twenty-fourth amendments, the last as recently as 1964).

In that remarkable formulation, the crucial adjective is "of"—generally misunderstood by almost everyone, among whom are many who should know better. Clearly, it does not mean that the people are the subjects of government, as the British people were subjects of the king, when they were government by the monarch. That meaning of the preposition "of" occurs when we say, the history "*of* the United States." The United States is then the *objective* reference of the adjective.

But in Lincoln's formulation, we have a very different meaning for "of," the genitive or possessive meaning, as when we say "the hat of my aunt"—in English or French—the equivalent phrasing of which is "my aunt's hat." So, when we say "government of the people," we are saying that this government *belongs* to the people, they possess it; it comes *from them* and therefore *is theirs.*

The significance of this simple point cannot be overestimated. It means, first of all, that the people who are citizens (some or all) are the *constituents* of the government, as well as its *participants* through suffrage. As the Declaration says: it is government with their *consent, deriving* its just powers from that consent. They give it its authority, without which there can be no government that is not by force or might and without right.

It tells us more. It tells us that the government is not in Washington, D.C.—not in the White House, not in the Capitol and the buildings that surround it, not in the office buildings of the departments of government, not in the Supreme Court. All those buildings in Washington do not house *our* governors, but only officeholders, most of them transient, who are the administrators of *our* government.

When at a national election we put new persons into office and into those office buildings, we are not changing our government. We can do that only by amending the Constitution. We are only changing our government's administration. The old administration is out; the new administration is in.

Where then is the government of the United States? With us—with "we the people," the enfranchised citizens, wherever we are. Most of us do not recognize this. Most of us do not live and act as if we understood this. Most of us do not speak properly about our relation to the government of the United States—*the government which is our most precious possession.*

But Lincoln understood this, always and deeply, when he said over and over again, sincerely and not just as a rhetorical flourish, that he was a servant of the people. Indeed he was, as every president is; but most of them who think of themselves as good leaders of the people seldom conceive of their leadership as a *service* to the people.

I said earlier that the second movement in American history is the movement from liberty—liberty for the few—to equality and, with it, equal freedom for all. That march began, in Lincoln's words at Gettysburg, with "a new birth of freedom." As I said before, our Constitution with the six amendments mentioned above has approached becoming a democratic charter as recently as 1964. But it is not completely there as yet. What remains to be done?

To answer this question, I must expand one crucial phrase in the Declaration, the phrase that says "among these rights"—the "unalienable" rights that are inherent in human nature, the rights with which all human beings are endowed—"are life, liberty, and the pursuit of happiness."

First of all, the words "among these" signify clearly that all the rights have not been explicitly named. Second, "the pursuit of happiness" must be correctly understood, not as meaning getting anything an individual wants and thus achieving contentment, but rather as meaning living a morally good life, a life enriched by all the real goods that any human being needs. [1]*

With these two points clear, that phrase in the Declaration can be expanded to say "among these rights are life, liberty, and anything else that human beings need"—need, not want—"in order to lead a decent human life."

What, in addition to life and liberty, does anyone need to lead a decent human life? The answer is a decent standard of living—that minimum of economic goods (not just money) needed by everyone: schooling, health care, clothing, housing, food, sleep, and so forth. Everyone has, in short, an unalienable, natural right to a decent livelihood, earned if they are

---

*Endnotes for this chapter are on page 228.

able to earn it and are given the opportunity to do so, or received as a welfare payment if they suffer mental or physical disabilities that prevent then from earning it, even if there were opportunity to do so.

In my judgment, if Lincoln were alive in the twentieth century, he—unlike Judge Bork and other strict constructionalists of our day—would have appealed to the Ninth Amendment's implicit reference to the unalienable rights enumerated in the Declaration as the basis not only for the Nineteenth and Twenty-fourth amendments, but also for further constitutional amendment still to come—the unalienable economic right that the Constitution does not yet secure. [2]

Let me make this completely clear by another statement of the same point. A society is politically democratic if it is one in which all are political haves and there are no political have-nots (no one disfranchised except infants, hospitalized mental incompetents, and incarcerated felons).

In such a society comprising all haves and no have-nots, some should have more power than others: citizens in public office should have more; citizens not in office, less. Apart from this, justice requires the equality of all haves. It also requires an inequality between the have-mores and the have-lesses that is based on their different political responsibilities and functions.

A society is economically socialist in exactly the same sense. It is a society in which all are haves—having a decent livelihood, by earning or receiving it—and in which some have more and some have less, justly so when that more or less is based on their differential contribution to the economic welfare of society, not on the personal greed that drives them to make more and more money, without increasing the wealth and economic welfare of society.

The ultimate ideal toward which we should aim is a socialist democracy, a society in which the rights of all to be *political and economic* haves is constitutionally ensured, and in which there are no unjustly deprived have-nots.

*   *   *

Can this be done without further constitutional amendments? Possibly, but I doubt it; certainly not without explicit legislation. As Lincoln said: the government should do for the people what they cannot do for themselves, either individually or collectively, in their private associations.

It should be clear to everyone that it is very unlikely that socialism will come about solely through private initiative—the socialism that Theodore Roosevelt embraced in his great New Nationalism speech in 1910, when he said that human rights must take precedence over property rights. His Progressive Party Platform in 1912 contained many measures that Wilson's government adopted, such as inheritance taxes and graduated income taxes. Many more of his planks became legislative in Franklin Delano Roosevelt's New Deal in 1932 and thereafter.

Unfortunately, most Americans do not realize that the first Roosevelt aimed at, and the second Roosevelt succeeded in, socializing bourgeois capitalism in this country. Why are they so blind to this obvious fact? Because they, and most of the Western world, have failed to understand that socialism is an end to be aimed at, quite distinct from communism, which is totalitarian state capitalism. By abolishing the private ownership of the means of production, totalitarian communism is the wrong means for trying to achieve socialism as the end in view. The past five years has persuaded all of us, including Soviets, that *communism does not work at all as a means, or as the only means, for achieving socialism.*

The last great words of the Gettysburg Address ring in our ears as we contemplate what has happened in Eastern Europe in 1990: "that government of the people, by the people, for the people" (with truly universal suffrage and securing all human rights, economic as well as political; in short, socialist democracy) "shall not perish from the earth."

I cannot refrain from spending a moment more on a

prophecy I made in 1978. A dispute took place at the Aspen Institute that summer. Its participants were Anthony Quinton, Maurice Cranston, and me. The subject of the debate was the future of democracy. It focused on three specific questions:

1. Should democracy survive, be perfected, and spread globally?
2. Can it survive, be perfected, and spread globally?
3. Will it?

My affirmative reply to the third question was prophetic so far as Hungary, Poland, Czechoslovakia, Romania, and East Germany are concerned. [3] I think that in the next ten years, or certainly in the next century, the prophecy will also become true in the Soviet Union, in mainland China, and even in Albania and North Korea. *Why* do I think so? Because people deprived of their political liberty will not long endure their oppression without fighting for and achieving the freedom to which they are entitled, and because people deprived of a decent livelihood, a decent standard of living, will not long endure the hardships of their daily deprivations and their economic misery.

The future of the whole human race belongs to socialist democracies or, if you prefer to say it another way, to democratic socialism. Totalitarian communism, born in this century, is self-defeated, self-destroyed, as bourgeois capitalism destroyed itself after the First World War and in the subsequent Great Depression.

Finally, one word more about the Declaration. Toward the end of that magnificent second paragraph, Thomas Jefferson wrote that when a government fails to secure everything to which the people are entitled, it is their right—*it is their duty*—to overthrow it and replace it by a just government, one that does secure all their human rights.

There is no question about their rebellion being *justified* by the violation of their human rights, but why does Jefferson also say that it is their duty—their *moral obligation*—to rebel?

The answer is: Because all human beings have a moral obligation to try to lead morally decent human lives. From that derives their obligation, their duty, to overthrow any government that frustrates or prevents them from doing so, and so fails to assist them in the pursuit of the happiness to which they are entitled.

ENDNOTES

1. I have fully explained why the text must be so understood (quite contrary to the popular and prevailing misunderstanding of it) in Chapters 8 and 9 of *We Hold These Truths* (New York, 1987).

2. Here is the wording of Article Nine: "The enumeration in the Constitution, of certain rights, shall not be construed to deny or disparage others retained by the people."

3. See my argument for Thesis III in Chapter Two.

FIVE

Human Nature, Nurture, and Culture

On July 1, 1950, I gave the first formal lecture at the opening of the Aspen Institute for Humanistic Studies. The title was "The Nature of Man," a subject I thought appropriate for that occasion. Now, forty years later, I am going to attempt a summing up of my views on human nature, nurture, and culture.

The issue falls into three related parts: first, the unity of the specific nature of the human race and its place in the world of living organisms. Second, differences within the human world—between human individuals and between human groups—that are nurtural, not natural in their origin and overlay the natural sameness of all human beings, and especially the natural sameness of the human mind. Which leads, finally, to the third and concluding section of this discourse about cultural pluralism and cultural unity.

THE NATURE OF THE HUMAN SPECIES AND ITS DIFFERENCE FROM THAT OF OTHER ANIMAL SPECIES

I must begin by commenting on an extraordinary error made by twentieth-century social scientists and by the existentialist philosophy that arose in France in this century. It consists in denying that man has a specific nature comparable to the specific natures to be found in the zoological taxonomy—in the classification of animals according to their generic and specific natures. As the existentialists put it, man has an existence, but no essence: the essence of each human being is of his or her own making. As the social scientists put it, the differences among human groups—racial, ethnic, or cultural—are primary; there is no common human nature in which they all share. The French existentialist Merleau-Ponty sums up this error by saying, "It is the nature of man not to have a nature."

Before I explain how this profound mistake came to be made, let me call your attention to its serious consequences. If moral philosophy is to have a sound factual basis, it is to be found in the facts about human nature and nowhere else. Nothing else but the sameness of human nature at all times and places, from the beginning of *Homo sapiens* 45,000 years ago, can provide the basis for a set of moral values that should be universally accepted. Nothing else will correct the mistaken notion that we should readily accept a pluralism of moral values as we pass from one human group to another or within the same human group. If the basis in human nature for a universal ethic is denied, the only other alternative lies in the extreme rationalism of Immanuel Kant, which proceeds without any consideration of the facts of human life and with no concern for the variety of cases to which moral prescriptions must be applied in a manner that is flexible rather than rigorous.

I turn now to the explanation of the mistaken denial of human nature, which while conceding that all human beings have certain common anatomical and physiological traits—number of bones, number of teeth, blood type, number of chromosomes, the period of parturition, and so on—denies their psychological sameness—the sameness of the human mind and its behavioral tendencies. How was that mistake made?

Consider other animal species. If you were to investigate any one of them as carefully as possible, you would find that the members of the same species, living in their natural habitats, manifest a remarkable degree of similarity in behavior. You might find differences in size, weight, shape, or coloration among the individuals you examined. You might find behavioral deviations here and there from what would have become evident as the normal behavior of that species. But, by and large, you would be impressed by the similitudes that reigned in the populations you examined.

The dominant likeness of all members of the species would lead you to dismiss as relatively insignificant the differences you found, most of which can be explained as the result of slightly different environmental conditions. That dominant likeness would constitute the nature of the species in question.

Now consider the human species. It inhabits the globe. Its members live in all hemispheres and regions, under the most widely divergent environmental conditions. Let us suppose you were to take the time to visit human populations wherever they existed—all of them. Let the visit not be a casual one, but one in which you lived for a time with each of these populations and studied them closely. You would come away with the very opposite impression from the one you took away from your investigation of the populations that belonged to one or another animal species. You were there impressed by the overwhelming similitude that reigned among its members. Here, however, you would find that the behavioral differences were dominant rather than the similarities.

Of course human beings, like other animals, must eat, drink, and sleep. They all have certain biological traits in common. There can be no doubt that they have the nature of animals. But when you come to their distinctive behavioral traits, how different one human population will be from another. They will differ in the languages they speak, and you will have some difficulty in making an accurate count of the vast number of different languages you will have found. They will differ in their dress, in their adornments, in their cuisines, in their customs and manners, in the organization of their families, in the institutions of their societies, in their beliefs, in their standards of conduct, in the turn of their minds, in almost everything that enters into the ways of life they lead. These differences will be so multitudinous and variegated that you might, unless cautioned against doing so, tend to be persuaded that they were not all members of the same species.

In any case, you cannot avoid being persuaded that, in the human case, membership in the same species does not carry with it the dominant behavioral similitude that you would find in the case of other animal species. On the contrary, the behavioral differences between one human race and another, between one racial variety and another, between one ethnic group and another, between one nation and another, would seem to be dominant.

It is this that might lead you to the conclusion that there is no human nature in the sense in which a certain constant nature can be attributed to other species of animals. Even if you did not reach that conclusion yourself, you might understand how that conclusion is plausible.

Unlike most other species of animals, the members of the human species appear to have formed subgroups that differentiated themselves, one from another. Each subgroup has a distinctive character. The differences that separate one subgroup from another are so numerous and so profound that they defy you to say what remains, if anything, that might be regarded as a human nature common to all.

Let me be sure it is understood that the denial of human nature rests ultimately on the striking contrast between the dominant behavioral *similitude* that prevails among the members of other animal species and the dominant behavioral *differentiation* that prevails among the subgroups of the human species.

Looked at one way, the denial of human nature is correct. The members of the human species do not have a specific or common nature *in the same sense* that the members of other animal species do. This, by the way, is one of the most remarkable differences between man and other animals, one that tends to corroborate the conclusion that man differs from other animals in kind, not in degree. But to concede that the members of the human species do not have a specific or common nature in the same sense that the members of other animal species do is not to admit that they have *no specific nature whatsoever.*

An alternative remains open, namely, that the members of the human species all have the same nature *in a quite different sense.*

In what sense then is there a human nature, a specific nature that is common to all members of the species? The answer can be given in a single word: "potentialities." Human nature is constituted by all the potentialities that are the species-specific properties common to all members of the human species.

It is the essence of a potentiality to be capable of a wide variety of different actualizations. Thus, for example, the human potentiality for syntactical speech is actualized in thousands of different human languages. Having that potentiality, a human infant placed at the moment of birth in one or another human subgroup, each with its own language, would learn to speak that language. The differences among all human languages are superficial as compared with the potentiality for learning and speaking any human language that is present in all human infants at birth.

What has just been said about one human potentiality applies to all the others that are the common, specific traits of the human being. Each underlies all the differences that arise among human subgroups as a result of the many different ways in which the same potentiality can be actualized. To recognize this is tantamount to acknowledging the superficiality of the differences that separate one human subgroup from another, as compared with the samenesses that unite all human beings as members of the same species and as having the same specific nature.

In other species of animals, the samenesses that unite the members and constitute their common nature are not potentialities but rather quite determinate characteristics, behavioral as well as anatomical and physiological. This accounts for the impression derived from studying these other species—the impression of a dominant similitude among its members.

Turning to the human species, the opposite impression of dominant differences among subgroups can also be accounted for. The explanation of it lies in the fact that, as far as behavioral characteristics are concerned, the common nature that all the subgroups share consists entirely of species-specific potentialities. These are actualized by these subgroups in all the different ways that we find when we make a global study of mankind.

The mistake that the cultural anthropologists, the sociologists, and other behavioral scientists make when they deny the existence of human nature has its root in their failure to understand that the specific nature in the case of the human species is radically different from the specific nature in the case of other animal species.

Having established the sameness of the human species, which consists in its common human potentialities, psychological and behavioral, in addition to its common anatomical and physiological traits, let us now consider the difference between the human species and other animal species.

That we differ from other nonhuman animals in many respects is doubted by no one. But among these differences, are *some* differences in kind, or are *all* differences in degree? Differences in degree are all differences of more and less with resp ct to the same property or trait. For example, all animals mature from infancy at different rates, humans more slowly than other animals. That is a difference in degree. Two things differ in kind rather than degree if one has a property that the other totally lacks: it is a difference between *haves* and *have-nots*. For example, the difference between animals that have and lack backbones is a difference in kind.

In a book I wrote in 1967, *The Difference of Man and the Difference It Makes*, and in a book I have just written in 1990, *Intellect: Mind Over Matter*, I think I have shown, beyond a reasonable doubt, that mentally and behaviorally, human beings differ in kind from nonhuman animals. All the differences between humans and nonhumans are not differences in degree.

I shall not state all these differences in kind, but only the most important and obvious ones.

Intellect is a unique human possession. Only human beings have intellects. Other animals may have sensitive minds and perceptual intelligence, but they do not have intellects. No one is given to saying that dogs and cats, horses, pigs, dolphins, and chimpanzees lead intellectual lives; nor do we say of nonhuman animals that they are antiintellectual, as some human beings certainly are. Other animals have intelligence in varying degrees, but they do not have intellectual powers in the least degree.

Free will or free choice, which consists in always being able to choose otherwise, no matter how one does choose, is an intellectual property, lacked by nonintellectual animals. Some of their behavior may be learned and thus acquired rather than innate and instinctive, but however it is determined by instinct or by learning, it is determined rather than voluntary and freely willed.

A person is a living being with intellect and free will. That is both the jurisprudential and the theological definition of a person. Everything else, animate or inanimate, totally lacking intellect and free will, is not a person but a thing.

Only persons have natural and unalienable rights. These we call human rights. There are no comparable animal rights. Morally, human beings may be obliged to treat some, but not all, other animals humanely. We are not obliged to treat a coiled rattlesnake about to strike or a charging tiger humanely.

In addition to the foregoing basic differences in kind between human and nonhuman animals, there are the following behavioral differences in kind.

Other animals live entirely in the present. Only human individuals are time-binders, connecting the present with the remembered past and with the imaginable future. Only man is a historical animal with a historical tradition and a historical development. In the case of other species, the life of succeeding generations remains the same as long as no genetic changes occur. Human life changes from one generation to another with the transmission of cultural novelties and with accretion of accumulated cultural changes and institutional innovations. Nothing like these innovations and changes can be found in any other species.

Other animals make things, such as hives, nests, dams, and, in the case of birds, songs. It may even be that in doing so, other animals use rudimentary tools as well as their own appendages.

But only man makes machines, which are not hand tools, for the purpose of making products that cannot be produced in any other way. It is not enough to say that man is the only manufacturing animal. We must add that he is the only machine-facturing animal. The kind of thought that is involved in designing and building a machine betokens the presence of an intellect in a way that the use of hand tools does not.

Among the things that man makes are works of art that we regard as fine rather than useful because they are made for the pleasure or enjoyment they afford rather than to serve some further purpose. Are the songs made by birds comparable? No, because even if the songs birds make serve no biological purpose and are simply made to be enjoyed, the songs made by a given species of bird remain the same for all members of that species generation after generation. In contrast, in the making of drawings or paintings, from the sketches drawn on the walls of the Cro-Magnon caves down to the present day, the extraordinary variety in human works of art shows that human artistry is not instinctive, and therefore not the same for all members of the species from one generation to the other.

As I see it, all the differences in kind so far mentioned cannot be explained except by reference to man's exclusive possession of an intellect, with its power of conceptual thought and its power of free choice. If any doubt about man's difference in kind remains in your minds, let me try to persuade you by the following distinctive, unique human performances that I think you will find unquestionable.

Only human beings use their minds to become artists, scientists, historians, philosophers, priests, teachers, lawyers, physicians, engineers, accountants, inventors, traders, bankers, statesmen.

Only among human beings is there a distinction between those who behave ethically and those who are knaves, scoundrels, villains, criminals.

Only among human beings is there any distinction between those who have mental health and those who suffer mental disease or have mental disabilities of one sort or another.

Only in the sphere of human life are there such institutions as schools, libraries, hospitals, churches, temples, factories, theaters, museums, prisons, cemeteries, and so on.

I hope you are now persuaded that human and nonhumans differ in kind, not merely in degree, but you may still ask what difference—what practical difference—it makes. I have already answered that question in part by calling your attention to the meaning of human personality—that only humans are persons, not things, and have the dignity and worth that belongs only to persons, the rights that belong only to persons, and the moral obligations that belong only to persons.

There is, in addition, one further consequence that I have

not yet mentioned. The Declaration of Independence asserts that all human beings are, by nature, equal, and that they are *equally* endowed with the *same natural or unalienable rights*. All of us know, as a matter of fact, that any two individuals that we may compare with one another will be unequal in a large variety of respects. How shall we understand the equality that all humans possess—all, with no exception whatsoever—and how shall we understand their myriad individual inequalities?

What do we mean by equality and inequality? Most persons, I have found, do not know the answer to this question, yet it is both short and simple. Two things are equal in a given respect, if in that respect, one is neither more nor less than the other. Two things are unequal in a given respect if in *that* respect, one is more and the other less than the other.

There is *only one* respect in which all human beings—all without any exception—are equal; that is as members of the human species. One human being is neither more nor less human than another. They all have the same species-specific common properties—the innate potentialities that constitute their human nature.

But individual human beings may differ from one another in the degree to which they possess these common human properties, and with respect to such differences, they may be unequal in many respects. These individual differences in degree may be due either to their different innate endowments or to their different individual attainments. Thus understood, there is no incompatibility between the statement that all human beings are equal in only one respect and the statement that they are also unequal in many other respects.

Finally, there is one other consequence of man's difference in kind from all nonhuman animals. Human and *some* other nonhuman animals are gregarious and are naturally impelled to associate with one another. But while man is not the only *social* animal, humans are the only *political* animals. Because they have intellects and free will, they voluntarily constitute the societies in which they live—their domestic, tribal, and political associations. All animal societies or groupings are instinctively determined, and thus they are all purely natural societies, differing from species to species but everywhere the same in the same species. Only human societies are both natural and conventional, natural by natural needs, not by instinctive determination. Motivated by natural need, they are conventionally instituted by reason and free will; and so, within the same species, they differ at different times and places.

THE ROLE OF NURTURE IN HUMAN LIFE

What is the role of nurture in human life?

All the knowledge we acquire, all the understanding we develop, everything we learn, is a product of nurture. At birth, we have none of these. All the habits we form, all the tastes we cultivate, all the patterns of behavior we accumulate, are products of nurture. We are born only with potentialities or powers that are habituated by the things we do in the course of growing up. Many, if not all, of these habits of behavior are acquired under the influence of the homes and families, the tribes or societies in which we are brought up. Some are the results of individually chosen behavior.

What nurture adds to nature in the development of human beings should be so clear to all of us that we do not make the serious mistake that results from the failure to distinguish what human nature is from all of its nurtural overlays. That serious mistake has been made again and again during the last 4,000 years. We found it being made in the twentieth century by those sociologists and existentialists who deny the existence of human nature itself because of the pluralism they find in differently nurtured groups of human beings. Equally serious is the mistake of regarding human inequalities that result from nurtural influences as if they were the manifestation of unequal natural endowments.

To be sure this is clear, let me repeat once more the difference between human nature and that of all other animal species. In the case of other animal species, the specific nature common to all members of the species is constituted mainly by quite determined characteristics or attributes. In the case of the human species, it is constituted by determinable characteristics or attributes. An innate potentiality is precisely that—something determinable, not wholly determinate, and determinable in a wide variety of ways.

Man is to a great extent a self-made creature. Given a range of potentialities at birth, he makes himself what he becomes by how he freely chooses to develop those potentialities by the habits he forms. It is thus that differentiated subgroups of human beings came into existence. Once in existence, they subsequently affected the way in which those born into these subgroups came to develop the acquired characteristics that differentiate one subgroup from another. These acquired characteristics, especially the behavioral ones, are the results of acculturation; or, even more generally, results of the way in which those born into this or that subgroup are nurtured differently.

No other animal is a self-made creature in the sense indicated above. On the contrary, other animals have determinate natures, natures genetically determined in such a way that they do not admit of a wide variety of different developments as they mature. Human nature is also genetically determined; but, because the genetic determination consists, behaviorally, in an innate endowment of potentialities that are determinable in different ways, human beings differ remarkably from one another as they mature. However they originated in the first place, most of those differences are due to differences in acculturation, to natural differences. To confuse nature with nurture is a philosophical mistake of the first order. That philosophical mistake underlies the denial of human nature.

The correction of the philosophical mistake just mentioned is of the greatest importance because of the consequences that follow from not doing so. Most important of all is overcoming the persistent prejudices—the racist, sexist, elitist, even ethnic prejudices—that one portion or subgroup of mankind is distinctly inferior by nature to another. The inferiority may exist, but it is not an inferiority due to nature, but to nurture.

When, for most of the centuries of recorded history, the female half of the population was nurtured—reared and treated—as inferior to the male half, that nurturing made them apparently inferior when they matured. To have correctly attributed that apparent inferiority to their nurturing would have instantly indicated how it could be eliminated. But when it is incorrectly attributed to their nature at birth, it is accepted as irremediable.

What I have said about the sexist prejudice concerning inequality of men and women applies to all the racist and ethnic prejudices about human inequality that still exist among mankind. All these apparent inequalities are nurtural. None is a natural inequality between one human subgroup and another. In the centuries prior to this one, the elitist view taken by the propertied class about the inferiority of the working class was similarly grounded in grave deficiencies in the nurturing of workers who went to work at an early age without schooling and who often toiled fourteen hours a day and seven days a week.

Thomas Jefferson was right in declaring that all human beings are created (or, if you will, are by nature) equal. They are also, in terms of their individual differences, unequal in the varying degrees to which they possess the species-specific potentialities common to all. When inequalities between human subgroups that are entirely due to nurture are taken for natural inequalities, that mistake must be overcome and eradicated for the sake of social justice.

The correction of the mistake that confuses nature with nurture leads to certain conclusions that many individuals may find disconcerting. All the cultural and nurtural differences that separate one human subgroup from another are superficial as compared with the underlying common human nature that unites the members of mankind.

Although our samenesses are more important than our differences, we have an inveterate tendency to stress the differences that divide us rather than the samenesses that unite us. We find it difficult to believe that the human mind is the same everywhere because we fail to realize that all the differences, however striking, between the mind of Western man and the mind of human beings nurtured in the various Eastern cultures are, in the last analysis, superficial—entirely the result of different nurturing.

If a world cultural community is ever to come into existence, it will retain cultural pluralism or diversity with respect to all matters that are accidental in human life—such things as cuisine, dress, manners, customs, and the like. These are the things that vary from one human subgroup to another accordingly as these subgroups differ in the way they nurture their members. When that happens, we will have at last overcome the nurtural illusion that there is a Western mind and an Eastern mind, a European mind and an African mind, or a civilized mind and a primitive mind. There is only a human mind and it is one and the same in all human beings.

CULTURAL UNITY AND CULTURAL PLURALISM

The unity of mankind and of the human mind underlies all the differences that are caused by differences in nurture and by their consequences—differences among diverse human creatures.

That being the case, should not an ultimate desideratum of human life on earth be the formation of a single cultural community to which all human beings belong—a single, global cultural community?

You may ask why this should be an ultimate desideratum.

My answer to this question is twofold. First, because world government is necessary not only for world peace, but also—and now more urgently—to preserve the planet as a viable place for human life. In 1943, I wrote a book that argued for world government as indispensable to permanent world peace, and predicted that it would occur in about 500 years. In the years subsequent to 1945, after the destruction of Hiroshima by the first atomic bomb, I changed my prediction of world government to 200 years because of the then threatening nuclear holocaust that would make life unlivable on a large portion of this planet. Now as we near the end of the century and the threat of a nuclear holocaust has dwindled almost to disappearance, another and more serious threat has loomed up—the prospect of climatic and environmental changes that, when they become irreversible, will make the whole planet unlivable for human beings.

It is clear that without worldwide enforced control of all human activities that pollute the environment, its degeneration will continue to the point where lethal disabling environmental conditions are irreversible. To enforce such worldwide control of human activities world government is necessary. The United Nations will not suffice. Nor will the global commons.

This leads to the second reason: world government is impossible without world community; but the existence of world community requires a certain degree of cultural unity—unity of civilization. These things being so, the problem to be solved can be stated as follows. What is the kind and the degree of cultural unity that is required for world community as a basis for world government? How much cultural diversity or pluralism should persist? How much is appropriate and tolerable? What is the basis for determining the matters with regard to which it is reasonable to expect worldwide cultural unity, as well as the basis for determining the matters with regard to which cultural diversity or pluralism should be tolerated because it is not incompatible with the unity of mankind and of the human mind?

The key to the solution of the problem as stated is to be found in a fundamental difference between matters that belong to the sphere of truth and matters that belong to the sphere of taste, together with the moral obligations imposed upon us by our commitment to the pursuit of truth with regard to all matters that properly fall in the sphere of truth. We must also take account of a principle that should regulate our pursuit of truth—the principle that the sphere of truth is itself unified, that it is not divisible into a plurality of separate and incompatible domains.

To illustrate the difference between matters of truth and matters of taste, let me offer you some examples. There is a spectrum of matters some of which clearly belong to the sphere of truth and some as clearly belong to the sphere of taste. Let us start with clear cases at the extreme ends of the spectrum. At one extreme, clearly belonging to the sphere of truth, is mathematics, and associated with it the exact sciences, especially the experimental sciences. Placing these disciplines in the sphere of truth does not mean that there is perfect agreement among all mathematicians or experimental scientists about everything in their fields. But it does mean, that, when they disagree, we expect them to be able to resolve their disagreements by rational processes. An irresolvable disagreement about any matter that properly falls in the sphere of truth would constitute an intellectual scandal. Not only would we find an irresolvable disagreement scandalous and intolerable, not only do we expect mathematicians and experimental scientists to be able to resolve whatever disagreements exist among them, but we also think that it is their obligation not to rest in their efforts to resolve such disagreements until they finally succeed in doing so.

At the opposite extreme, clearly belonging to the sphere of taste, are such matters as cuisine, social manners, styles in dress or dance, and so on. Here we do not expect that men should be able to resolve their differences in taste. We do not expect them to seek to achieve uniformity. On the contrary, we would regard as monstrous any attempt to impose conformity upon all with regard to any one culinary program or set of social manners or style of dress. Here the adoption of one style rather than another is an act of free choice, not an act of the intellect necessitated by completely objective considerations.

Between these extremes, where there is no doubt that we are dealing with matters of truth on the one hand and with matters of taste on the other, philosophy and religion represent a difficult middle ground. The prevalent view today, in academic circles at least, tends to place philosophy and religion on the side of taste rather than the side of truth. In what follows, I will take the opposite view—that philosophy belongs to the sphere of truth, not of taste. With regard to the very difficult problem of locating the position of religion on one or the other side of the line that divides matters of truth from masters of taste, I reserve comment for later.

I turn now to the bearing of the points so far considered on the problem of cultural unity and cultural pluralism. Two things should be immediately obvious. There is no question about worldwide cultural unity with regard to mathematics and the exact and experimental sciences. We have already achieved a high degree of transcultural agreement in these fields, and we should expect it to continue and approach completeness. Nor is there any question about worldwide cultural unity with respect to the principles of technology that are now also transcultural—adopted worldwide. Unity with respect to these principles is, after all, nothing but an extension by application of the agreements achieved in mathematics and the exact sciences.

Tabling for the moment the insistent question about the status of religion, we can say that in all other matters which are matters of taste, we should both expect and tolerate cultural diversity and pluralism, even in a world community when that comes into existence.

There is one whole of truth, no matter how many diverse

parts there are and no matter how diverse the methods by which the truth of the parts is attained. The irrefragable unity of the sphere of truth is merely an extension, but nonetheless a very important extension, of the principle of contradiction: that two propositions—or sets of opinions or beliefs—cannot both be true if they contradict one another. Truth in these different parts may be attained by quite different methods: investigative and experimental, noninvestigative and nonexperimental, intuitive, mystical, or even by the acknowledgment of divine revelation.

Staying within the boundaries of Western civilization or culture, the principle of the unity of truth entails the consequence that the several parts of the one whole of the truth to be attained must coherently fit together. As we have already seen, there cannot be irreconcilable contradictions between one segment of the whole truth and another. What is regarded as true in philosophy and religion must not conflict with what is regarded as true in science.

Since it is only in the spheres of mathematics and experimental science that doctrinal agreement has been achieved in large measure, if not completely, the truths agreed upon in those areas at a given time test the claims to truth that are made in philosophy. In other words, a particular philosophical view must be rejected as false if, at a given time, it comes into conflict with the scientific truths agreed upon at that time.

The same mandate that has been operative within the Western tradition should, therefore, be operative when we go beyond the Western tradition and consider the philosophies of the Far East as well as the philosophies of the West. Just as, within the Western tradition, the truths of mathematics and science that are agreed upon at a given time have been employed as the test for accepting or rejecting Western religious beliefs or philosophical views, so, in exactly the same way, they should be employed as the test for accepting or rejecting Far Eastern religious beliefs or philosophical views.

The principle that whatever is inconsistent or incompatible with the truths of mathematics and science that are agreed upon at a given time must, at that time, be rejected as false is universally applicable—to Eastern as well as to Western culture.

There are only two ways in which this consequence can be avoided. One is to deny the principle of contradiction and, with it, the unity of truth. The other is to regard Eastern religions and philosophies as making no cognitive claims at all, thus putting them along with cuisine, dress, manners, and customs on the side of taste rather than on the side of truth.

However, if the several Far Eastern cultures regard philosophy as an area in which the criteria of truth and falsity are applicable, and if the criteria are operative in the same way in philosophy as they are in science and mathematics, then it must be possible to establish a measure of dialectical agreement, as between the Far East and the West as well as between the several Far Eastern cultures, a measure sufficient to make some progress toward resolving the doctrinal disagreements that exist.

In conclusion, let me repeat the point that constitutes the nerve of my argument. The fruits of technology are now universally put to use. This confirms the universal acknowledgment of a worldwide transcultural doctrinal agreement about the best approximations to truth that we have made so far in mathematics and experimental science. That agreement involves an agreement about the rules of logic and of discourse which enables men to pursue the truth cooperatively and to resolve their disagreements. The logic of science and of mathematics is, like science and mathematics, global, not Western.

Though the method of philosophy may not be the same as that of mathematics or science, the basic framework of its logic is the same. A contradiction is a contradiction whether it occurs in philosophy, in mathematics, or in science. Unchecked equivocation in the use of words generates fallacious arguments, whether in philosophy or in science and mathematics.

The problem of religion is much more difficult than that of philosophy. If religion claims to involve knowledge, then we must face a further question. Is it distinguishable from philosophy as a branch of natural knowledge, or does it regard itself as quite distinct from philosophy and all other branches of natural knowledge because its beliefs are articles of faith, not conclusions supported by empirical evidence and rational arguments? The problem thus raised is so difficult that it requires a separate discourse on the plurality of religions and the unity of truth, a subject addressed in a book of mine, *Truth in Religion*, published in late 1990.

SIX

The New World of the Twenty-first Century: USDR

1. THE SEEDS OF THE FUTURE IN THE PAST

In the century in which two world wars changed the political landscape—the second more than the first an engagement of global extent—and in 1943, the darkest summer in the European theater of war, the summer of the siege of Stalingrad, I wrote a book entitled *How to Think About War and Peace.* [1]*

As I prepared in June to write that book, I asked myself the question, what had others thought about war and peace? I learned two things. First, I discovered that the journalists of the press and radio, the pundits, and even the statesmen, so misused the words "war" and "peace" that they blinded themselves to the realities of the matter. The phrase "cold war" had not yet come into circulation and without the insight that stems from that phrase, they clearly did not understand the intricacies of war and peace.

Second, I also discovered what I had not learned in college

---

*Endnotes for this chapter begin on page 266.

or in the early years of my teaching career, that the idea of world peace through world government was not of recent origin. In 1943, and in the few years immediately preceding, Walter Lippmann, John Foster Dulles, Clarence Streit, Sir Norman Angell, the reigning Pope, and others had mentioned world government as a remote and then unfeasible remedy for future world wars, but they did not appear to know that the idea of world government first emerged with Dante in the thirteenth century and that it had been developed in subsequent centuries by Charles Saint-Pierre, Jean-Jacques Rousseau, Immanuel Kant, Jeremy Bentham, Thorstein Veblen, and others; nor did I know that until I had carefully examined the great books on the subject. [2]

In the almost fifty years that have elapsed since 1943, I joined the World Federalists and campaigned for world government; I was appointed by President Robert M. Hutchins of the University of Chicago to his Committee to Frame a World Constitution, established by him immediately after atomic bombs were dropped on Hiroshima and Nagasaki; I conducted a seminar for the Ford Foundation on war and peace, world peace, and world government in 1951; and I wrote two books (*The Common Sense of Politics*, 1971, and *A Vision of the Future*, 1984), in which these subjects are treated with a maturity acquired by years of thinking about them. [3]

I have placed in Appendix 1, with brief comments, eloquent statements relevant to the meanings of the words "war" and "peace." These, when understood, show that in the present world of international affairs there are only three possible relationships, one of which does not yet exist.

I have placed in Appendix 2 a sampling of expressions of the idea and ideal of perpetual world peace and its implementation through world government, beginning with Dante in the thirteenth century and coming down to John Strachey in 1963.

I recommend to readers that they read carefully both of

these appendixes as preparation for reading my own brief summary of the matter in the following sections of this essay.

Section 2 will be concerned with the fundamental understanding of war and peace, and with the clarification of current misconceptions about them.

Section 3 will briefly summarize the argument for world government as both the necessary and sufficient condition of permanent world peace. It will also deal with the possibility, the probability, and the desirability of world government.

Section 4 will deal with the major obstacles to world government, the most serious of which may be overcome in the last decade of this century by the steps being taking by the technologically advanced nations to approach homogeneity in their political institutions and in their economic arrangements. [4]

Finally, in Section 5, I will close with a vision of the new world of the twentieth century, in which the conflict between the two great superpowers—the USA and its NATO allies vs. the USSR and its Warsaw Pact satellites—will be replaced by the USDR (a union of socialist democratic republics). This will be a penultimate stage of progress toward a truly global world federal union that will eliminate the remaining potentially threatening conflict between the have and the have-not nations. [5]

2. THE UNDERSTANDING OF WAR AND PEACE

Journalistically, popularly, and academically, the words "war" and "peace" are used with meanings that do not account for all the realities of the matter. To think adequately and clearly about the relationships involved, we must distinguish between two meanings of the word "peace" and, correspondingly, two meanings of the word "war."

We say that the United States is currently at peace with its adjacent neighbors, Canada and Mexico; that it is also at peace with England, Iran, and the Soviet Union. When we speak thus, we are using the word "peace" negatively to mean the absence of actual fighting—no use of military force in any kind of military engagement. It is only in this negative sense that we speak of international peace.

We might qualify this negative meaning of the word "peace" by adding that Canada and England are friendly nations in their relation to the United States; that Iran is hostile; and that the relationship between the Soviet Union and the United States, which for many years of this century was hostile, has now become friendly, though both countries still persist in trying to achieve something like a balance of military power, which is not the case in the relation of Canada or England to the United States.

This difference in the relation between friendly and hostile nations—nations that are at peace in the sense of *not* being engaged in actual military action against each other—clearly affects the conduct of their foreign policies and the actions of their diplomats. As the great German military strategist Carl von Clausewitz observed in his book *On War*, it is only when the diplomats fail to serve the interests of their countries about seriously disputed issues that the military take over, to carry out the foreign policies in which the diplomats could not succeed.

In sharp contrast to this purely negative meaning of the word "peace," there is the positive meaning of the word when we use it to say that peace exists among the citizens of the United States, a peace that is breached by criminal actions of all sorts and by all acts of violence or terrorism. What do we have in mind when we use the word "peace" in this other way?

We mean much more than just the absence of military action. That kind of peace did not exist among the people of the United States when in the last century the citizens of its Northern and Southern states engaged in a bitter civil war with one another. It is most unlikely that anything like that internecine strife will ever occur again in this country. Since then the people of our fifty states have lived peacefully with one another in the sense that all the disputes or quarrels that may arise between one state and another can be settled without resort to the violence of military action. How? By the action of our federal judiciary and our federal legislature.

In short, when constitutional and legal means for settling all disputes are available and effective between the states of a federal union such as ours, the people live at peace with one another—a peace not threatened by the seriousness of the quarrels that may break out among them.

The same kind of peace exists in each of the states of our federal union; not only in Massachusetts, Pennsylvania, and California, but also in the great cities of those states—in Boston, Philadelphia, and Los Angeles. There, too, it is not the absence of serious disputes or quarrels that constitutes such peace, but the presence of judicial and legislative remedies for effectively settling issues without having to resort to the use of force, violence, or fighting in order to do so. The disputes or quarrels can be settled by speech, by voting, by available political means, by all the resources of civil government that, according to the great German jurist Hans Kelsen, exercises a monopoly of authorized force when it exercises its police powers to enforce the judgments of its courts or its legislative enactments.

To remember the difference between (a) the negative meaning of "peace" that is merely the absence of military action between states that have foreign policies and engage in diplomacy to carry them out, and (b) the positive meaning of the word when we say that people living in civil society under civil government are at peace with one another, let us always call the latter state of affairs "civil peace." Where civil peace exists, as in the United States, in California, or in Los Angeles, it is established and preserved by civil government.

How do we use the word "war" in senses corresponding to the negative and positive meanings of "peace" that we have just noted? In the War of 1812, England made war upon the United States, a war that was settled by a so-called peace treaty. With that one exception, England and the United States have been at peace with one another, but only in the negative sense of no actual warfare between them, not in the positive sense that all serious disputes between them can be settled by diplomatic means and without recourse to the violence of military action. Being completely sovereign states, they have only diplomacy or warfare as means for settling disputes. Both are members of the United Nations, but that is not an effective civil government with either the authority or the power to settle serious disputes among its members.

The positive sense of the word "war" signifies actual warfare—the kind of military engagement that occurred between England and the United States in 1812. But the word also has a negative sense in which it connotes the absence of civil peace between states, especially those hostile to one another, when they have no means of settling their disputes without resort to actual warfare after all diplomatic efforts fail to do so.

As readers will discover by examining Appendix 1, the great writers of the past about war and peace used the phrase "state of war" to distinguish the negative sense of the word "war" from the positive sense in which it signifies actual warfare. They maintained that a state of war always exists among human beings living in what they called "a state of nature," by which they mean living anarchically—not in civil society under civil government. Even when they concede that there may never have been a time on earth when human beings lived in a state of nature, they call our attention to the fact that sovereign princes and sovereign states that are not federated are always in a state of nature in relation to one another (or, what is the same, in a state of war), because when serious disputes occur and diplomatic measures fail to resolve them, the only option left is fighting—actual warfare.

As Cicero, Machiavelli, and Locke point out in amazingly

parallel statements, when disputes cannot be settled by talk or law (which are the means available to human beings but not to brutes), the only option remaining is to employ the methods of the jungle (see Appendix 1).

The use of the phrase "cold war" to designate the relation between the United States and the Soviet Union during much of this century shows that we have learned to use the word "war" for a relationship between hostile sovereign states that is neither one of civil peace nor one of actual warfare. This indicates that the negative meaning of the word "peace" (that is, the absence of actual warfare) is, in the case of hostile nations, identical with the state of affairs described by the phrases "cold war" or "state of war." That peace is negative in two senses: it is not only the absence of actual warfare; it is also the absence of civil peace. It is a state of affairs intermediate between actual warfare and civil peace.

As such, it is the only peace that has ever existed between sovereign princes or sovereign states, whether they happen to be friendly or hostile. There never has been international peace in any sense except this purely negative meaning of the word "peace" (see Appendix 1).

3. THE NECESSITY OF CIVIL GOVERNMENT FOR CIVIL PEACE

When the difference between civil peace and international peace—between peace in the positive sense and peace in the negative sense—is fully understood, the argument for civil world government as necessary for world civil peace can be stated in a few unquestionable propositions.

Disarmament, partial or complete, does not and cannot preserve or perpetuate peace between sovereign nations that have been or have become hostile. It cannot do so because the only peace that exists between sovereign states, especially nations that are hostile, is one that involves conflicting foreign policies and the attempts of diplomacy to resolve matters at issue. As we have seen, when diplomacy fails, and the matters at issue are regarded as crucial to national interests, military action is inevitable. When conversations completely break down, fighting begins.

In any community in which civil peace is present, government is necessary not only to prevent recourse to violence as a means for settling quarrels, because the existence of government makes law and talk available as effective non-violent means. Government is also necessary to decide matters of policy and of conduct concerning which reasonable persons can disagree, even such simple matters as the regulation of traffic. In any community, small or large, if driving on the left or right side of the road and a safe speed of driving were not regulated by law and were left instead to the decision of differing individuals, pandemonium would result and the civil peace of that community would be shattered.

Here, then, are the unquestionable propositions, referred to above, that constitute the nerve of the argument for the necessity of world civil government to preserve and perpetuate world civil peace. They are all hypothetical propositions.

1. *If* civil government is necessary for civil peace in any organized community, small or large—in villages, towns, and metropolitan municipalities, and in sovereign states, either independent states or states that are members of a federal union—*then* civil government is necessary for civil peace in that largest of all possible communities, the global community that includes all the peoples on earth.

2. *If* world civil government is necessary for world civil peace, *then* it must also be *possible* to unite all the sovereign states that now exist in a federal union, in which those states would relinquish their external sovereignty (namely, their power to engage in diplomacy with one another, to engage in warfare, and to contract treaties) while retaining their internal sovereignty (as do the fifty states in the federal union that is the United States of America). The categorical proposition implicit in this hypothetical proposition asserts that what is necessary cannot be impossible.

3. *If* world civil government is possible, then a world cultural community must also be possible. That possibility is quite compatible with the continued existence of pluralism with regard to diverse languages and ethnic diversity in customs and conventions, in mythologies and religions, and in all matters about which reasonable men and women may reasonably disagree. The only things that now prevail which would be precluded by world government from continuing to exist are foreign policies, diplomacy, military installations and personnel, customs and immigration barriers, and the existence of persons called foreigners.

The rule of logic applicable to hypothetical propositions is that affirmation of the antecedent clause, the *if* clause, entails affirmation of the consequent clause, the *then* clause. Denial of the consequent entails denial of the antecedent.

Those who argue against the possibility of world civil peace and the possibility of a global civil government, concluding that neither is necessary, tend to confuse the possible and the probable. To say that something is unlikely or improbable is not to say that it is impossible.

When we consider all the obstacles and difficulties that must be overcome in order to constitute a world federal union and to establish world civil peace, we are led to make different estimates of the probability that world civil government can be established at some foreseeable time in the future; but whether those estimates are short-term or long-term in no way affects the possibility of its occurrence, and certainly not the necessity of it.

At various times in the last fifty years, in arguing for the necessity and possibility of world federal government, I have made different estimates of the probability of its occurrence. When I wrote *How to Think About War and Peace* in 1942, I predicted that we might establish world government in 500 years. That was before the dropping of atomic bombs on Hiroshima and Nagasaki. After that, the desirability of establishing world federal government to prevent a thermonuclear holocaust, which might make a large portion of the globe uninhabitable, shortened my prediction to 300 years or less. In the sixties and seventies, as the cold war between the US and USSR intensified and the two superpowers strove to exceed each other in building nuclear weapons, that prediction was further shortened.

In the last decade, though the threat of a thermonuclear holocaust diminished, the threat of irreversible damage to the environment, which might make the planet inhospitable to life, increased. The need for world civil government to prevent that from happening has still further shortened the time in which it must be established in order to deal effectively with the viability of this planet as a dwelling place for the human race.

All these considerations affect different estimates of the desirability and probability of world government, but have no bearing on its necessity or possibility. It remains possible without being probable at any time in the foreseeable future. It can also be necessary for world civil peace without also being sufficiently desirable to motivate human beings to pay the price for it and to make the effort to surmount all the obstacles and difficulties that stand in the way of its establishment.

There are many arguments concerning the desirability and undesirability of world civil government. In the opinion of many, all governments are necessary evils. World government, in their view, would be the worst of such necessary evils, not to mention its undesirability in terms of the surrender of national sovereignty to constitute a world federal union.

Readers will find these arguments, pro and con, considered in Appendixes 3 and 4, where they will also find much more ample statements of the argument for the necessity of world civil government to establish world civil peace, which has been briefly summarized here in three hypothetical propositions.

The establishment of world civil government at some future time may preclude the occurrence of the kind of international warfare that from the beginning of independent sovereign states has always existed on earth. But it does not preclude the possibility of a war between the states of a world federal union, something like the war between the Northern and Southern states that, in the history of the United States, is often called a civil war.

However, that war did not end with a peace treaty, but with a declaration of amnesty, which restored the civil peace that had been sundered. When international wars end with peace treaties, the peace established by those treaties is the negative peace of a truce. [6] The fighting ceases, but the diplomats go to work again and the military prepare for the next outbreak of warfare when the diplomats fail.

It has been said that if world government were to come about, it would eventuate either through world conquest or through a world constitutional convention. Only the latter would serve the purpose of world peace. Government must be constitutional, not despotic, if it is to be the indispensable condition of peace.

In any community ruled despotically, insurrection and rebellion are forever brewing among those who are oppressed by the injustice of the despot. [7] The peace of the community is fragile and perishable. If world civil peace is to be stable and perpetual, the world government required for its establishment must be constitutional, not despotic. A military conquest of the world by a superpower, ending in despotic world government, could not establish stable and perpetual world civil peace.

4. THE FOUR MAJOR OBSTACLES TO WORLD GOVERNMENT

Of the four major obstacles to world government, two have been overcome or are now in the process of being overcome. Two still remain to be surmounted. They are the most obdurate and intractable.

In the long march toward world government until this

century, a major obstacle was the size of the global community. It appeared to be ungovernable. But the technological advances made in the twentieth century, especially in travel and communication time, have shrunk the size of the globe to an extent less than the travel and communication time that prevailed in the eighteenth century among the thirteen independent states on the Atlantic seaboard of this country. After the Philadelphia convention in 1787, the anti-Federalists argued that the domain for which a federal constitution was being drafted and was submitted to the people for adoption was too large to be governable.

Until very recently, as recently as the closing months of 1989 and the succeeding months of 1990, another serious obstacle remained, one that appeared to be insurmountable. Once again our own experience in constitutional construction helps us to define the character of this second obstacle. The opening clause of Section 4 of Article IV of the Constitution reads as follows: "The United States shall guarantee to every State in this Union a republican form of Government. . . ." This applies not only to the thirteen states that were called upon to ratify or reject the Constitution as drafted; it also applied in the future to any of the Western territories that would apply for admission to the federal union.

The significance of this clause is that it calls for political homogeneity of the states comprising the union. If the national government of the federal union is to be a republican, which is to say a constitutional, form of government, its member states must also be constitutional in their forms of government. What is being rejected as unfeasible is political heterogeneity, some of the federating states being constitutional in their form of government, while others were despotic—governments by might rather than by right, governments with force but without authority derived from the consent of the governed.

The economic homogeneity of the federating states did not even have to be mentioned, because in the eighteenth century all the states had agrarian, preindustrial economies, with private ownership of the farmlands, of hand tools and simple machines, and of beasts of burden, including chattel slaves in the Southern states.

In the middle years of the twentieth century, the technologically advanced, industrial countries of what came to be called the First and Second worlds were both politically and economically heterogeneous in radically opposing respects. On the one hand, the private property, capital-intensive economies of nations that were politically democratic in varying degrees formed one bloc of nations. On the other hand, capital-intensive economies of the countries in which all capital was owned by totalitarian states that were governed despotically formed another bloc of nations. This radical heterogeneity, both political and economic, so long as it persisted, would have remained an insurmountable obstacle to a federal union that included the states of the First and Second worlds.

That obstacle is now being surmounted and there is every reason to hope and believe that it will be more and more effectively surmounted in the decade immediately ahead. As pointed out in Endnote 13 to the first chapter of this book, the technologically advanced industrialized countries either are or are becoming democratic republics. They also either are or are becoming free-enterprise market economies, with private ownership of capital.

What once was a conflict between antagonistic governments and economies, radically heterogeneous, is now moving toward fraternal and cooperative relationships among states that are or are becoming politically and economically homogeneous. What once was an unbridgeable chasm between the First and Second worlds promises to become a new First World order in the next century, with no inherent obstacle to the membership of these states in a federal union.

The despotically ruled oil-producing countries of the Arabic and Islamic Middle East have now become a Second World in conflict with the First and the technologically retarded, insufficiently industrialized countries have now become a Third World. Many or most of them are also democracies in name only or are despotically governed. Here is the political and economic heterogeneity that remains an obstacle to global world government and remains to be surmounted.

It is still too early to outline the ways and steps by which to overcome this third major obstacle to world civil peace through world civil government. A federal union including all the states in the First World may have to precede the solution of this problem; for it may be that only by the united action of these states can conflict, and even possible warfare, between the have and the have-not nations be avoided or ameliorated. The difficult problem to be solved is complicated by the fact that 75 percent of the world's population live, or merely subsist, in the have-not nations, and it is there that population increase is on the rise.

A whole world of haves without have-nots, both political and economic haves, may look like an utterly impracticable utopian dream, even to those who are persuaded that it is feasible to socialize private-property capitalism more completely and to make democracy more effective than it now is in the technologically advanced, industrialized nations of the new First World.

Finally, we come to the fourth and most intractable of the four major obstacles to a world civil government by a global federal union. It is most intractable because it is the only one of the four major obstacles that is entirely emotional and irrational.

Of the three others, two are either now solved or are in the process of being solved and one is subject to rational consideration. But thinking about this fourth obstacle can do no good, for those whose emotions generate it are deaf to the voice of reason and blind to the necessity and desirability of world civil peace.

Everywhere in the world we now see resurgent nationalism rampant, filled with the passion for preserving ancient ethnic identities, with virulent racial prejudices and hatreds, with passion for the illusory purity of bloodlines that must be protected against infection by outsiders. This rising tribalism and ethnocentrism in Europe, in the Near East, in Africa, in India and Pakistan, and in the Far East involves what appears to be an incurable xenophobia, an inveterate attachment to locality, an emotional provincialism or parochialism that is totally incompatible with thinking about the need to abandon the external sovereignty of independent states in order for them to enter into a federal union, not to mention their taking actual steps to do so. As Arnold Toynbee observed, it was this inveterate attachment to locality that frustrated the efforts of the Delian League to resolve the issues that, unresolved, lead to the Peloponnesian War in the fifth century B.C.

5. THE MOTIVATION NEEDED TO OVERCOME THE EMOTIONAL OBSTACLE

When the opening papers of *The Federalist* argued for the ratification by the citizens of New York of the constitution that had been drafted at the convention in Philadelphia, they gave what they thought were two compelling reasons for doing so. The first was that without federal union, actual warfare between the states could not be prevented; in fact, hostilities were at that time brewing between New York and New Jersey about rights to the waterways that separated them and about commerce between them. [8]

Their second argument, which they thought might be even more persuasive, was the common defense of the eastern seaboard from invasion from abroad. The thirteen independent states, by surrendering their external sovereignty to form a federal union, would be better able to secure themselves from subjugation by a foreign power than each of them alone could effect.

These two reasons proved to be sufficiently persuasive to

overcome the emotional obstacles (which operated less strin-
gently than they are operating in the world today) to preserve
the separate identity of local groups and their inveterate attachment to locality. The prevention of war between the states
and protection from conquest from outside was sufficient
motivation for the people of the thirteen former British colonies to pay the price they had to pay for peace and national
security.

Peace—not merely the absence of fighting, but civil peace
where there are are effective means for settling disputes without diplomacy or military action—is an ideal state of affairs
toward which human beings, for the most part, aspire, or to
which they at least pay lip service as a desirable goal. But
when they count the costs of actually establishing such peace
to replace the anarchy of sovereign states and the state of
nature and of war between them that such anarchy maintains,
most human beings find themselves emotionally unwilling to
pay the price. That is increasingly evident in the world today.

What motivation is needed for the peoples of the world
—both in the new First World and in the new Second
World—to overcome their emotional reluctance or even passionate resistance to move in the direction of world civil
government? What will make them willing to pay the price
for it?

Fortunately or unfortunately, there is no threat of invasion
from outer space to impel them to unite for the common
defense of this planet. The threat of a thermonuclear holocaust that would create an unlivable nuclear winter on most
of this planet's surface has now dwindled. With these two
threats nonexistent or lessened as motivations for overcoming
the emotional impediments to thinking about and acting for
peace on earth, is there any threat that can operate with
sufficient force?

Yes, a threat that has emerged with growing awareness
in the last half of this century. It is the threat of irreversible
damage to the environment that will make this planet inhos-

pitable to human life. To operate as it should to overcome worldwide emotional reluctance and resistance, that threat must be clearly understood and emotionally felt by more and more of the world's peoples, in the have-not as well as in the have nations.

Not only is this less likely to occur in the have-not nations, but it must also be recognized that, if the have-not nations must speedily industralize in order to become socialist democracies, their industrialization will itself hasten the deterioration of the environment to the point where irreversible lethal changes will occur. In other words, the time it will take for the environmental threat to become effectively operative in both the have and the have-not nations will itself be shortened by the industrialization of the have-not nations.

Be that as it may, the threat of lethal environmental change is the only threat that can have the persuasive power to overcome the emotional obstacles that now are as raging and rampant as they have ever been in the past. It is a sad but true commentary on mankind that human beings may be compelled to do on their knees, groveling in despair, what they should do for sound reasons, upright and hopeful, by the exercise of their minds.

That all human beings participate in one and the same human nature and that the human mind is essentially the same everywhere on earth is the last, best hope for the fraternity among all the peoples of the earth that is needed for world civil peace through world civil government. All the differences that have arisen among human subgroups, ethnic or national, are of nurtural origin, and like all the cultural differences that remain, are superficial as compared with the profound sameness of human nature and the unity of the human mind.

The preceding chapter in this book, on human nature, nurture, and culture, explains the origin of the widespread twentieth-century error about the nonexistence of human nature along with the equally important mistake of regarding the differences, especially the inequalities, between human subgroups as being natural, instead of being nurtural and, therefore, eradicable.

The twentieth century had seen three elements in human life and society become globally transcultural: technology and the mathematics and natural science that underlie it. Philosophy and religion are still not transcultural. However much one may hope that they, too, become transcultural if, like natural science, they claim logical and factual truth for themselves, their not ever becoming transcultural is not an impediment to global federal union.

We know this from the fact that, where smaller federal unions have come into existence and have endured, pluralism in the spheres of philosophy and religion have not been disruptive. Even with an irreducible pluralism in the spheres of philosophy and religion, a worldwide cultural community in technology, mathematics, and natural science may be a sufficient foundation for world civil government. It can come into being and endure with pluralism in all matters of taste about which human beings can reasonably differ without disputing, or in matters of public policy about which they can reasonably differ, engage in dispute, and resort to majority rule in order to settle their disputes. (See Appendix 5 on the vision of what is possible in the future.)

ENDNOTES

1. Published in New York in 1944.
2. See Chapter 2 of *How to Think About War and Peace*. After being defeated for the presidency by Franklin Delano Roosevelt, Wendell Willkie later made his world tour and wrote a best seller entitled *One World* (1943).

Here is a brief bibliography of the major works on the idea of world peace through world government.

Dante Alighieri: *On World Government or De Monarchia* (1310–13), New York, 1949.

Charles Saint-Pierre: *Scheme for Lasting Peace* (1739), London, 1939.

Jean-Jacques Rousseau: *A Lasting Peace* (1756), London, 1917.

Immanuel Kant: *Perpetual Peace* (1795), New York, 1939.

Jeremy Bentham: *A Plan for a Universal and Perpetual Peace* (1789), London, 1939.

Thorstein Veblen: *An Inquiry into the Nature of Peace and the Terms of Its Perpetuation*, London, 1917.

3. The Committee to Frame a World Constitution had the following membership:

ROBERT M. HUTCHINS, Chancellor of the University of Chicago; Chairman of the Board of Editors of the *Encyclopaedia Britannica*

G. A. BORGESE, Professor in the Division of the Humanities, University of Chicago; author of *Goliath*

MORTIMER J. ADLER, Professor of the Philosophy of Law, University of Chicago; Associate Editor of the *Great Books of the Western World*; author of *How to Think About War and Peace*

STRINGFELLOW BARR, former President of St. John's College

ALBERT LEON GUÉRARD, Professor Emeritus of General Literature, Stanford University; author of *Europe Free and United*

HAROLD A. INNIS, Professor and Chairman of the Department of Political Economy, University of Toronto

ERICH KAHLER, Visiting Professor at Cornell University; author of *Man the Measure*

WILBER G. KATZ, Dean of the Law School, University of Chicago

CHARLES H. MCILWAIN, Professor Emeritus of Science of Government, Harvard University; author of *The Growth of Political Thought in the West* and *Constitutionalism, Ancient and Modern*

ROBERT REDFIELD, Professor and Chairman of the Department of Anthropology, University of Chicago, member of the Board of the American Council on Race Relations

REXFORD GUY TUGWELL, Professor of Political Science, University of Chicago; former Governor of Puerto Rico; author of *Battle for Democracy*

An extensive excerpt from the preliminary draft of a world constitution, as written and published in 1947–48, will be found at the end of Appendix 2.

4. On this matter of political and economic homogeneity, see Endnote 13 attached to the first chapter in this book.

5. See ibid.

6. In his account of the beginning of the Peloponnesian War, Thucydides tells us that the envoys from each country returned home and did not return again. Then at the opening of Book II of his history, he writes as follows:

> The war between the Athenians and Peloponnesians and the allies on either side now really begins. For now all [communication] except through the medium of heralds ceased, and hostilities were commenced and prosecuted without intermission (Thucydides, *History of the Peloponnesian War*, Chapter 6).

The actual fighting was interrupted for a little more than twenty years. Thucydides refers to this period of time as a truce rather than as a period of peace, because both sides were then preparing to resume the military contest.

7. John Locke, in his *Second Treatise on Civil Government*, comments on the meaning of the word "rebellion" (*rebellare*). Those who transgress lawful civil government and rule despotically return to a state of war with their subjects (which is the literal meaning of the word *rebellare*).

In another place in his treatise, Locke adds the following statement:

> Whosoever uses force without right—as every one does in society who does it without law—puts himself into a state of war with those against whom he so uses it, and in that state all former ties are cancelled, all other rights cease, and every one has a right to defend himself, and to resist the aggressor (John Locke, *Second Treatise on Civil Government*, Chapter XIX, Section 232).

Aquinas goes further. In his view, any injustice imposed by force renders a civil peace defective:

> For if one man enters into concord with another, not by a spontaneous will but through being forced, as it were, by the fear of some evil that threatens him, such concord is not really peace. . . . (Thomas Aquinas, *Summa Theologica*, Part II-II, Q. 29, A. 1, Reply 1).

> . . . there is no peace when a man agrees with another man counter to what he would prefer. Consequently, men seek by means of war to break this concord, because it is a defective peace, in order that they may obtain a peace in which nothing is contrary to their will (Ibid., Q. 29, A. 2, Reply 2).

> [Hence] peace is the work of justice . . . insofar as justice removes the obstacles to peace (Ibid., Q. 29, A. 3, Reply 3).

8. In *The Federalist, No. 6*, Alexander Hamilton writes:

> To look for a continuation of harmony between a number of independent, unconnected sovereignties in the same neighbourhood, would be to disregard the uniform course of human events, and to set at defiance the accumulated experience of ages.

Appendix 1. On the Meanings of the Words "War" and "Peace"

Three strikingly parallel passages from Cicero, Machiavelli, and Locke:

> There are two ways of settling disputed questions; one by discussion, the other by force. The first being characteristic of man, the second of brutes, we should have recourse to the latter only if the former fails.
> —CICERO, *De Officiis*, bk. I, sec. XI, chap. 34 (44 B.C.)

> There are two ways of contesting, the one by law, the other by force; the first method is proper to men, the second to beasts;

but because the first is frequently not sufficient, it is necessary to have recourse to the second.
                —MACHIAVELLI, *The Prince*, chap. XVIII (1513)

There are two sorts of contests among men, the one managed by law, the other by force; and these are of such nature that where the one ends, the other always begins.
                —JOHN LOCKE, *Letter Concerning Toleration* (1706)

In antiquity, Plato on war and peace:

. . . What men in general term peace would be . . . only a name; in reality every city is in a natural state of war with every other, not indeed proclaimed by heralds, but everlasting.
                —PLATO, *Laws*, I, 626 (5th century B.C.)

In modern times, Hobbes, Rousseau, and Locke on war and peace:

. . . It is manifest that during the time men live without a common power to keep them all in awe, they are in that condition which is called *war*; and such a war as is of every man against every man. For war consisteth not in battle only, or the act of fighting, but in a tract of time, wherein the will to contend by battle is sufficiently known: and therefore the notion of *time* is to be considered in the nature of war, as it is in the nature of weather. For as the nature of foul weather lieth not in a shower or two of rain, but in an inclination thereto of many days together: so the nature of war consisteth not in actual fighting, but in the known disposition thereto during all the time there is no assurance to the contrary. All other time is *peace*.
                —THOMAS HOBBES, *Leviathan*, chap. XIII (1651)

. . . Though there had never been any time wherein particular men were in a condition of war one against another, yet in all times kings and persons of sovereign authority, because of their independency, are in continual jealousies, and in the state and posture of gladiators, having their weapons pointing, and their eyes fixed on one another; that is, their forts, garrisons, and

guns upon the frontiers of their kingdoms, and continual spies
upon their neighbours, which is a posture of war.
    —THOMAS HOBBES, *Leviathan*, chap. XIII (1651)

War between two Powers is the result of a settled intention,
manifested on both sides, to destroy the enemy State, or at least
to weaken it by all means at their disposal. The carrying of this
intention into act is war, strictly so called; so long as it does
not take shape in act, it is only a state of war. . . . The state of
war is the natural relation of one Power to another.
    —JEAN-JACQUES ROUSSEAU, *A Lasting Peace* and
        The State of War (c. 1756)

Want of a common judge with authority puts all men in a state
of Nature. . . . [If, in a state of nature, men fail to settle their
differences by reason, they enter into a state of war which is
the realm of force] or a declared design of force . . . where there
is no common superior on earth to appeal to for relief. . . .
    —JOHN LOCKE, *Second Treatise Concerning
        Civil Government*, chap. XIX, sec. 19

[Writing about Saint-Pierre's scheme in his essay on *A Lasting
Peace Through the Federation of Europe* (1761), Rousseau argued for federation as the only way to procure such peace on
the continent. We must admit, he declared,] that the powers of
Europe stand to each other strictly in a state of war, and that
all the separate treaties between them are in the nature of a
temporary truce rather than a real peace. [This is due to the
fact that the only] recognized method of settling disputes between one prince and another [is] the appeal to the sword; a
method inseparable from the state of anarchy and war, which
necessarily springs from the absolute independence conceded to
all sovereigns under the imperfect conditions now prevailing in
Europe.
    —JEAN-JACQUES ROUSSEAU, *A Lasting Peace* (c. 1756)

Emery Reves and E.B. White on the misuse of the words
"war" and "peace" in the twentieth century:

All those brief respites from war which we called "peace" were
nothing but diplomatic, economic, political, and financial wars

between the various groups of men called "nations," with the only distinction that these conflicts, rivalries, and hostilities have been fought out with all the means except actual shooting.
    —EMERY REVES, *A Democratic Manifesto*, p. 64 (1942)

Nothing is more frightening than to hear what is not law called law, what is not peace called peace. . . . To speak as though we had peace when what we've got is treaties and pacts, to use the word "peace" for non-peace, is to lessen our chance of ever getting world peace, since the first step toward getting it is to realize with dazzling clearness that we haven't got it and never have had it.
    —E. B. WHITE, "Talk of the Town,"
    The New Yorker, May 6, 1943

Appendix 2. On World Peace Through World Government

In the 13th century, Dante in *On World-Government, or De Monarchia*:

Wherever there can be contention, there judgment should exist; otherwise things would exist imperfectly, without their own means of adjustment or correction, which is impossible, since in things necessary, God or Nature is not defective. Between any two governments, neither of which is in any way subordinate to the other, contention can arise either through their own fault or that of their subjects. This is evident. Therefore there should be judication between them. And since neither can know the affairs of the other, not being subordinated (for among equals there is no authority), there must be a third and wider power which can rule both within its own jurisdiction. This third power is either the world-government or it is not. If it is, we have reached our conclusion; if it is not, it must in turn have its equal outside its jurisdiction, and then it will need a third party as judge, and so *ad infinitum*, which is impossible. So we must arrive at a first and supreme judge for whom all contentions are judiciable either directly or indirectly; and this will be our world-governor or emperor. Therefore, world-government is necessary for the world.

—Dante Alighieri, *De Monarchia*,
bk. I, chap. 10 (c. 1313)

World-government . . . must be understood in the sense that it governs mankind on the basis of what all have in common and that by a common law it leads all toward peace. This common norm or law should be received by local governments in the same way that practical intelligence in action receives its major premises from the speculative intellect. To these it adds its own particular minor premises and then draws particular conclusions for the sake of its action. These basic norms not only can come from a single source, but must do so in order to avoid confusion among universal principles. Moses himself followed this pattern in the law which he composed, for, having chosen the chiefs of the several tribes, he left them the lesser judgments, reserving to himself alone the higher and more general. These common norms were then used by the tribal chiefs according to their special needs. Therefore, it is better for mankind to be governed by one, not by many; and hence by a single governor, the world ruler; and if it is better, it is pleasing to God, since He always wills the better. And when there are only two alternatives—the better is also the best, and is consequently not only pleasing to God, but the choice of "one" rather than "many" is what most pleases Him. Hence it follows that mankind lives best under a single government, and therefore that such a government is necessary for the well-being of the world.

—Dante Alighieri, *De Monarchia*,
bk. I, chap. 14

. . . The proper work of mankind taken as a whole is to exercise continually its entire capacity for intellectual growth, first, in theoretical matters, and, secondarily, as an extension of theory in practice. [This function] cannot be achieved by a single man, or family, or neighborhood, or city, or state, [but only by] the whole of mankind as an organized multitude. . . . [Therefore], *to achieve this state of universal well-being, a single world-government is necessary.*

—DANTE ALIGHIERI, *De Monarchia,*
bk. I, chaps. 3–5

Comment on Immanuel Kant's essay "Perpetual Peace" (1795), excerpted from the *Syntopicon* chapter on War and Peace:

Not only does Kant definitely dismiss the notion of a world union formed along American lines, but even that less perfect union of states which would have the form of a *"Permanent Congress of Nations"* seems to him an impracticable idea in the world as it is at the end of the eighteenth century. "With the too great extension of such a Union of States over vast regions," he writes, "any government of it, and consequently the protection of its individual members, must at last become impossible; and thus a multitude of such corporations would again bring round a state of war."

Nevertheless, Kant refuses to yield completely to this conclusion. "The morally practical reason," he affirms, "utters within us its irrevocable *Veto: 'There shall be no War.'* . . . Hence the question no longer is as to whether Perpetual Peace is a real thing or not a real thing, or as to whether we may not be deceiving ourselves when we adopt the former alternative, but we must *act* on the supposition of its being real. We must work for what may perhaps not be realized . . . and thus we may put an end to the evil of wars, which have been the chief interest of the internal arrangements of all States without exception."

And in his *Idea of a Universal History on a Cosmo-Political Plan*, Kant does more than urge upon us our moral duty to work for perpetual peace as prerequisite to "the highest political good." He engages in prophecy. He pictures the nations of the world "after many devastations, overthrows, and even complete internal exhaustion of their powers" as "driven forward to the goal which Reason might well have impressed upon them, even without so much sad experience. This is none other than the advance out of the lawless state of savages and the entering into a Federation of Nations. . . . However visionary this idea may appear to be . . . it is nevertheless the inevitable issue of the necessity in which men involve one another."

John Strachey on democracy and world government:

A CONCLUSION

My conclusion is, then, that while democracy is no cure-all, it will prove to be the political system of the future. It is no cure-all, first because it is not yet applicable to large parts of the world and, second, because, even if it were, it would still fail, in itself, to solve some of the more acute problems of our period.

Nevertheless, democracy is the political system of the future, because it is by far the best way—in the long run the only tolerable way—of managing complex, highly developed societies made up of well-educated people, capable of taking part in public affairs. As these societies are the most powerful and influential, they will set the pace for the rest of the world.

But this is to look at democracy in a utilitarian, cold-blooded sort of way. Democracy is not only the most practical way of running up-to-date communities. It is much more than that. It is the only political system which recognises the ultimate worth of every human being: which gives expression to the conviction that behind and beyond all the enormous inequalities, in education, in opportunity, and perhaps in innate ability, which today distinguish one man from another, there is yet an ultimate equivalence between all men, as men. Democracy gives expression to the conviction that no one of us, and certainly no government, is fit to say that one man is inherently better than another. In a word, democracy is a political system for free men instead of slaves.

WORLD DEMOCRACY

Democracy is simply the best way yet discovered of arranging the affairs of advanced modern societies. It is not a potential solution to the human problem, for there is none. For we had better learn to be modest in the demands we make on human institutions. One of my favourite quotations on democracy is a saying of old Churchill's: "Democracy," he used to say, stumping his way down the lobbies of the House of Commons, "democracy is the worst form of government in the world, except for all the others. . . ."

There is another reason why democracy is not in itself a cure-all. Even if all the existing states in the world could become effectively functioning democracies, which they can't, this would not in itself be enough. This is because a world of a hundred or more democratic states would still be a world of *states*; a world of *sovereign* states; and it is my considered opinion that sovereign states will not do in the nuclear age. This form of human organisation will not secure the survival of the human race in the desperate epoch in which we live.

This raises the whole question of democracy and war. War—the prevention of war—is the supreme question of our epoch. This is a far more cogent issue than whether we should organise our economic life on capitalist or socialist lines. After all, experience is showing that peoples can survive under either capitalism or socialism; but they cannot survive under nuclear war.

Writing as a life-long socialist, I must say that there is no question on which, looking back, we socialists have suffered more disillusion than on this question of war. I think that all socialists, whether of the left or the right, whether crusty old Social Democrats like myself, or active Communists, once believed, to a greater or lesser extent, that the essential cause of war lay in the economic rivalries of capitalist states. From this diagnosis of the causes of war arose the belief that once capitalism had been abolished and society organized on a socialist basis, the cause of war would have been removed and the establishment of world peace would be easy enough. I do not see how this argument can be maintained any longer.

We have now had 45 years' experience of the world policies of a major socialist society, the Soviet Union. And now we have had 14 years' experience of the behaviour of another vast country, organising its economic life on ultra-socialist lines, China.

What is their record on this supreme issue of peace and war? I am not one of those who allege that the socialist countries have been more warlike or aggressive than the capitalist countries. I think it is wrong to assert that Russia is determined to make the world Communist by means of military conquest. What is true is that the Russian Government believes that one day the whole world will be Communist; and it also believed, at any rate until recently, that war was by no means a thing of the past. But what is more important than the exact belief of the men who form governments, is the record of what they do. And, by and large, I would say that the record of the Communist countries, since they have come into existence, is neither worse nor better than the rest of us in the matter of peace and war. Russia has often been aggressive, in Finland, in Hungary, in annexing the Baltic states and on other occasions. But so have we in the West: at Suez, for example, in the case of my own country, Britain.

But this, for a socialist, is a profoundly depressing conclusion. It suggests that there is no solution for our overwhelmingly important problem of the maintenance of peace in the nuclear age by means of transforming our societies along socialist lines. Socialism is desirable in itself: I am convinced that it is. But there is no evidence that it will solve the problem of peace and war. China was recently engaged in a most wanton aggression against India, a Communist country attacking a semi-socialist country. It is really no longer open to socialists to claim that they have found the solution to the problem of the maintenance of peace. If they do so, they make a laughing-stock of themselves.

The Economic Causes of War

What was wrong, then, with the socialist diagnosis of the economic causes of war? I am still as convinced as ever I was that the original purpose of wars of conquest was predominantly economic. In the ancient world, in the world of the great slave empires—Assyria, Egypt, Rome, and the like—the purpose of conquest was essentially to enslave the conquered peoples and then exploit their labour. Either you physically took them and transported them to your own country as slaves and set them to work, as the Romans did on their great landed estates, or you left them in their own country and then, by one device or another, you took away from them almost everything they produced above subsistence.

After all, in the ancient world with its very low level of productivity, the only way in which the leisured class could live in luxury was to acquire an abundant supply of slave (or semi-slave) labour by means of conquest. However, that was all a long time ago. Nevertheless, socialists believed that by a different mechanism, the wars of capitalist society were still essentially economic. Lenin put forward his theory of the causation of war in his book *Imperialism*. He believed that capitalist societies must attack each other in order to expand and secure markets and spheres of investment. If they did not do so, they would stifle in their own "plethora of capital" and overproduced consumer goods. Every major capitalist society, Lenin taught, was a sort of pressure-cooker which sooner or later must burst out on the rest of the world or stifle.

Now I still believe that this thesis of Lenin's had a very large measure of truth in it, at any rate for the type of capitalism which existed when he wrote in 1917. It was true that this kind of capitalism, of which the essential characteristic was that the wage-earning masses were held down at near subsistence level, could only expand into the outside world. It had to seek its markets and its fields of investment outside itself because its own internal market was so limited by the poverty of the vast majority of its people. But all this is demonstrably no longer true of contemporary capitalist society. As I have noted previously, there is no doubt at all about the fact that they are able to, and actually have, raised steadily the standard of life of their wage-earning masses. And this of course has provided them with an ever-expanding internal market which made external expansion unnecessary.

LENIN'S OPINION

Curiously enough Lenin noticed this possibility. But he dismissed it as something which, if it could be done, would no doubt solve the problem, but which capitalism was inherently incapable of doing. In a little-noticed passage in Chapter 4 of his book *Imperialism* Lenin said quite clearly that *if* capitalism *could* raise the standard of life of the wage-earning masses and develop agriculture, then the outward pressure toward limitless expansion would be relieved. The capitalist powers would no longer need to collide with each other in bloody war.

Now there is no denying the fact that during the last 20 years, capitalism has done precisely these two things. It *has* developed agriculture and it *has* raised the standard of life of the masses in capitalist countries. It is still doing both of these things. Therefore, according to Lenin's argument, it is no longer capitalism. In fact there are economists who say that the economic system as it exists in the Western countries today has been so greatly changed by the reforms and modifications of the last 20 years that it cannot any longer really be called "capitalist." I think this is wrong; I think that the Western countries are still most conveniently classified as capitalist societies. What has been shown is that with limited, but important, changes capitalism can do precisely the two things which Lenin said it could never do. (As you will note we are back by another road at the fundamental question of Marx's forecast of the ever-increasing misery of the wage-earners. It is the fact that this forecast has been disproved which changes everything.)

No Inevitabilities

I conclude from all this that war is no longer inevitable between capitalist societies; they can manage all right while keeping the peace. But unfortunately this does not mean that they necessarily *will* keep the peace. Socialist societies, of course, are under no necessity to undertake aggression and expansion: they can occupy themselves indefinitely in raising the standard of life of their peoples, and with development in general. But, equally, experience shows that this is no guarantee that they *will*, in fact, abstain from aggression. For what are the Chinese armies doing on the southern slopes of the Himalayas? China, surely, on any rational calculation, should be devoting every ounce of her energies and resources to her desperate task of internal development. But, on the contrary, she sent some 14 divisions to attack India.

From this I conclude that all one can say about the causes of war is something simpler and more general than we socialists had supposed. The cause of war seems to be simply the existence of separate sovereign states, whether capitalist, socialist, feudal, or any other kind. It is the fact that the world is organised, or rather disorganised, into over one hundred sovereign states that is the cause of war.

ARE DEMOCRACIES PACIFIC?

I have gone into this whole question of the disillusionment which socialists have suffered on this issue of the economic causes of war in order to avoid a new disillusionment that I think democrats may well suffer unless they take care. Democrats are often accustomed to argue that the cause of war lies in tyrannies, autocracies, or other forms of arbitrary dictatorship, and that if only all the states of the world would become democracies, all governments would be pacific and there would be no danger of war. I am afraid that experience will show, if such a state of things as a world of democratic states ever comes into existence, that this belief in the inherent pacifism of democracies is also an illusion. I do indeed believe that democracies are, on the whole, rather less aggressive and bellicose than tyrannies, autocracies, or other forms of arbitrary government. A government which is responsible to its electors does, from time to time at any rate, experience pressures for peace. But I am afraid that it is far from true that democracies are always and completely pacific. On the contrary, a majority of democratic electors sometimes suffers moods in which it is unreasonable and bellicose. If we study the history of, say, the last 100 years, in which alone we can find states with democratic governments in the sense in which I have been using the words, it will not, alas, be difficult to find examples in which undoubtedly democratic states have been aggressive and bellicose. You will readily call to mind examples of this in the case of Britain. Most left-wing people, at any rate, consider that the United States today is a rather aggressive country. Yet undoubtedly the

United States Government is one of the most effectively functioning democracies in the world. I do not myself think that America is specially aggressive but I agree that she is not absolutely, or even particularly, pacific either.

No, a world of democratic states would still be a world subject to war. The most that we can claim for such a world would be that it would be less likely to go to war than a world of states ruled by arbitrary, autocratic governments. Unless we face these unpleasant facts we shall, I think, suffer an analogous disillusionment with democracy to that which socialists have suffered over this question of peace and war.

Is War Inevitable?

War, then, would still be possible in a world of democratic states. In fact I am afraid that I must go further than this and say that, in the long run, war would be inevitable in a world of separate sovereign, democratic states. It might be postponed for a long time. Indeed I believe that the series of crises through which the world is passing at the present time—Cuba, Berlin, Vietnam, the Indo-Chinese conflict, to name a few—are by no means so immediately dangerous as many people think. I do not think that it is at all likely that, say, the next, or the next but one, of these crises will precipitate us into a world nuclear war and so blot us out. Nevertheless how can we deny that if the world goes on living like this: if crisis succeeds crisis in endless succession, sooner of later one of them *will* erupt into world nuclear war?

After all, we are living in an international anarchy. There is no power whatever superior to the sovereign state today. That is the essence of sovereignty. And anarchy has its own laws. They are statistical laws and for that very reason they are not subject to human control, but they are subject to human calculation and forecast. So we can forecast only too confidently that if you leave a state of anarchy in existence indefinitely, it will, sooner or later, erupt into conflict—or else all historical experience is at fault.

I conclude, therefore, that something more than a world of separate democratic states is necessary for the survival of man in the nuclear age. If mankind had not developed these fantastic powers of destruction, a world of separate sovereign democratic states might have been a possible and a tolerable world. No doubt there would have been periodic wars; but then there always have been periodic wars throughout human history and, somehow or other, civilisation has survived them. The development of nuclear weapons has changed all that. I do not see how we can possibly escape the conclusion that full-scale nuclear war is incompatible with the maintenance of human civilisation.

WORLD UNITY

What is necessary and indispensable for human survival is not merely the spread of democracy from one country to another until the world consists of democratic states. What is necessary, on the contrary, is *world democracy*. And I mean by this nothing less than the unification of the world under one democratic government. I cannot see how, in the long run, human civilisation can survive unless within a few generations it somehow produces a government which is both worldwide in extent and responsible directly or indirectly to a world electorate. By "responsible" I mean that it must be possible for the peoples of the world, by one means or another, to hire and fire that government. And that means that it must be possible for them to choose between different kinds of government; and it must be possible for them at least to influence their government while it is in power. In a word, those essential institutions of democracy which I defined earlier in respect of any particular state, must be applied on a world-wide scale.

Of course all this is a long distance off. It cannot possibly come into existence immediately. But many of you I am sure will go much further in scepticism than this and say that world democracy can never come into existence; or at any rate that it is extremely unlikely. Well, maybe. If you say that, what you are really saying is that human survival in the nuclear age is very unlikely. You may well be right. But I should like to hear of any other aim, goal, cause, or ideal which can offer mankind the hope of survival in the nuclear age. I think that it is world democracy or nothing. After all, the fact that a goal is distant and difficult of attainment has never prevented man from giving his allegiance to it.

If you ask me for details of how a world unity might come about I cannot give them. It may be that the only way to the achievement of world unity soon enough to prevent world destruction will prove to be a very undemocratic way. It may be that, initially, it will have to be done by a virtual dictatorship of the major nuclear powers. Nevertheless that would not be tolerable in the long run. A unified world would have in the end to become a world democracy. Nor do I think it particularly important to try and imagine how a world democracy would be organised. I suppose that, for many decades, it might be organised indirectly upon the basis of the election of a world government by national governments (no doubt on some weighted system) which were themselves democratically elected.

But surely in the end it must be voted for directly by the peoples of the world. I regard the United Nations as a precious expression of man's aspirations toward some sort of world government, rather than as anything closely resembling a world government itself. The United Nations is a forum of debate and discussion and as such indispensable. But is is not in any sense a government. A world democratic government must have two characteristics—responsibility and power: the United Nations by its very nature can have neither.

A General Conclusion

In the light of 20th-century experience, I may conclude that countries may have many sorts of economic systems, ranging from decidedly capitalist systems to completely socialist systems. With good luck and skill, any or all of these systems may be made to work tolerably well—though in my opinion the more socialistic systems will prove much the more satisfactory. Two things, therefore, have become even more important than the exact way in which we organise our economies. The first is whether or not we organise the political life of our nations upon a democratic basis. The second is the search for that worldwide unity of the human race without which we are all bound

to perish in the nuclear age. The political arrangements which
we establish within our own countries matter vitally, because
experience shows that unless they are democratic, all sorts of
injustices, instabilities, and outright disasters occur. Our capacity to unite the world matters more vitally still because the
lesson of the nuclear age is this. "Unite or perish!"

—JOHN STRACHEY, *The Challenge of Democracy,*
Encounter, Pamphlet No. 10 (1963)

Preliminary Draft of a World Constitution (1947–1948):

PREAMBLE

The people of the earth having agreed
        that the advancement of man
in spiritual excellence and physical welfare
is the common goal of mankind;
        that universal peace is the prerequisite
for the pursuit of that goal;
        that justice in turn is the prerequisite of peace,
and peace and justice stand or fall together;
        that iniquity and war inseparably spring
from the competitive anarchy of the national states;
        that therefore the age of nations must end,
and the era of humanity begin;
the governments of the nations have decided
        to order their separate sovereignties
in one government of justice,
to which they surrender their arms;
        and to establish, as they do establish,
this Constitution
as the covenant and fundamental law
of the Federal Republic of the World.

DECLARATION OF DUTIES AND RIGHTS

A.

The universal government of justice as covenanted and pledged
in this Constitution is founded on the Rights of Man.

The principles underlying the Rights of Man are and shall be permanently stated in the Duty of everyone everywhere, whether a citizen sharing in the responsibilities and privileges of World Government or a ward and pupil of the World Commonwealth:

to serve with word and deed, and with productive labor according to his ability, the spiritual and physical advancement of the living and of those to come, as the common cause of all generations of men;

to do unto others as he would like others to do unto him;

to abstain from violence,

except for the repulse of violence as commanded or granted under law.

B.

In the context therefore of social duty and service, and in conformity with the unwritten law which philosophies and religions alike called the Law of Nature and which the Republic of the World shall strive to see universally written and enforced by positive law:

it shall be the right of everyone everywhere to claim and maintain for himself and his fellowmen:

release from the bondage of poverty and from the servitude and exploitation of labor, with rewards and security according to merit and needs;

freedom of peaceful assembly and of association, in any creed or party or craft, within the pluralistic unity and purpose of the World Republic;

protection of individuals and groups against subjugation and tyrannical rule, racial or national, doctrinal or cultural, with safeguards for the self-determination of minorities and dissenters;

and any such other freedoms and franchises as are inherent in man's inalienable claims to life, liberty, and the dignity of the human person, and as the legislators and judges of the World Republic shall express and specify.

C.

The four elements of life—earth, water, air, energy—are the common property of the human race. The management and use of such portions thereof as are vested in or assigned to particular ownership, private or corporate or national or regional, of definite or indefinite tenure, of individualist or collectivist economy, shall be subordinated in each and all cases to the interest of the common good.

GRANT OF POWERS

I.

The jurisdiction of the World Government as embodied in its organs of power shall extend to:

a) The control of the observance of the Constitution in all the component communities and territories of the Federal World Republic, which shall be indivisible and one;

b) The furtherance and progressive fulfillment of the Duties and Rights of Man in the spirit of the foregoing Declaration, with their specific enactment in such fields of federal and local relations as are described hereinafter (Art. 27 through 33);

c) The maintenance of peace; and to that end the enactment and promulgation of laws which shall be binding upon communities and upon individuals as well,

d) the judgment and settlement of any conflicts among component units, with prohibition of recourse to interstate violence,

e) the supervision of and final decision on any alterations of boundaries between states or unions thereof,

f) the supervision of and final decision on the forming of new states or unions thereof,

g) the administration of such territories as may still be immature for self-government, and the declaration in due time of their eligibility therefor,

h) the intervention in intrastate violence and violations of law which affect world peace and justice,

i) the organization and disposal of federal armed forces,

j) the limitation and control of weapons and of the domestic militias in the several component units of the World Republic;

k) The establishment, in addition to the Special Bodies listed hereinafter (Art. 8 and 9), of such other agencies as may be conducive to the development of the earth's resources and to the advancement of physical and intellectual standards, with such advisory or initiating or arbitrating powers as shall be determined by law;

l) The laying and collecting of federal taxes, and the establishment of a plan and a budget for federal expenditures,

m) the administration of the World Bank and the establishment of suitable world fiscal agencies for the issue of money and the creation and control of credit,

n) the regulation of commerce affected with federal interest,

o) the establishment, regulation, and, where necessary or desirable, the operation of means of transportation and communication which are of federal interest;

p) The supervision and approval of laws concerning emigration and immigration and the movements of peoples,

q) the granting of federal passports;

r) The appropriation, under the right of eminent domain, of such private or public property as may be necessary for federal use, reasonable compensation being made therefor;

s) The legislation over and administration of the territory which shall be chosen as Federal District and of such other territories as may be entrusted directly to the Federal Government.

2.

The powers not delegated to the World Government by this Constitution, and not prohibited by it to the several members of the Federal World Republic, shall be reserved to the several states or nations or unions thereof.

THE FEDERAL CONVENTION, THE PRESIDENT,
THE LEGISLATURE

3.

The sovereignty of the Federal Republic of the World resides in the people of the world. The primary powers of the World Government shall be vested in:

a) the Federal Convention,
b) the President,
c) the Council and the Special Bodies,
d) the Grand Tribunal, the Supreme Court, and the Tribune of the People,
e) the Chamber of Guardians.

4.

The Federal Convention shall consist of delegates elected directly by the people of all states and nations, one delegate for each million of population or fraction thereof above one-half million, with the proviso that the people of any extant state . . . ranging between 100,000 and 1,000,000, shall be entitled to elect one delegate, but any such state with a population below 100,000 shall be aggregated for federal electoral purposes to the electoral unit closest to its borders.

The delegates to the Federal Convention shall vote as individuals, not as members of national or otherwise collective representations [except as specified hereinafter, Art. 46, paragraph 2, and Art. 47].

The Convention shall meet in May of every third year, for a session of thirty days.

5.

The Federal Convention shall subdivide into nine Electoral Colleges according to the nine Societies of kindred nations and cultures, or Regions, wherefrom its members derive their powers, such Regions being:

1) the continent of Europe and its islands outside the Russian area, together with the United Kingdom if the latter so decides, and with such overseas English- or French- or Cape Dutch-

speaking communities of the British Commonwealth of Nations or the French Union as decide to associate (this whole area here tentatively denominated *Europa*);

2) the United States of America, with the United Kingdom if the latter so decides, and such kindred communities of British, or Franco-British, or Dutch-British, or Irish civilization and lineage as decide to associate (*Atlantis*);

3) Russia, European and Asiatic, with such East-Baltic or Slavic or South-Danubian nations as associate with Russia (*Eurasia*);

4) the Near and Middle East, with the states of North Africa, and Pakistan if the latter so decides (*Afrasia*);

5) *Africa*, south of the Sahara, with or without the South African Union as the latter may decide;

6) *India*, with Pakistan if the latter so decides;

7) China, Korea, Japan, with the associate archipelagoes of the North- and Mid-Pacific (*Asia Major*);

8) Indochina and Indonesia, with Pakistan if the latter so decides, and with such other Mid- and South-Pacific lands and islands as decide to associate (*Austrasia*);

9) the Western Hemisphere south of the United States (*Columbia*).

Each Electoral College shall nominate by secret ballot not more than three candidates, regardless of origin, for the office of President of the World Republic. The Federal Convention in plenary meeting, having selected by secret ballot a panel of three candidates from the lists submitted, shall elect by secret ballot one of the three as President, on a majority of two-thirds.

If three consecutive ballots have been indecisive, the candidate with the smallest vote shall be eliminated and between the two remaining candidates a simple majority vote shall be decisive.

6.

Each Electoral College shall then nominate by secret and proportional ballot twenty-seven candidates, originating from the respective Electoral Area or Region, for the World Council; with the proviso that one-third and not more than one-third of the nominees shall not be members of the Federal Convention; and the nine lists having been presented to the Federal Convention, the Federal Convention in plenary meeting shall select by secret and proportional ballot nine Councilmen from each list, with the same proviso as above.

The Federal Convention shall also elect by secret and proportional ballot, on nominations, prior to the opening of the Convention, by such organizations of world-wide importance and lawfully active in more than three Regions as shall be designated [for the first election by the United Nations Assembly and subsequently] by the Council, eighteen additional members, regardless of origin; and the total membership of the World Council shall be thus ninety-nine.

7.

The primary power to initiate and enact legislation for the Federal Republic of the World shall be vested in the Council.

The tenure of the Council shall be three years.

The Council shall elect its Chairman, for its whole tenure of three years.

Councilors shall be re-eligible.

8.

Within the first three years of World Government the Council and the President shall establish three Special Bodies, namely:

a) a House of Nationalities and States, with representatives from each, for the safeguarding of local institutions and autonomies and the protection of minorities;

b) a Syndical or functional Senate, for the representation of syndicates and unions or occupational associations and any other corporate interests of transnational significance, as well as for mediation or arbitration in non-justiciable issues among such syndicates or unions or other corporate interests;

c) an Institute of Science, Education and Culture;

each of the three bodies with such membership and tenures and consultative or preparatory powers as shall be established by law and with no prejudice to the establishment of other advisory or technical agencies in accordance with the purposes stated hereinbefore (Art. 1, k).

9.

Within its first year the World Government shall establish a Special Body, to be named Planning Agency, of twenty-one members appointed by the President, subject to vetoes by two-thirds of the Council, for tenures of twelve years [except that the terms for the initial membership shall be staggered by lot, with one-third of it, seven members, ceasing from office and being replaced every fourth year].

It shall be the function of the Planning Agency to envisage the income of the Federal Government and to prepare programs and budgets for expenditures, both for current needs and for long-range improvements. These programs and budgets shall be submitted by the President, with his recommendations, to the Council, as provided hereinafter (Art. 13).

Plans for improvement of the world's physical facilities, either public or private, and for the productive exploitation of resources and inventions shall be submitted to the Agency or to such Development Authorities or regional subagencies as it may establish. The Agency shall pass judgment on the social usefulness of such plans.

Members of the Planning Agency shall not be re-eligible nor shall they, during their tenure in the Agency, have membership in any other federal body.

10.

The executive power, together with initiating power in federal legislation, shall be vested in the President. His tenure shall be six years.

The President shall not have membership in the Council.

The President shall not be re-eligible. He shall not be eligible to the Tribunate of the People until nine years have elapsed since the expiration of his term.

No two successive Presidents shall originate from the same Region.

11.

The President shall appoint a Chancellor. The Chancellor, with the approval of the President, shall appoint the Cabinet.

The Chancellor shall act as the President's representative before the Council in the exercise of legislative initiative. The Chancellor and the Cabinet members shall have at any time the privilege of the floor before the Council.

But no Chancellor or Cabinet member shall have a vote or shall hold membership in the Council, nor, if he was a member of the Council at the moment of his executive appointment, shall he be entitled to resume his seat therein when leaving the executive post unless he be re-elected at a subsequent Convention.

No one shall serve as Chancellor for more than six years, nor as Cabinet member for more than twelve, consecutive or not.

No three Cabinet members at any one time and no two successive Chancellors shall originate from the same Region.

The Council shall have power to interrogate the Chancellor and the Cabinet and to adopt resolutions on their policies.

The Chancellor and the Cabinet shall resign when the President so decides or when a vote of no confidence by the absolute majority of fifty or more of the Council is confirmed by a second such vote; but no second vote shall be taken and held valid if less than three months have elapsed from the first.

12.

The sessions of the Council, as well as those of the Grand Tribunal and the Supreme Court, shall be continuous, except for one yearly recess of not more than ten weeks or two such recesses of not more than five weeks each, as the body concerned may decide.

13.

The budget of the World Government, upon recommendation by the Planning Agency, shall be presented every three years by the President to the Council, which shall pass it, or reject it in whole titles, by majority vote; the same procedure to apply when at other intervals the President requests additional appropriations or approval of changes.

14.

Any legislation of the Council can be vetoed by the President within thirty days of its passage. But the Council can overrule the veto if its new vote, by a majority of two-thirds, finds support, within sixty days of the President's action, in the majority of the Grand Tribunal [and no such support shall be required during the tenure of the first President].

15.

The President can be impeached on grounds of treason to the Constitution, or usurpation of power, or felony, or insanity, or other disease impairing permanently his mind.

The vote of impeachment shall be final when three-quarters of the Council and three-quarters of the Grand Tribunal concur and the majority of the Supreme Court validates the legality of the proceedings.

If a President is impeached or resigns or dies in the interval between two sessions of the Federal Convention, the Chairman of the Council shall become Acting President until the new Convention elects a new President; and the Council shall elect a new Chairman.

THE GRAND TRIBUNAL AND THE SUPREME COURT

16.

The supreme judiciary power of the World Republic shall be vested in a Grand Tribunal of sixty Justices, with the President of the World Republic as Chief Justice and Chairman, and the Chairman of the Council as Vice-Chairman ex officio.

The President as Chief Justice shall appoint the Justices of the Grand Tribunal and fill the vacancies, subject to vetoes by the Council on majorities of two-thirds. He shall have power to overrule any such veto if he finds support in a two-thirds majority of the Justices in office [except that no such power shall be vested in the first President].

No one, except the Chairman of the Council, shall hold membership at the same time in the Council and the Tribunal; nor shall a Chancellor or Cabinet member hold membership in the Tribunal or be eligible to it until six years have elapsed from the termination of his executive office.

17.

The tenure of the Chief Justice and Chairman and of the Vice-Chairman of the Grand Tribunal shall be the time of their tenure of office respectively as President of the World Republic and as Chairman of the Council.

The President shall have power to appoint an Alternate, subject to approval by the Grand Tribunal, for the exercise of such of his functions in the judiciary branch and for such a time within his tenure as he may decide.

The tenures of the sixty Justices shall be fifteen years [except that the terms for the initial membership shall be staggered by lot, with one-fifth of it, twelve Justices, ceasing from office and being replaced every third year].

Justices of the Grand Tribunal shall not be re-eligible, except that a Justice appointed as Chancellor or Cabinet member, having resigned his membership in the Tribunal, shall be re-eligible to it for the unfulfilled portion of his tenure when six years have elapsed from the termination of his executive office.

18.

The sixty Justices shall be assigned twelve to each of five Benches:

the First Bench to deal with constitutional issues between the primary organs and powers of the World Government as well as with all issues and cases in which the Tribune of the People shall decide to appear in his capacity of World Attorney and defender of the Rights of Man;

the Second Bench to deal with issues and conflicts between the World Government and any of its component units, whether single states or unions thereof or Regions, as well as with issues and conflicts of component units of the World Republic among themselves;

the Third Bench to deal with issues and conflicts between the World Government and individual citizens or corporations or unions or any other associations of citizens;

the Fourth Bench to deal with issues and conflicts among component units, whether single states or unions of states or Regions, and individual citizens or corporations or unions or any other associations of citizens when such issues and conflicts affect the interpretation or enactment of federal law;

the Fifth Bench to deal with issues and conflicts, when they affect the interpretation and enactment of federal law, either among individual citizens or among corporations, unions, syndicates, or any other collective organizations of citizens and interests.

Each Region shall be represented in each Bench by at least one member and not more than two.

19.

The Supreme Court shall be of seven members: five representing one each Bench, with the Chief Justice as their Chairman and the Chairman of the Council as their Vice-Chairman ex officio; and the active membership of the Benches shall thus remain of eleven each.

No two members of the Supreme Court shall originate from the same Region.

The representatives of the Benches in the Supreme Court shall be elected by secret vote of the Grand Tribunal in plenary session, with each Justice casting a ballot for five candidates, one from each Bench, and with those candidates elected who have obtained the largest vote, except that any presumptive electee shall be held ineligible whose assignment to the Court would duplicate the representation therein of any one Region or Bench.

If the first vote fails to fill all seats, the vote shall be repeated according to the same regulations.

The tenures of the members of the Supreme Court shall be: for the Chairman and Vice-Chairman the same as their tenures of office respectively as President of the World Republic and as Chairman of the Council, and for the other members six years, at the end of which each of the five elected by the Grand Tribunal may be re-elected or shall be restored to the Bench whereof he was the delegate; but no Justice shall sit in the Court beyond his regular term of membership in the Tribunal; and when the latter term expires before the regular six-year term in the Court is completed, or when an elective member of the Court resigns or dies, the Grand Tribunal shall fill the vacancy for the unfulfilled portion of the term by secret partial election in plenary session, with the same proviso as above in regard to the representation of Regions.

Regions which have not been represented in the Supreme

Court for two successive six-year terms shall have mandatory precedence in the elections for the third term.

20.

The Supreme Court shall distribute the cases among the five Benches of the Grand Tribunal according to competences as specified hereinbefore [Art. 18].

Cases where competences overlap or are otherwise doubtful shall be referred to such Bench or Benches jointly as the Supreme Court shall decide.

The Supreme Court shall have power to modify the rules of assignment for the five Benches as specified in Art. 18, subject to approval by the majority of the Council and by a two-thirds majority of the Grand Tribunal concurrently.

21.

It shall be the office and function of the Supreme Court to review the decisions of the Benches, within three months of their issuance, said decisions to become effective upon registration by the Court, or, when annulled, to be returned for revision each to the Bench which judged the case, or to another, or to others jointly as the Court may decide; annulment to be pronounced in cases of unfair trial or faulty procedure, and also for reasons of substance when final appeal was filed by the losing party, if the Court at its own discretion choose to take cognizance thereof, or by the Tribune of the People, whose demand shall be mandatory.

22.

The Grand Tribunal, with the approval of the Supreme Court, shall establish Lower Federal Courts in such number and places as conditions in the component units of the World Republic shall require, and a Federal Appellate Court in each Region. It shall also determine the rules and competences of such courts, and appoint their officials on the basis of competitive examinations.

23.

The President or his Alternate and the Chairman of the Council shall not sit as judges in cases affecting the solution of conflicts between the President and the Council.

The President or Acting President or Alternate, or a Justice or the Chairman of the Council in his capacity of Justice, shall not sit as a judge in cases involving his appointment or impeachment or demotion or tenure or in any other way affecting his particular interest.

24.

No member of the Council or the Grand Tribunal shall be liable to removal from office until a criminal sentence on charges of felony or grave misdemeanor is final. But he shall be suspended from office, pending last recourse to the Grand Tribunal, when a sentence of guilty, issued by a lower court, has been confirmed by a Federal Appellate Court.

The Supreme Court shall pronounce final judgment on the legality of the proceedings. It shall also pronounce final judgment on the legal validity of elections and appointments to the Council and the Tribunal, and to the offices of President and of Tribune of the People.

25.

The President in his capacity of World Chief Justice shall have power of pardon over sentences passed under federal law.

THE TRIBUNE OF THE PEOPLE AND THE WORLD LAW

26.

The Federal Convention, after electing the Council, shall elect by secret ballot the Tribune of the People as a spokesman for the minorities, this office to be vested in the candidate obtaining the second largest vote among the eligible candidates; ineligible to the office of Tribune being any candidate having also been nominated by any Electoral College for the office of President in the current Convention, or having been a President or Acting President or Alternate or a member of the Grand Tribunal at any time in the nine years preceding said Convention, or originating from the same Region as the President simultaneously in office.

The Tribune of the People shall not have membership in the Council.

The tenure of the Tribune of the People shall be three years. He shall have power to appoint a Deputy, subject to the same ineligibilities as above, with tenure to expire not later than his own.

He shall not be re-eligible, nor shall he be eligible to the office of President or Alternate or Justice of the Grand Tribunal, until nine years have elapsed from the expiration of his present term.

The Tribune, or his appointed Deputy, shall have the privilege of the floor before the Grand Tribunal and, under such regulations as shall be established by law, before the Supreme Court; but no vote in either; and he shall not be present when a vote is taken.

27.

It shall be the office and function of the Tribune of the People to defend the natural and civil rights of individuals and groups against violation or neglect by the World Government or any of its component units; to further and demand, as a World Attorney before the World Republic, the observance of the letter and spirit of this Constitution; and to promote thereby, in the spirit of its Preamble and Declaration of Duties and Rights, the attainment of the goals set to the progress of mankind by the efforts of the ages.

28.

No law shall be made or held valid in the World Republic or any of its component units:

1) inflicting or condoning discrimination against race or nation or sex or caste or creed or doctrine; or

2) barring through preferential agreements or coalitions of vested interests the access on equal terms of any state or nation to the raw materials and the sources of energy of the earth; or

3) establishing or tolerating slavery, whether overt or covert, or forced labor, except as equitable expiation endured in state or federal controlled institutions and intended for social service and rehabilitation of convicted criminals; or

4) permitting, whether by direction or indirection, arbitrary seizure or search, or unfair trial, or excessive penalty, or application of ex post facto laws; or

5) abridging in any manner whatsoever, except as a punishment inflicted by law for criminal transgression, the citizen's exercise of such responsibilities and privileges of citizenship as are conferred on him by law; or

6) curtailing the freedom of communication and information, of speech, of the press and of expression by whatever means, of peaceful assembly, of travel;

paragraphs 5 and 6 to be subject to suspension according to circumstances, universally or locally, in time of emergency imperiling the maintenance and unity of the World Republic; such state of emergency, world-wide or local, to be proposed by the Chamber of Guardians and proclaimed concurrently by a two-thirds majority of the Council and a two-thirds majority of the Grand Tribunal for a period not in excess of six months, to be renewable on expiration with the same procedure for successive periods of six months or less but in no case beyond the date when the time of emergency is proclaimed closed, on the proposal of the Chamber of Guardians by simple majority votes of the Council and of the Grand Tribunal concurrently or, if the Guardians' proposal is deemed unduly delayed, by three-quarters majority votes of the Council and of the Grand Tribunal concurrently.

29.

Capital punishment shall not be inflicted under federal law.

30.

Old age pensions, unemployment relief, insurance against sickness or accident, just terms of leisure, and protection to maternity and infancy shall be provided according to the varying circumstances of times and places as the local law may direct.

Communities and states unable to provide adequate social security and relief shall be assisted by the Federal Treasury, whose grants or privileged loans shall be administered under federal supervision.

31.

Every child from the age of six to the age of twelve shall be entitled to instruction and education at public expense, such primary six-year period to be obligatory and further education to be accessible to all without discrimination of age or sex or race or class or creed.

Communities and states unable to fulfill this obligation shall be assisted by the Federal Treasury with the same proviso as in Art. 30.

32.

All property or business whose management and use have acquired the extension and character of a federal public service, or whereon restrictive trade practices have conferred the character and power of a transnational monopoly, shall become the property of the Federal Government upon payment of a just price as determined by law.

33.

Every individual or group or community shall have the right of appeal against unjust application of a law, or against the law itself, gaining access through the inferior courts, local or federal, to the superior and the Grand Tribunal, and securing the counsel and support of the Tribune of the People when the Tribune so decides; and, if a law or statute is found evidently in conflict with the guarantees pledged in the foregoing articles or irreparably in contradiction with the basic principles and intents of the World Republic as stated in the Preamble to this Constitution and in its Declaration of Duties and Rights, the Grand Tribunal shall have power to recommend to the Supreme Court that such law or statute be declared, and the Supreme Court shall have power to declare it, null and void.

34.

The Tribune of the People cannot be impeached except on the same grounds and with the same procedure as specified for the President in Art. 15.

If the Tribune of the People is impeached or resigns or dies, his substitute for the unfulfilled portion of his tenure shall be the candidate to the Tribunate who was next in line in the last Federal Convention, with the same provisos in regard to eligibility as in Art. 26, first paragraph.

The Chamber of Guardians

35.

The control and use of the armed forces of the Federal Republic of the World shall be assigned exclusively to a Chamber of Guardians under the chairmanship of the President, in his capacity of Protector of the Peace. The other Guardians shall be six Councilmen elected by the Council and the Grand Tribunal in Congress assembled, for terms of three years. [But the Grand Tribunal shall not participate in the first election.]

One former President shall also sit in the Chamber of Guardians, the sequence to be determined term for term, or, if he resign or die, for the fractional term, according to seniority in the presidential office; he shall have the privilege of the floor in the deliberations of the Chamber, but no vote in its decisions.

Officers holding professional or active rank in the armed forces of the Federal Republic, or in the domestic militia of any component unit thereof, shall not be eligible as Guardians.

36.

The election of the six elective Guardians shall be by secret and proportional vote, with each Elector casting a ballot of six names or less; but no three Guardians of the seven, including the President and excluding the ex-President, shall originate from the same Region; and any presumptive electee whose election would contravene this norm shall be declared ineligible and replaced by the candidate fulfilling the norm and having obtained the next largest vote.

Regions which have not been represented among the seven Guardians referred to above for two successive three-year terms shall have mandatory precedences in the subsequent elections; but the Guardian or Guardians originating from a nation or Region where sedition against the World Republic is actual or, according to the majority of the Chamber, imminently expected shall cease from office and be replaced; unless the other Guardians decide unanimously otherwise.

No Guardian can be impeached or in any way suspended or removed from office for any other reason, except on such grounds and with such procedure as specified for the President and the Tribune of the People hereinbefore (Art. 15 and 34), and for the Guardians hereinafter (Art. 38).

If a Guardian resigns or dies or is in any way suspended or removed, his substitute for the unfulfilled portion of the term shall be chosen by partial election, with the same rules and provisos as in the first two paragraphs of this article, each elector casting a ballot of one or more names as the number of vacancies may be.

37.

The Chancellor shall have access to the Chamber of Guardians as Deputy of the President whose vote he shall cast by proxy if the President so decides.

38.

Appropriations for the budget of Peace and Defense, under control of the Chamber of Guardians, as proposed by the Chamber at the beginning of each term for the whole duration thereof, shall be submitted by the President to the Council, in conformity with Art. 13. But if a state of emergency is declared, in the manner and limits as specified hereinbefore (Art. 28, last paragraph), the Chamber shall have power to demand and appropriate such additional funds as the emergency demands, subject to auditing and sanction by the Council when the emergency is closed; whereafter, if sanction is denied, the Guardians responsible shall be liable to impeachment and prosecution for usurpation of power with the same procedure as specified for the President and the Tribune of the People hereinbefore (Art. 15 and 34).

39.

The Chamber shall have power to propose by absolute majority, subject to approval by two-thirds majority votes of the Council and of the Grand Tribunal concurrently, extraordinary powers, world-wide or local, to be conferred on the President beyond those assigned to him by this Constitution, when a state of emergency, as provided in Art. 28, is proclaimed; such powers not to be granted for periods exceeding six months each and to be relinquished before the expiration of any such period as soon as the state of emergency, in conformity with Art. 28, is proclaimed closed.

40.

The Chamber of Guardians shall answer interrogations from the Council on its general and administrative directives, but no vote shall be taken after discussion thereof, except as otherwise provided in Art. 28 and 39; and the decisions of the Chamber in matters technical and strategic shall be final, and withheld from publicity when the Chamber so decides.

41.

The Chamber of Guardians, assisted by a General Staff and an Institute of Technology whose members it shall appoint, shall determine the technological and the numerical levels that shall be set as limits to the domestic militias of the single communities and states or unions thereof.

Armed forces and the manufacture of armaments beyond the levels thus determined shall be reserved to the World Government.

THE FEDERAL CAPITAL AND FEDERAL LANGUAGE AND STANDARDS

42.

Within one year of its foundation the World Republic shall choose a Federal Capital, or a site therefor, with eminent domain over it and an adequate Federal District.

43.

Within three years of its foundation the Federal Government shall designate one language, which shall be standard for the formulation and interpretation of the federal laws; and for analogous purposes, relative to communication, taxation, and finances, it shall establish in its first year a federal unit of currency with a federal system of measures and a federal calender.

THE AMENDING POWER

44.

Amendments to this Constitution, recommended concurrently by a two-thirds majority of the Council and of the Grand Tribunal, shall be in force when approved by a two-thirds majority of the Federal Convention in the Constitutional Session following the recommendation.

Constitutional Sessions, of thirty days or less, as the discussion may require and the majority may decide, shall be held immediately after the ordinary electoral session in the third Federal Convention and thereafter every ninth year.

[But no amendment altering the electoral units as listed in Art. 5, or the assignment to them of seats in the Council and the other Federal bodies, shall be recommended to the first of such Sessions.]

Appendix 3

NOTE: The following sections on the necessity of government and on war and peace are taken from my book *A Vision of the Future* (New York, 1984), no longer in print.

THE NECESSITY OF GOVERNMENT

If human beings could engage in their pursuit of happiness more effectively without living in states and under the auspices of government, then neither the state nor its government would be necessary as a means to the ultimate objective at which human beings should aim—living decent human lives.

In the preceding chapter, I argued that the goodness of the state or civil society lies in its being indispensable to living a civilized life and obtaining all the real goods that individuals cannot obtain by themselves alone or under the conditions of family and tribal life. The goodness of the state or civil society was thus seen to be inseparable from its necessity as an indispensable means to the ultimate good we should seek.

What holds for the state holds also for government. Its goodness resides in its necessity—in its indispensability as a means. But a means to what? Is it not possible for human beings to achieve good lives for themselves without the constraints imposed by government through its sanctions and the coercive force of its laws? Is not the road to happiness on earth more open to those who pursue that goal without being subject to government?

Those who call themselves anarchists—philosophical, not bomb-throwing, anarchists—answer such questions with resounding affirmations. When they call for the immediate abolition of the state or for its gradual withering away, they identify the state itself with government by might, that is, by the coercive force of its various sanctions. This is what they abominate.

They think that it is quite possible for human beings, either as they are now or as they might become under altered conditions, to live peacefully and harmoniously together in society and to and to act in concert for a common good in which they all participate, and to do this without the restraining force exercised by the state or its government. They do not see in the complete autonomy that everyone would have under anarchy any threat to the peace, harmony, and order of social life.

Why are they profoundly wrong? One answer was given by Alexander Hamilton when he said that if men were angels, no government would be necessary for social life. Spelled out in a little more detail, Hamilton's reference to angels expressed his understanding of angels as completely virtuous, and so obedient by free choice to just laws. When he rejected as illusory the attribution to mankind of angelic virtue, he did not thereby intend to deny that some men have sufficient, if not angelic, virtue to obey just laws out of respect for their authority and without responding to the threat of coercive force.

Some men, yes, but not all! That is precisely why some portion of the individuals living together in society must be constrained by coercive force from injuring their fellows or acting against the common good of all. Hence, government with its sanctions is as necessary for social life as that, in turn, is necessary for the pursuit of happiness.

Hamilton's argument is not only sound, but unanswerable by philosophical anarchists in the light of all the known historical realities. Their only out is to appeal, beyond the facts about human beings as they now are, to what human beings might become under radically altered future circumstances.

The hope for a new type of man, with a different human nature that has been altered by external circumstances, is bizarre and groundless. The specific nature of any living organism is gene-determined, not determined in any essential respect by external circumstances. Human nature may be overlaid by all the nurtural influences imposed by the environment, but that natural overlay does not alter the underlying nature.

There is one point with respect to which one must concede some soundness to the philosophical anarchist's position. The coercive force that is exercised by a tyrannical and despotic government is an evil from which human beings should be emancipated. But constitutional and just governments also exercise coercive force; and then, as Hamilton argued, that confers a benefit to be sought, not an evil to be avoided.

Sound and answerable as Hamilton's argument may be, it is not the only or complete answer to the position of the philosophical anarchist. The other part of the answer consists in seeing that the authority of government, quite apart from its exercise of coercive force, is necessary for the concerted action of a number of individuals for a common purpose.

Let us consider the simplest possible case of three individuals—scientists engaged in the exploration of the far reaches of the Amazon. Before they embark on their expedition, must they not all agree on the method by which decisions will be reached about matters upon which they, as reasonable individuals, can possibly disagree? Without such agreement, do they not stand in danger of having unresolved differences of opinion among them frustrate, even ruin, their concerted efforts?

Granted affirmative answers to these two questions, what are their options? Only two appear to be available. To insist upon unanimity in the solution of all problems they are likely to face is to deny that reasonable differences of opinion are likely to arise. Grant that likelihood and then the only options left are twofold: (1) the choice of one of the three as the leader whose decisions about all matters shall prevail; and (2) the adoption of the principle that decisions will be reached by a majority of two against one.

Either principle of decision-making must be adopted unanimously on the part of the three explorers. It cannot be imposed by one of them upon the other two; it cannot be selected by a majority of two against one, because the problem of how matters should be decided must first be solved by the agreement of all three. Leadership by one can be set up by that one only through force. This we have excluded in our imaginary case. The principle of majority rule cannot be set up by a majority vote, not unless the majority imposes it by force.

Decision-making can, of course, be avoided entirely by tossing a coin. That, however, is an abdication of government, leaving everything to chance instead of putting reason to use.

Our hypothetical example of the three explorers setting up some instrument of government for their expedition has excluded the use of force either to institute government in the first place or to exercise it, once it has been set up. Here, then, we have government with voluntarily established authority and with no recourse to might. We also have government that serves a necessity other than that of preventing or reducing antisocial or unjust conduct on the part of some portion of society's population.

This picture portrays government as an indispensable means to the concerted action of a number of individuals for a common purpose. That is the essence of social life. Many of the decisions that have to be made may be morally indifferent; such as traffic ordinances about driving on the left-hand or the right-hand side of the road. There is nothing just or unjust about either alternative. But when the circumstances are such that traffic control becomes necessary for the security of life and limb, one or the other alternative must be chosen. Government is necessary to decide which, and to render that decision with the requisite authority.

WAR AND PEACE

Implicit in the preceding pages are insights about war and peace that are the best fruits of thinking about the idea of government.

Our conventional and colloquial use of these two terms has for centuries obscured the difference between a state of war and warfare, and between civil peace and the mere absence of warfare.

In the vocabulary of daily usage, we speak of making war as an engagement in battle by the employment of weapons. When victory by one side or exhaustion on the part of both brings warfare to a conclusion, we refer to the cessation of violent hostilities as the onset of peace. Arrangements are then entered into by treaties or other devices to prolong the armistice which we think of as preserving peace.

To enlarge and improve our understanding of these matters, we need only remember what has been said in the preceding pages about the benefit that government confers upon any society by ensuring its domestic tranquility, which is the condition of civil peace. Civil peace is not just the absence of warfare, nor is it the absence of serious conflicts between individuals or groups of individuals who comprise the population of a society. It consists rather in the possibility of resolving all the conflicts that may arise in a society without resort to illicit violence and an illegitimate use of force.

There are only two ways in which human conflicts can be resolved: either by talk or by force. When talk fails, and the conflict is serious enough to demand resolution, resort to force—or the threat of force—is the only alternative. When the apparatus of government is adequate for the purpose, it provides the machinery for settling all conflicts or disputes by talk. It thus eliminates the need to have recourse to force and violence.

The adjudication of disputes in courts, the resolution of conflicts of opinion about public policy in legislative or other assemblies, the enforcement of the law, referenda, plebiscites, and elections, with one exception, are operations in which human beings talk about and talk away the differences that bring them into conflict.

The one exception to be noted is the enforcement of law. Here it would seem that talk alone does not suffice and the use of force must be employed. What force? Force employed by whom? The force that is vested in an arm of government, the force that a government employs, to prevent disruptions or breaches of the peace by criminal conduct that involves an illicit or illegitimate use of force.

A great German jurist, Hans Kelsen, pointed out that a de jure government, a rightfully established government, exercises a monopoly of authorized force. All other force, the resort to violence on the part of members of a society, either individually or in groups, is unauthorized force and, therefore, illicit or illegitimate.

As we have already observed, there are de facto as well as de jure governments—governments that rule by might alone, and rightfully established governments that have authority as well as power, an authority that includes an authorized use of force to preserve peace.

Do both modes of government provide adequate machinery for preserving peace? In one sense, yes; in another, no.

Government by might alone, without legitimate authority, preserves peace by means of an unauthorized use of force. It succeeds, of course, only to the extent that the force at its disposal has overwhelming weight as against the force that can be employed by any dissident groups in the population.

Furthermore, to the extent that the government itself lacks justice and rules unjustly, the peace that it establishes and preserves by illegitimate force is a fragile and unstable condition. Sedition, insurrection, riot, and rebellion are always seething below the surface in any society in which gross injustices are inflicted upon the population.

What appears to be peace is really a state of war between rulers and ruled, for when long-standing abuses and a train of injustices bring them into serious conflict with one another, actual warfare breaks out between them. A state of war is that condition in which actual warfare is always latent. It is the ever-present possibility of which warfare is the actualization.

Perfect peace, in contrast, is that condition in which the possibility of actual warfare is totally eliminated by the adequacy of governmental means for settling all disputes by talk, by lawful devices, by government's monopoly of authorized force, and by providing all dissident groups within the population with legal means of dissent so that, where injustices exist, the abused or oppressed can seek to redress their grievances without resort to violence.

Perfect peace is obviously an ideal that may never be fully realized on earth. But it is also an ideal that is realized in some degree wherever rightfully instituted governments exist. It is approximated to whatever extent such governments govern justly, provide machinery adequate for the purpose of resolving all disputes, and exercise authorized force.

Three great political philosophers—Cicero, Machiavelli, and John Locke—have pointed out, in almost identical phraseology, that there are only two ways of settling disputes. One is by talk, by law, and by law enforcement. The other is by force or violence.

The first is the uniquely human method of settling conflicts. The second is the method of brutes, of the beasts of the jungle.

When the first method prevails and succeeds, we have the civil peace of civilized life. When it fails or is totally lacking, we have a state of war in which actual warfare is always below the surface of a merely apparent peace that is nothing but the temporary absence of fighting, of bloodshed, of violence.

Another great political philosopher, Thomas Hobbes, completes the picture by pointing out that peace exists only within the boundaries of a state and among individuals living together under the benign auspices of a legitimate government. Between completely autonomous sovereigns—sovereign princes or sovereign states—there is always a state of war.

It is only in this century that we have come finally to recognize the soundness of his insight. We have invented the phrase "cold war" to refer to the state of war that sovereign states are in vis-à-vis one another. This is manifest in the conduct of foreign policy, in the actions of diplomats, in the subterfuges of espionage, and in the aggressive potency of the military installations that we call defense establishments. Lurking beneath the surface, ready to break out, is the hot war of the generals and the admirals, who are called upon to achieve the results that have been unsuccessfully sought by all the devices of the cold war.

Anarchy—the jungle in which all sovereign states find themselves—is identical with the alternatives of cold war and hot war. It is never a condition of peace, even when sovereign states appear to be friendly rather than hostile in relation to one another. What we miscall peace between states is nothing but the absence of actual warfare between them. Genuine peace exists only when government replaces anarchy.

From the beginning of history to the present time, there has never been world peace, but only a plurality of peaces— as many as, at a given time, there are separate societies. In each of these, some mode of government establishes some degree of civil peace by the machinery it provides for settling disputes without resort to violence. The plurality of peaces is smaller or larger according to the number of separate societies in which individuals live under government. The size or extent of each of these plural peaces varies with the size of the domain and of the population that is governed.

In the course of history, mankind has passed from tribal peaces and tribal wars to the peaces of separate city-states and the wars between them. When city-states became empires with colonies, the extent of the peace units became enlarged, and so also did the wars in which imperial dominions engaged. When in modern times, national states emerged from and replaced the anarchy that existed among the petty principalities of the feudal system, the size of the peace units once again enlarged, and enlarged still further as national states became empires with colonies under their dominion. What was called the Pax Romana in the ancient world and has been called the Pax Britannica in the modern world represent such enlarged peace units.

In the twentieth century, the first century in which anything that deserves to be called a world war first occurred, world peace has not yet come into existence, though its possibility is presaged by the occurrence of world wars. The creation of the League of Nations after the First World War and the formation of the United Nations after the Second created inadequate devices for the establishment of world peace.

They may have served to inhibit the cold war, which always exists among sovereign states, from turning into the hot war that is always latently present. But precisely because the League of Nations was not and the United Nations is not a government with a monopoly of authorized force, neither can be regarded as an instrument for establishing and preserving genuine peace. That the United Nations is not a government and cannot be one is plainly indicated by the fact that its members are all sovereign states, each completely autonomous, each able to withdraw at will or to exercise a nullifying veto over any action taken.

The Charter of the United Nations is analogous to the Articles of Confederation, under which the thirteen sovereign states on our Eastern Seaboard were associated with one another between the time they won their independence from Great Britain and the time they entered into a more perfect union by adopting a federal Constitution. With that transition, the civil peace of the United States of America replaced the state of war that prevailed among the thirteen sovereign states under the Articles of Confederation.

The lesson to be learned should be patently plain. If government is the indispensable means for establishing and preserving genuine peace wherever it is found on earth in the plural peaces that exist (however small or large their extent may be, varying with the size of the domain and the population that is governed), then it inexorably follows that genuine world peace requires world government.

The obstacles to the establishment of world government are many and various. The probability of its being realized can be estimated in terms of the difficulty of overcoming those impediments. The two ways in which it may be brought about in the first instance are identical with the two ways available for resolving human disputes or conflicts—by talk and by force.

The first way would involve the framing of a constitution by a world constitutional convention and the adoption of that constitution by all sovereign states, which would then relinquish their external sovereignty vis-à-vis one another.

The second way would involve a world war that resulted in world conquest without, at the same time, making the earth uninhabitable.

However unlikely the first way may appear to be, the second is even more unlikely. But the improbable, in whatever degree, is never the same as the impossible. However improbable may be the establishment and preservation of world peace by the institution of world federal government, its possibility remains untouched—for, since world government is *necessary* for world peace, and world peace is *necessary* for the survival and welfare of mankind, both must also be *possible.*

Appendix 4

NOTE: The following discussion of world government is excerpted from Chapter 16 in my book *The Common Sense of Politics* (New York, 1971), no longer in print.

WORLD GOVERNMENT

(1)

The discussion so far has indicated the need for world government to overcome the defects intrinsic to parochial communities, defects that are not remediable by local governments. I would now like to treat this subject more extensively, for the formation of a world political community is the second major development required for the realization of the ideal that we can now project as possible.

[In an earlier chapter,] I pointed out that nothing short of the world state can adequately serve the end that the state, teleologically defined, should aim at, since peace in the fullest sense of that term is an essential condition of the good human life. Nothing less than the world state, therefore, perfectly realizes the idea of the state.

Peace must be understood in positive, not negative, terms. If it were merely the absence of overt violence, then we would have to admit that peace exists between sovereign states during such periods as they are not engaged in actual fighting. But we also know that peace in this purely negative sense is often replaced by actual warfare, especially if the sovereign states have conflicting interests that put them in the posture of hostility toward one another.

Positively conceived, peace exists only when institutions are operative to resolve conflicting interests and settle all serious differences without recourse to violence. It is in this positive sense of peace that civil peace—the peace that obtains within the boundaries of a state—is one of the boons conferred upon the members of a society by its institutions of government. They have ways of settling their differences without recourse to violence.

In sharp contradistinction to peace in this positive sense, the negative use of the word "peace" to signify nothing but *the absence of overt violence* conceals the fact that what is being described is a state of war—what we have come to call the "cold war," in which military establishments, active espionage, and propaganda are manifest threats of violence that has not yet become overt. While it is true that the cold war is an active enterprise only between hostile rather than between friendly nations, it is always present in some degree between sovereign states. Between sovereign states, whether friendly or hostile, peace in the positive sense of that term has never existed and cannot exist; the alternatives for them are not peace and war, but only cold war and hot war— threatening violence that cannot be prevented from turning into overt violence, because the relation of sovereign states precludes the one factor that is required for the preservation of civil peace—government.

In the history of mankind up to this moment, peace—or what I shall call *civil peace* to signify the positive sense of that term—has existed only within states, not between states. Even there, as we shall presently observe when we come to consider the violence of revolutions, it may be illusory to the extent that the institutions of the society are unjust and breed revolution. Nevertheless, such civil peace as has obtained on earth, to whatever degree, has been the product of civil government.

If civil government is necessary for civil peace within the boundaries of a parochial society, then, for exactly the same reason, world civil government is necessary for world civil peace; and to achieve this we must replace the plurality of parochial societies, each a sovereign state, with the unity of a world state. The elimination of war between states—hot war or cold war—is identical with the elimination of a plurality of independent states, each of which is sovereign or subject to no superior in its external relations with other states. The elimination of war between states is not identical with the elimination of all forms of violence, for injustice may still breed revolution in a world community, as it has and does in parochial societies. Nevertheless, if we regard revolutionary violence as civil war, whether within the confines of a parochial society or in a world community, the replacement of international war by civil war through the formation of a world state is an advance, because civil war can lead to the restoration and improvement of civil peace, as international war cannot.

(2)

The foregoing constitutes an answer to the question, why world government is necessary for world civil peace, and, in part at least, it also answers the question of its desirability; for if worldwide civil peace is an indispensable means to the happiness of mankind, and if world government is an indispensable means to worldwide civil peace, then its necessity as a means makes it as desirable as the end it is needed to serve. But this leaves quite open the question whether world government is possible, as well as fails to touch on other considerations with regard to its desirability.

However appealing or persuasive it may be to say that if something is necessary as a means to an end that we are morally obligated to seek, it must be possible, that proposition by itself need not be our only answer to the question about the possibility of world government. The feasibility of world government depends on our being able to overcome two formidable obstacles. One of these is technological, the other political. Let me deal with each of these briefly.

The technological obstacle to world government appeared to be insurmountable in earlier centuries when the geographical barriers to communication and interaction among the peoples of the earth were of such an order that they could not function as fellow-citizens in a single community under one government. Technological advances have now shrunk the world, not in geodesic space, but in social space, to a size small enough to make its political as well as its economic unification feasible. If we are persuaded that the economic interdependence of the peoples of the world has now reached the point that makes their political unification desirable, we should also be able to see that the same technological factors that have produced global economic interdependence now make political unification feasible. Another sign pointing in the same direction is the advent of world wars, new in the twentieth century. The same technological advances that ushered in the era of world war—conflicts that have been and threaten to become more and more global in their extent— also provide the underpinnings for world peace by reducing the distances in social space and in communication and transportation time that were, in the past, obstacles to world political unification, as in the past they were also obstacles to global war.

The technological obstacles to world government being overcome, the only question of its feasibility concerns the political obstacles that remain. The difficulty of the problem that these present is such that one cannot be assured of its solution in the immediate future. All we can be sure of is that, in principle, it is solvable, which is tantamount to saying that world government is, in principle, politically feasible, as well as being, in fact, technologically feasible.

If world government is to be, as it should be, the de jure government of a republic, the best hope for its coming to be lies in the adoption of a federal constitution for the world state, creating a federal union of participating states that have surrendered every vestige of external sovereignty in dealing with one another. The chief political obstacle to the adoption of a constitution for a world federal republic lies in the requirement that all the participating states must themselves be republics. I would go further and say that if the world state is to embody the political ideal to which we are committed, the participating states must not only be republics, but also socialist, democratic republics. This requisite degree of political homogeneity among all the participating members of a world federation—a union of socialist, democratic republics—may be extremely difficult to achieve in a relatively short time, though there is no reason whatsoever to suppose that it cannot be achieved if sufficient time is allowed for revolutions and reforms to occur in the parochial societies that now exist. . . .

(3)

But can the political obstacles, which represent real difficulties of a high order, be surmounted in the immediate future, or will it take several centuries or more of revolutionary changes and institutional reforms to remove the social, economic, and political heterogeneities that stand in the way of world government? That is a factual question and one that calls for a prediction which lies beyond the scope and competence of political philosophy as a normative discipline. However, one consideration can be mentioned as having a bearing on the question of time.

Twenty-five years ago, when the preliminary draft of a world constitution was published, the urgency to create a world government rested solely on the need to prevent a third world war—more nearly global in its extent and, with the advent of atomic weapons, irremediably destructive of life on earth. Today there is the additional urgency that stems from the even more desperate need to prevent the destruction of the biosphere which, according to leading technologists, cannot be effectively accomplished by the action of parochial governments. A third world war has been postponed for twenty-five years and may be postponed indefinitely by the widespread fear of its cataclysmic consequences; but the destruction of the biosphere in the next twenty-five or fifty years can be prevented only by strenuous positive measures undertaken rapidly and carried out globally. The urgency of mounting and effectuating this program does more than reinforce the urgency of preventing global war: it sets a relatively short time as the period allowed us for doing what must be done. Men and nations everywhere may not be able much longer to close their eyes to the inexorable alternatives of one world or none.

I said earlier that the necessity of world government as an indispensable means to worldwide civil peace is only one point in answer to the question about its desirability as a political objective. Its indispensability as a means to preserving a life-sustaining and life-enhancing environment for mankind is another positive consideration. But there are still other considerations that should be mentioned before we face the objectionable features of a world state that might make it undesirable. Let me mention three briefly.

(1) The formation of a world community under world government is needed to eliminate the inequitable distribution of resources and wealth that has allowed the rich nations to dominate and exploit the poor nations. The same reforms that have been operative to overcome poverty within the technologically advanced welfare states must become operative on a worldwide basis to rectify the injustices suffered by the have-not nations. We must, in the words of Gunnar Myrdal, go beyond the parochial confines of the welfare state to extend participation in general economic welfare to all the peoples

of the world; and this can be done only by the regulation of a world economy by a world government that aims at the economic welfare of men everywhere. It should be added here that so long as the cold war exists and the hot war threatens, the wasteful employment of our productive powers to maintain military establishments can prevent us from producing enough wealth to remove poverty, no matter how far our productive technology may advance.

(2) What is true of poverty on a worldwide basis is similarly true of racism on a worldwide basis. This, like poverty, is not an evil confined within the borders of this or that parochial society. It is an evil that pervades a world in which nationalism generates ethnic and racial hatreds and hostilities. The elimination of racism requires a world community in which all men, of whatever stock or complexion, are fellow citizens, and no one is a foreigner, a barbarian, an enemy, or a subhuman alien.

(3) The formation of a world community under world government is needed to safeguard constitutional government and democratic processes from the political schizophrenia that besets parochial states whose foreign policies undermine or conflict with their domestic programs. The machinations of international politics usually evade or violate the principles of justice that the best parochial societies attempt to apply within their own borders. In addition, with the advent of war on a global scale, the so-called military-industrial complex has grown to such power that it has become a serious threat to the institutions of political democracy; but so long as parochial states remain in the posture of war toward one another, there may be no cure for this evil, which afflicts all the great powers—China and Russia as much as the United States.

(4)

With all these things in its favor, what disadvantages attach to world government that might raise a serious question for us about its desirability?

Certainly not that world government would require the abolition of the external sovereignty and independence of the parochial national states in existence today. That, as we have seen, counts as one of the great benefits world government would confer, not only serving the cause of peace but also helping to eliminate poverty and racism. Only myopic provincialism or, what is worse, an overriding commitment to short-term gains for a favored few against the interests of all the rest would lead anyone to regard the loss of national sovereignty as an unmitigated evil that overbalances all other considerations.

The only respectable objection with which I am acquainted derives from the fear that a monolithic world state would embody a centralization of authority and a concentration of power so massive that if it were converted into an instrument of despotism and tyranny, it would be one against which no countervailing force could ever prevail.

In reply to this objection, let me say, first, that the same constitutional safeguards that prevent a republic from becoming a despotism can be built into a world constitution in a manner that is appropriate to the organization of the government it sets up. Once again I would refer to the *Preliminary Draft of a World Constitution* for a vision of how constitutional limitations on public officials and departments of government can safeguard the citizens of a world republic from abuses of authority or power, as these have been safeguarded by comparable devices in parochial societies.

In the second place, everything that has already been said about the preservation of residual autonomy for individuals and subordinate associations applies to world government, and with even greater force because of the number, variety, and size of the subordinate communities, corporations, and associations that would not only be included but would also be granted some measure of local autonomy in the organization of a world federal republic. In other words, the centralization of ultimate authority in the organs of a world government should be counterbalanced by a decentralization of the functions to be performed by its subordinate components, each exercising the measure of residual autonomy that is requisite for an effective performance of its special function.

Finally, with all military power abolished, and with the only implements of authorized force available to government those which can be justified as means of preserving peace and protecting individuals against criminal violence, the power at the disposal of the world government might be considerably less than that provided by the armaments under control of the national governments of parochial societies. One of the great advances that will come about with the formation of a world republic will be the substitution of a legally constituted and civilly controlled police power for all the other forms of force that have been available to government. The only authorized force will be that of police operating solely to protect rights and to render the acts of government efficacious.

If injustice of one sort or another still persists in the world community after world government is instituted, or creeps back into it, and if the legal means for the redress of grievances are not adequate to rectify serious wrongs, revolutionary violence would still remain the only option, and having recourse to it would not be precluded; for world government, if properly constituted, would not have overwhelming force at its disposal, as it might if it were empowered with a vast military establishment proportionate to its global scope, rather than confined to the use of a civil police force designed primarily to preserve civil peace.

Appendix 5

NOTE: The following discussion of future possibilities is excerpted from Chapter 19, "Our Limited Vision of the Possible," in my book *The Common Sense of Politics* (New York, 1971), no longer in print.

I have proceeded throughout this book in terms of the vision of the possible that is now available to us in the light of past and present experience. Our enlarged conception of the possible, I have said, has enabled us to project a political ideal far beyond anything that our ancestors would have thought attainable. But I have also said that political philosophy is always conditioned by the historic limitations of the time in which it is being formulated. This is as true of any twentieth-century effort as it was true of the political formulations made in earlier centuries. The same mote that clouded the vision of earlier political philosophers still clouds our own, even if we are not so aware of it.

In the uprising that took place at the Sorbonne a few years ago, a student chalked up on the wall the following graffito: *Be realistic; attempt the impossible*! On the face of it, considered soberly and strictly, the statement is, of course, false. The impossible is that which cannot be done; and, therefore, it should not be attempted by anyone in his right mind. Nevertheless, the statement is a witty way of expressing the truth that the determination of what is possible or impossible is an extremely difficult matter, involving more knowledge of facts than is generally available at any time; and so, as this student was really saying, the spirit of progress should always challenge those who seek to preserve the status quo by claiming that the changes called for by justice lie beyond the bounds of the possible.

The same insight applies to our vision of a future state of affairs that precludes the possibility of further progress because all the institutional improvements that are needed for the happiness of mankind have been achieved. That vision may be defective, because we cannot foresee the effect on human life of factors that have not yet become operative. The further development of space exploration, for one thing, and, for another, the development of our power to manipulate the genetic code may bring with them social problems and social opportunities so novel and so consequential that the possibility of progress may be enlarged beyond anything that we can now conceive. This, however, suggests the conclusion, not that institutional progress is without limits, but only that our present view of what its limits are may be inaccurate.

On the assumption, which it seems reasonable to make, that institutional progress has a definite limit even if we cannot correctly define it at this point in history, we are left with the question: Would reaching that limit mean the end of progress in human affairs? The answer is clearly no.

Before elucidating that answer, let me say a word in defense of the assumption on the basis of which the question is asked. There is nothing in the nature of man or of society and its institutions that makes it impossible to rectify all injustices and to remove all deprivations. If the limit of institutional progress is defined formally as the best possible society, in which all men will have the opportunity to make good lives for themselves, then that limit will be reached, or at least very closely approached, when revolutionary or civil progress has brought into existence a classless society that embraces all men in a world state under a world government that is constitutional, democratic, and socialistic. Nothing less than this will completely abolish war, racism, and poverty from the face of the earth; or maximize, through justice, freedom and equality for all.

Let us further suppose that the fullest realization of this political ideal is accompanied by satisfactory solutions of the population problem, the problem of preserving a healthful ecological balance in the environment, and the problem of providing effective liberal schooling for all. What then? What does the future hold for man beyond the point at which his institutions are perfected so that no injustices remain to be rectified and no deprivations remain to be remedied? What is the ultimate goal toward which the human race can and should collectively strive after all the external conditions of human life are optimal and stable?

Only one answer seems to be possible. Progress in human affairs will shift from the realm of externals—the realm of social, economic, and political institutions—to the interior life of man, the life of the mind and the spirit. Progress in institutions will be replaced by progress in individuals. The ultimate goal of human striving ought to be the fullest development of the potentialities of the human mind and spirit, a development that will not begin in earnest until the realization of the political ideal provides all men with the external conditions under which they can devote themselves to the highest pursuits of which the human race is capable—teaching and learning.

When no obstacles or barriers stand in the way of the effective and sustained communication of the members of the human race with one another, and when the human mind is no longer distracted from concentration on what is important by the urgency of practical problems that press for solution, then the cooperative engagement of men in teaching and learning as lifelong pursuits should be the chief source of progress toward fulfilling the capacities for understanding and wisdom, for friendship and love, that are the distinctive powers of the human mind and spirit.

Index

Abortion rights, 188–89, 210–11
Absolutism, absolute government, 109,
    112, 115, 117, 118, 119, 150–51,
    169, 176
Adams, John, 105, 130
American Revolution, 219, 221, 227
Anarchy, 71, 96, 100, 305–6;
    international, 101, 132–35, 157,
    264, 281, 311–13; Marxist-Leninist
    utopian version of, 54, 65, 69;
    "state of nature," 254
Aquinas, Thomas, 110, 196, 269
Aristocracy, 148, 180; elitist
    pretensions, 122, 128, 148
Aristotle, 51, 95, 110, 111–12, 114–
    15, 154, 167, 171, 176, 177, 178–
    79, 180, 196
Articles of Confederation, 313
Aspen Institute for Humanistic Studies,
    5–8, 62, 73, 105, 195, 227, 229
Associations, private, 44–45, 46, 57,
    81, 168
Athenian Democracy (Jones), 139
Athens, ancient, 111–12, 138–40,
    145, 159, 268
Attlee, Clement, 26
Augustine, Saint, 196
Austin, John, 196

Bacon, Sir Francis, 147
Bakunin, Mikhail, 69, 100
Banking, 29, 74
Benevolent despotism, *see* Despotism
Bentham, Jeremy, 147, 196, 198, 250,
    267
Berlinguer, Enrico, 153
Bill of Rights, US, 35, 179, 200,
    201–2
Binary theory, 35, 42, 50, 76, 89
Blackmun, Harry, 197, 210
Blacks: discrimination against, 207–8;
    disenfranchisement of, 20, 189, 205,
    206, 222

Bork, Robert: and abortion rights,
    188–89; and civil rights, 189, 207;
    confirmation hearing, 187–89;
    enemy of Ninth Amendment, 202,
    225; a legal positivist, 190, 197; on
    liberty and equality, 194; principles
    of justice and natural law denied by,
    188, 191, 193–94, 205, 213; and
    right to privacy, 203, 209–10, 217;
    a strict constructionist, 200, 225;
    view of judicial review vs. restraint,
    188, 191, 192–95, 200, 211; *The
    Tempting of America*, 187, 212,
    216, 217
Bourgeois capitalism, 21–25, 49, 52,
    63, 81, 87, 131; demise of, 21, 26–
    30, 34, 36, 63, 226, 227
Bowers v. Hardwick, 209, 217
Brandeis, Louis, 197
Brennan, William, 197
Brezhnev, Leonid, 56
Brownson, Orestes, 48
Brown v. Board of Education . . .,
    207
Bureaucracy, professional, 87, 115–17
Burke, Edmund, 162
Bush, George, 8; Administration, 89

Calhoun, John C., 17, 97, 121
Capital: classless distribution, 50;
    defined, 12, 38; extension of
    ownership to the many, 41–42, 63,
    131; as instrument of production of
    wealth, 12–13, 15, 16, 27–28, 37,
    64, 76, 86–87; Marxist view of, 13
    –14, 28, 37–39, 64; private
    ownership of, 46, 81, 86–87, 89.
    See also Property; Property rights,
    private; Wealth
Capital-intensive economy, 14, 42, 73,
    79, 261
Capitalism, 91; disappearing, Lenin's
    view of, 55–56, 279; exploitation of

Capitalism (cont.)
 labor by, 14, 15–16, 21–25, 37–38,
  41; forms of, 81; socialized, 6, 21,
  26–34, 36, 81, 92–94, 131, 226;
  standard of living under, 32–33, 47,
  278, 279; terminology, 6, 36, 79;
  universal, 87, 88, 89, 94;
  unsocialized, 130–31; wars of, 278,
  279. *See also* Bourgeois capitalism;
  Private-property capitalism; State
  capitalism
*Capitalism, Communism and
 Coexistence* (Galbraith-Menshikov),
  45–46
"Capitalism, Communism, and Their
 Future" (Aspen seminar), 5–66;
 Dictionary and Thesaurus, 6, 79–
 82; reading list, 77–78
Capitalism, Socialism and Democracy
 (Schumpeter), 42
Capitalist Manifesto, The (Kelso and
 Adler), 89
Capitalization, 81–82; of communist
 socialism, 36, 68
Cardozo, Benjamin, 197
Challenge of Democracy, The
 (Strachey), 31–32, 48, 57–58, 68
*Challenge of Facts and Other Essays,
 The* (Sumner), 16–18
China, 72, 227; attack on India, 276–
 77, 279–80, 281
Churchill, Sir Winston, 276
Cicero, 196, 215–16, 254, 269, 311
Citizenship, 20, 80, 83, 95, 108, 111,
 114–15, 122, 174–75, 217; active,
 prerequisites for, 86–87, 107–8,
 114, 119, 126, 129–30; education
 for, 125–29, 132, 155, 157;
 property qualifications for, 111,
 118, 130, 139; unjust exclusions
 from, 49, 109, 111, 113, 120, 130,
 139, 175, 176, 204–5
Civil government, 253, 316; necessity
 of, 255–56; world, 256–59
Civil peace, 253, 254–59, 264, 311–
 12, 322; defined, 308–9, 315
Civil rights, 35, 183, 185, 201; Bork
 and, 189, 207
Civil War, 222, 252, 259
Class distinctions and conflict, 30, 48–
 49, 50–54, 56, 63, 66, 69, 94–102;
 economic, 48–49, 95, 96, 98, 121;
 factional, 58, 95–99, 100, 102, 121;
 nonfactional, 100; political, 52–54,
 95, 97–98, 111, 121, 138; and
 political parties, 58; social, 95, 98–
 100, 102
Classless society, 80–81, 82–83, 121;
 achieving, 66, 88, 100–101; ideal

of, 30, 45, 48–51, 53–57, 64, 65,
 69, 94–104; question of political
 parties in, 57–58
Clausewitz, Carl von, 252
Coexistence, 8, 46, 47, 59
Cold war, 5, 101, 249, 255, 258, 311,
 312, 315, 316, 320
Collective ownership, 28–29, 37–39,
 40, 92. *See also* Common property;
 State ownership
Coming Struggle for Power, The
 (Strachey), 68
Common property, 9–11, 38, 40, 92
Common Sense of Politics, The
 (Adler), 67, 69, 250; excerpts, 69–
 72, 82–89, 94–104, 314–25
Communism, 3–5, 36–37, 87, 131,
 153, 226; blinded by theory, 33;
 Cranston on, 153; expansionism and
 war, 276–77, 279–80; Marxist, 36,
 45, 79–80, 81, 90; rise and fall of,
 65; vs. socialism, 8, 21, 65, 226;
 terminology, 6; totalitarian, 3, 5, 6,
 8, 21, 43, 226, 227
Communist Manifesto, The (Marx and
 Engels), 4, 9, 15, 21, 27–28, 30,
 36–37, 38–39, 40–41, 42, 48, 50,
 62
Communist party, 87; USSR, 43, 47,
 52–53, 56–57, 60, 61, 62
Communist revolution, two phases
 postulated, 52–53, 54–55, 56–57
Communist socialism, 3, 65;
 capitalization and demise, 34–45,
 68
Concurrent majority, 97
Confederation, American, 260, 313
Conflict resolution, 69–70, 253, 255–
 56, 269–70, 309, 310–11, 315
Congealed labor, 13–14, 28, 38, 64
Consent of the governed, 107, 118,
 119, 175, 181, 198, 223
Conservatism, 141; in Bork
 confirmation hearings, 187; 19th-
 century European, 146
Constitutional democracy, 109, 111,
 118, 119, 174, 176–77, 183, 211,
 222; Bork's views, 192–93;
 Cranston on, 136, 138, 140–51
Constitutional government, 19–20, 80,
 107–8, 109–13, 115, 116, 117–19,
 142, 146–47, 150, 161, 174–75,
 180, 306; limits on, 164, 165–67,
 175, 192, 201–4, 211; oligarchical
 vs. democratic, 109, 111, 118, 119,
 222; without democracy, 111, 148,
 165; with power of judicial review,
 190; with universal suffrage, 108,
 111, 113, 124, 163–65, 174, 176–

77. *See also* Constitutional democracy
Constitutionalism, 133, 148–50, 153, 161, 165–68, 179–80; nondemocratic, 165, 174, 175
Constitutionalism, Ancient and Modern (McIlwain), 179
Constitutional oligarchy, 109, 111, 118, 119, 222
Convergence, East-West, 8, 47, 59, 73–77; philosophical gap, 246–47
Courts, in conflict resolution, 253, 309
Cranston, Maurice, 105, 106, 108, 135–55, 157–58, 160, 165, 167, 176, 177, 180, 182–86, 227
Creeping socialism, 28–30
Crime, 57, 65; against humanity, 200; victimless, 210
Critique of the Gotha Program (Marx), 50, 51
Cromwell, Oliver, 111
Culturalization of man, 154
Culture: transmission of, 236; world, unity vs. diversity in, 242–43, 245–48, 265–66

Dante Alighieri, 250, 266, 272–74
Decent livelihood: components of, 67, 83–84, 104, 224; right to, 20, 26, 34–35, 49, 80, 183, 224–25, 227
Declaration of Independence, 18, 198, 199, 201–2, 218, 223, 224–25, 227, 238; Lincoln and, 218–22
De Gaulle, Charles, 116
De jure vs. de facto government, 71, 119, 309–10
Delian League, 236
Democracy, 19–20, 27, 59–60, 88, 97, 99, 102, 107, 180, 275; absolute unlimited, 169, 174, 176; American movement toward, 110, 143, 222; ancient Greek, 109, 111–12, 138–40; Churchill on, 276; conservative vs. liberal orientations, 141; definitions, 108, 124, 137, 158–59, 162–65, 174–75; direct, 97, 139–40, 141, 144–45, 161, 177; economic, 82, 88, 130–31, 225; essence of, 119, 126, 174; extension of, 125, 131–32, 136, 141–42, 146, 153, 227, 261; hamstrung in foreign affairs, 133–34; infirmities of, 120, 137; as just government, 116, 119–20, 123, 124, 136, 149, 156–57, 165, 175; in name only, 144, 149, 159, 262; nonegalitarian, 74; obstacles to perfection and survival, 125–35, 146–47, 157, 165; perfection of, 125, 130–32, 134,

135–36; political, 19–20, 80, 82–83, 88, 107–9, 110–14, 116, 117–25, 130–31, 136, 138, 157, 177; representative, 80, 97, 110–11, 144–46, 177; social, 116, 125, 131, 157, 168; and socialism, 3–5, 19–21, 30, 63–64; socialist, 3, 57, 61, 102, 225, 226–27; standard of living in, 32–33; still only a goal, 113–14, 143; superiority of, 120–23, 124; survival of, 107, 125, 130, 132, 134, 135–36, 154–55, 157–58, 177–78, 227; terminology, 8, 107–14, 136, 158–65; Tocqueville on, 43, 116, 190, 212–13; unconstitutional, 176; viability of, 107, 123–25; and war, 280–81; world, Strachey on, 275–77, 282–84. *See also* Constitutional democracy
Democracy in America (Tocqueville), 23–24, 43, 212–13
Democratic Manifesto, A (Reves), 272
Democratic peoples' republics, 149
Democratic socialism, 3–5, 8, 227
Democratic society, 108, 113–14, 136, 142; term, 108
Denaturization of man, 154, 177
De Officiis (Cicero), 269
Despotism, 43, 109–10, 117–18, 120, 138, 321; benevolent, 115–17, 118, 119, 125, 131, 147; communist, 53; monarchic, 109, 119; populistic, 149; totalitarian, 116 (*see also* Totalitarianism; Totalitarian State); tyrannical, 117, 118, 122, 306
Difference of Man and the Difference It Makes, The (Adler), 235
Discrimination, 98, 99–100, 102, 118; against blacks, 207–8; sex, 241
Dividend income, 13, 34–35, 42, 50
Djilas, Milovan, 56, 87
Douglas, Stephen A., 220–21
Dred Scott case, 194, 214, 220, 221
Dulles, John Foster, 250
Dworkin, Ronald, 108, 213

Earned income, 13, 34–35, 74, 75; binary sources of, 42, 50, 76
Eastern Europe, 3, 61, 62, 68, 73, 75, 159, 227; economic reforms, 76, 89–94; welfare benefits, 90
Economic Bill of Rights (FDR), 26
Economic democracy, 82, 88, 130–31, 225
Economic equality, *see* Equality
Economic independence, 86–87, 88, 157

Economic justice, 20, 44, 82, 95, 130, 183–84, 224–25; distributive, 49, 54, 65. *See also* Taxation; Wealth, redistribution of

Education, 29, 125–29, 154; of electorate, 121–22, 125–26; of elite, 128, 147; liberal, 126–29, 155, 157, 324; as a natural right, 83, 129; vocational, 126–27, 128–29

Egalitarianism, 17; extreme, 54, 72

Elitism, 148, 241; intellectual, 121, 122, 128

Engels, Friedrich, 3–4, 27–28, 30, 36, 48, 62

Entitlements, 29, 35, 42, 75

Environmental pollution, 104, 135, 243, 258, 264–65, 319, 324

Environmental/social conditioning, 71–72. *See also* Nature vs. nurture

"Equal but separate" rule, 208–9

Equality, 65, 71, 72, 82, 101, 121–22, 134, 135, 238; Bork on, 194; of conditions, 43, 115–16, 121, 135, 157; economic, 20–21, 30, 31, 43–44, 45–46, 63–64, 65, 80, 82–86, 88, 98, 99, 115–16, 130; in educational opportunity, 83, 128; and liberty, compatibility of, 17–18, 44, 135, 224; maximization of, 71, 102, 104, 324; natural, vs. nurtural inequality, 239, 241; of opportunity, 93, 128, 182; political, 20, 44, 45–46, 65, 82–83, 86, 98, 99, 108, 113, 114–17, 119, 130, 225; seen in Declaration, not Constitution, by Lincoln, 218, 220–21, 224; social, 98–100, 115–16, 130

Equal protection clause, 207–9

Establishment, 100; classless, 101–2

Ethnic groups, 98, 102, 265; nationalism, 61, 263, 320; pluralism and, 257; and prejudice, 241, 263

Eurocommunism, 153

Europe, 147, 153; continental, and popular sovereignty rationalism, 150–51, 162; former oligarchic monarchies of, 52, 53; imperialism, 152. *See also* Eastern Europe

Existentialism, 230, 239

Factionalism, 72–73, 95–99, 100, 102; and tyranny of the majority, 96–97, 121

Federalism, 266; need for economic/political homogeneity, 260–62, 318; US, 168, 252–53, 256, 260, 263–64, 313

Federalist, The: No. 6, 263, 269; No. 10, 72, 95, 97

Feudal system, 44, 49, 130, 312

Fifteenth Amendment, 189, 194, 205, 212, 222

First Amendment, 201, 206–7, 209–10, 216

First World, 75–76, 261–62, 264

Flag salute cases, 213–14

Foreign policies, 133–34, 252, 254, 255, 257, 311, 320

Fourteenth Amendment, 189, 194, 205, 207–8, 212, 222

Fourth Amendment, 203–4, 206–7, 209–10

France, governmental systems of, 150–51, 161–62

Franchise, *see* suffrage

Frankfurter, Felix, 190–91, 197, 213–14

Free choice, 204, 216, 235, 237

Freedom, 148; of association and assembly, 160, 163, 201; in democracies, 32, 71, 160; education for, 126–29; of press, 181, 201; of religion, 201; of speech, 160, 163, 201. *See also* Liberty

Free-enterprise economy, 21, 45, 46, 57, 79, 81, 261

Free-market system, 45, 46, 57, 74, 79, 91; Eastern European transition to, 90–94

Free will, 204, 217, 235, 238–39

French Revolution, 150, 161, 162, 174, 221

Friedman, Milton, 90, 91

"From each . . . to each" principle of communism, 54, 68–69

Fukuyama, Francis, 77

Galbraith, John Kenneth, 45–46, 59

Gandhi, Mahatma, 152

Gaullism, 116

Genetic determinism, 240, 306

Germany, 52, 53, 151–52; economic system, 91

Gettysburg Address, 218, 222, 224, 226

Gorbachev, Mikhail, 1–3, 4, 7, 42, 43, 45, 46, 47, 51, 61, 63–64

Government, 19–20, 44, 82; abolition, *see* Anarchy; absolute vs. relative justification of, 131–32; absolute unlimited powers, 150–51, 169, 174, 181; authority of, 70, 223, 253, 306–8, 310; authorized use of force, 57, 65, 167, 253, 306, 309–10, 322; best form of, 111, 120, 182; centralized, 46, 53, 64, 71, 88–89, 116; checks and balances, 211; decentralized, 44, 46, 71, 167–68,

322; illegitimate use of force, 71, 268, 310; infirmities of (incompetence, tyranny), 120; just, 82, 84–85, 101, 102, 113, 116, 118–20, 123, 124, 136, 149, 156–57, 164–65, 175, 182–84, 207, 306, 310; of laws, 110, 115, 119; limits on, 150–51, 164, 165–67, 175–76, 192, 201–4, 211; as "necessary evil," 258; necessity of, 69–71, 150, 167, 168–69, 256, 304–8, 313, 315–16; norms and criteria for, 124; parliamentary, 144; "of the people, by the people, for the people," 107–8, 116, 125, 137, 222–24, 226; "popular," term criticized, 112; scientific, 147; separation of branches and powers of, 167–68, 211; . . . which governs least . . . , 44, 151, 182, 184. *See also* Absolutism; Civil government; Constitutional government; Democracy; Despotism; Monarchy; Oligarchy; Representative government; Republic; Totalitarianism; Tyranny; World government
Greece, ancient, 109, 111–12, 137, 138–40, 143, 178–80, 185, 263
Griswold v. Connecticut, 209, 217

Habeas corpus, 166, 181
Hamilton, Alexander, 14, 142, 148, 269, 305–6
Hand, Learned, 190–91, 197
Happiness, *see* Pursuit of happiness
Have-lesses and have-mores, 21, 49, 54, 65, 69, 74, 76, 80, 225
Have-nots, 36, 49, 74, 80, 94, 95–96, 98; goal of eliminating, 20–21, 31, 54, 63–64, 76, 102, 225; nations, 251, 262, 265, 319
Haves, 20–21, 36, 49–50, 63–64, 65, 74, 76, 80, 94, 95–96, 98, 225; in classless society, 54, 102; nations, 251, 262, 265, 319
Hegel, Georg W.F., 110, 151
Hitler, Adolf, 159
Hobbes, Thomas, 110, 150, 196, 270–71, 311
Holmes, Oliver Wendell, 190–91, 197, 212
How To Think About War and Peace (Adler), 249, 257, 266
Human mind, 242, 265, 325
Human nature, common, 70, 229–42; behavioral differences compared to other animals, 236–37, 238–39, 240; behavioral/cultural differences

within, 231–32, 234, 239, 240, 242, 265–66; equalities of, vs. individual and subgroup inequalities, 238, 239, 241, 266; genetic determination, 240, 306; mistaken denial of, 71–72, 230–34, 239–40, 265–66; nurtural factors, 72, 239–42, 265–66, 306; potentialities, 72, 233–34, 238, 239, 240, 241
Human rights, 20, 122, 176, 190, 199–200, 235, 237; Cranston, 108, 148; vs. property rights, 25–26, 226; US defense of, 199–200, 204–5. *See also* Natural rights
Hume, David, 142
Hutchins, Robert M., 190, 250

Imperialism (Lenin), 278–79
Imperialism, 152, 312
Inalienable rights, 20, 198, 199–200, 201–4, 224–25, 235, 238
Income: forms of, 13, 34–35, 86–87; redistribution of, 29, 32, 226. *See also* Earned Income; Unearned income
Income-producing property, 86. *See also* Capital
Income tax, graduated, 29, 226
Industrialization, 132, 265
Industrial Revolution, 14–15, 37
Inequality: justifiable distinctions, 49, 54, 65, 74–75, 76, 238; as result of nurtural influences vs. natural endowment, 239, 241, 266
Inheritance right and tax, 29, 226
Intellect, 235, 236, 237, 238–39
Intellect: Mind Over Matter (Adler), 235
Intelligence, 69–70, 126–28, 235
International affairs, 250–52, 253–66, 320; anarchy, 101, 132–35, 157, 264, 281, 311–13. *See also* Peace; War; World government
Iron law of wages, 21, 33, 36, 63

Jefferson, Thomas, 140, 142, 182, 191, 228, 241
Jones, A.J.M., 139
Jouvenel, Bertrand de, 116, 150
Judicial restraint, 188, 192, 194; Bork's view, 192–95, 200, 211
Judicial review, 122, 181, 188, 190, 211; Bork's view, 192–95, 211; of unjust but not unconstitutional laws, 189, 190–91, 193–94
Justice, 17–18, 20, 44, 49, 85, 100–102, 103, 117, 120, 135; Bork's stance, 188, 191, 193–94, 205, 213; class distinctions inimical to, 94–95,

Justice (cont.)
  97–99; conflicting aims, 171, 182;
  distributive, 49, 54, 65; economic,
  20, 44, 82, 95, 130, 183–84, 224–
  25; essence of, 182–84, 198;
  political, 20, 82, 95, 117, 118, 119–
  20, 123, 124, 183; in positive (man-
  made) vs. natural law, 195–98;
  principles of, 208, 209; social, 95,
  98–100, 102, 183–84, 189;
  worldwide, 103–4, 132–33, 312–
  14, 319–20, 324. *See also*
  Government, just
Justification, absolute vs. relative,
  131–32

Kant, Immanuel, 87, 110, 113, 196,
  230, 250, 267, 274–75
Kapital, Das (Marx), 42, 50
Kelsen, Hans, 69, 253, 309
Kelso, Louis O., 35, 42, 50, 76, 89
Khrushchev, Nikita, 54, 68
Kropotkin, Pyotr A., 69

Labor, 86–87; in classless society, 50;
  congealed (accumulated), 13–14, 28,
  38, 64; division of, 22–23;
  exploitation of, 14, 15–16, 21–25,
  37–38, 41; as instrument of
  production of wealth, 11, 12, 13–
  16, 37–39, 76. *See also* Wage labor;
  Working class
Labor-intensive economy, 14
Labor theory: of property (Locke), 9–
  13, 76; of value (Marx), 9, 13–14,
  15, 16, 28, 37, 39–40, 64
Labor unions, 34, 44, 86
Laissez-faire economy, 42, 74, 81
Land ownership, 29, 49, 53, 261
Lassalle, Ferdinand, 21
Lasting Peace and The State of War, A
  (Rousseau), 271
*Lasting Peace Through the Federation
  of Europe, A* (Saint-Pierre), 271
Law, 133; equal protection of the,
  207–9; government of, 110, 115,
  119; international, 133; natural,
  193, 195–98, 200; positive (man-
  made), 190, 194, 195–98,
  200; relation to liberty, 110, 150,
  206–11
Law enforcement, 57, 65, 253, 309–
  10, 311
Laws (Plato), 270
League of Nations, 312–13
Legal naturalism, 195–98
Legal positivism, 190, 194, 195–98,
  200
Legal realism, 196, 212

Legislatures, in conflict resolution,
  253, 309
Lenin, Vladimir, 3–5, 61–64, 69, 72;
  classless society as goal of, 48–57,
  63–64; doctrine of withering away
  of state, 53–56, 64–65;
  Imperialism, 278–79
Leninism, 2–5, 48–49, 51. *See also*
  Marxism-Leninism
Letter Concerning Toleration (Locke),
  270
Leviathan (Hobbes), 196, 270–71
Liberal education, 126–29, 155, 157,
  324
Liberalism, 148; in Bork confirmation
  hearings, 187; 19th-century
  European, 146, 151
Libertarianism, 17, 149–50
Liberty, 134, 135, 142, 147–48, 149–
  51, 185, 222; absent in totalitarian
  state, 87; Bork on, 194; and
  equality, compatibility of, 17–18,
  44, 135, 224; maximization of, 71,
  102, 104, 182–83, 324; moral, 217;
  a natural right, 185, 194, 201–4,
  224; personal, 116; political, 19–20,
  35, 44, 61, 71, 72, 80, 88, 101,
  114–15, 117, 119, 176, 181, 185–
  86, 204–6, 217, 227; in relation to
  law, 110, 150, 206–11; seen in
  Declaration, not Constitution, by
  Lincoln, 218, 220, 221, 224; state
  as protector of, 149–51; without
  democracy, 147–48
Lincoln, Abraham, 44, 218–26
Lippmann, Walter, 116, 250
Locke, John, 40, 45, 110, 135, 142,
  148, 311; labor theory of property,
  9–11, 37, 76; on liberty, 150,
  202–3; and natural law, 196;
  *Second Treatise Concerning Civil
  Government*, 9–10, 51, 268, 271;
  "tacit consent," 175; on use of
  force, 254, 268, 269, 270, 271, 311
Louis Philippe, King, 148, 161

Machiavelli, Niccolo, 254, 269–70,
  311
Machinery, 14–15, 16, 22–23, 38–40,
  66–67, 73, 236; as congealed
  (accumulated) labor, 13–14, 28, 38
McIlwain, Charles, 179
Macpherson, C.B., 144
Madison, James, 60, 72–73, 95–96,
  97, 98, 121
Maine, Sir Henry, 147
Majority: educated vs. ignorant, 125–
  29, 132, 155, 157; rule, 122, 157,
  164, 175, 192–93, 206, 212–13,

266, 307; rule limited in US, 97, 166, 175–76, 190–91, 211; rule unlimited in UK, 166, 181; tyranny of, 96–97, 120, 121, 122, 163–64, 170–71, 174, 189, 190, 193, 195–96, 197, 198, 211
Mann, Horace, 23, 24, 49–50
Mao Tse Tung, 72
Market economy, 21, 45, 46, 57, 74, 79, 91; Eastern European transition to, 90–94
Marsilius of Padua, 110
Marx, Karl, 3–5, 21–23, 24, 27–28, 34, 36, 38–39, 42, 57, 61–62, 69, 72, 81, 95, 100; classless society goal of, 30, 48–54, 56, 63–64, 69; labor theory of value, 9, 13–14, 28, 37, 39–40, 64; nonsupportable doctrines of, 64–65; prophecy of ever-increasing misery of workers, 32–33, 41, 47, 63, 279; supportable doctrines of, 63–64
Marxism, 2–5, 6, 14, 48–49, 51, 92; critique of doctrines of, 13–14, 32–33, 36–42, 45, 54, 62, 63–65; failure of, 47
Marxism-Leninism, 50–54; valid vs. invalid assumptions, 4, 60–61, 62–66
Marxist communism, 81, 90; doomed to fail, 45; term, 36, 79–80
Marxist socialism, 43
Mechanics' Union *Preamble*, 15–16
Menshikov, Stanislas, 45–47, 59
Merleau-Ponty, Maurice, 230
Military establishments, 252, 256, 257, 259, 311, 320
Mill, John Stuart, 116, 147; concern about tyranny of majority, 96, 97, 121, 122, 163–64, 175, 190; and liberty, 202–3, 216; *Representative Government*, 110–11, 120, 177; and suffrage, 112, 113, 163, 171; for women's vote, 111
Minersville School District v. Gobitis, 213–14
Minority: disfranchisement of, 111, 118, 189, 205–6; legal protections for, 97, 122, 189, 190–91, 193–94, 211; rule of, 175; tyranny of, 96, 122–23
Mixed economy, 74, 79, 81, 87–88
Monarchy, 109, 137, 148, 180; absolute, 109, 112, 119; constitutional, 109, 111; oligarchical, 52, 53
Montaigne, Michel Eyquem de, 191
Montesquieu, Charles, 110, 141, 142
Moral duty, 227–28, 237
Moral liberty, 217, 237

Morality, private, 203, 209–10
Moral rights, 108. *See also* Human rights; Natural rights
Moyers, Bill, 105–6, 135, 155, 174, 178, 180–81, 182, 183, 184, 186
Myrdal, Gunnar, 319

Napoleon, Emperor, 151, 152, 161
Napoleon III, Emperor, 162
Nationalism, 101, 149, 152, 153, 154, 262–63, 320; in USSR, 61
Natural law, 193, 195–98, 200, 212, 215–16
Natural right(s), 18–19, 20, 80, 83–84, 108, 119, 122, 169–70, 182–83, 185, 195, 196, 198–200, 224, 235; Bork attitude toward, 192, 193–94, 205; Bork not questioned on, 188, 189; economic (decent livelihood), 20, 26, 34–35, 49, 67, 183, 224–25; to liberty, 18, 185, 194, 201–4, 216–17, 224 (*see also* Liberty); to life, 18, 201, 224; political, 19–20, 35, 113, 117, 119, 157, 181, 183, 185, 204–6, 225; protected by constitutional amendments, 201–6; pursuit of happiness, 19, 83–85, 104, 224; Supreme Court review of violations, 189, 190–91, 193–94
"The Nature of Man" (Adler), 229
Nature vs. nurture, 72, 239–42, 265–66, 306; and political man, 154, 177–78
New class (of oppressors), 56, 87
New Deal, 25, 226
"New man" fantasy, 57, 72, 306
New Nationalism, 25–26, 226
Nineteenth Amendment, 20, 189, 205, 212, 222, 225
Ninth Amendment, 201–2, 225, 228
Nonegalitarian democracy, 74
Nonegalitarian socialism, 49, 65–66, 74–75, 76
Nuclear threat, 134–35, 258, 264, 281–82, 319
Nurture, *see* Nature vs. nurture

"Of the people, by the people, for the people," 107–8, 116, 125, 137, 222–23, 226
Oligarchy, 110, 111, 115–16, 117, 120, 122, 137, 159, 175; benevolent, 131; constitutional, 109, 111, 118, 119, 222; elitism, 128, 130; tyrannical, 117, 120, 122; Western bourgeois, 52, 53–54, 64
One World (Willkie), 266
On War (Clausewitz), 252

334 Index

On World-Government (Dante), 272–74
Opportunity: of education, 83, 128; equality of, 93, 128, 182
O'Toole, James, 33, 34, 42, 45, 59, 72–73; essays, 59, 89–94
Owen, Robert, 33–34, 111

Parliament, UK, 142, 143, 151, 181
Parliamentary government, 144
Pax Romana, Pax Britannica, 312
Peace, 251–55, 308, 310–12; civil, 253, 254–59, 264, 308–9, 311–12, 315–16, 322; global, 103–4, 132–34, 243, 249–51, 255, 258–59, 276–77, 312–14, 316–17; negative meaning of term (cold war), 251–52, 253, 255, 259, 315; positive meaning, 252–54, 315; prerequisites for, 256–57, 313–14, 315–16; writings on term, 269–72, 308–14
Peloponnesian War, 263, 268
Peoples' democracies, 149, 159
Perestroika, 1, 3, 43, 47, 61, 64, 73
Pfaff, William, 1–3, 5, 59
Philosophy, 245, 246–48, 266
Plato, 48, 95, 110, 111, 116, 147, 176, 195, 214–15, 270
Plessy v. Ferguson, 208
Pluralism, 43–45, 46–47, 57, 59–60, 72, 74, 168, 257; cultural/behavioral, 230–32, 239, 243, 245–48, 266; feudal, 44
Plural voting, 97, 121, 122, 175
Political animal, proposition of, 114–17, 119–20, 157, 176–78, 238–39; Cranston's comments on, 154–55, 177, 185; Quinton's questioning of, 171–72
Political democracy, 19–20, 80, 82–83, 88, 107–14, 116–25, 130–31, 177; Cranston on, 136, 138; obstacles to, 125–35, 157
Political equality, *see* Equality
Political justice, 20, 82, 95, 117, 118, 119–20, 123, 124, 183
Political liberty, *see* Citizenship; Liberty; Natural rights, political; Suffrage
Political parties, 44, 46, 57–58, 146, 168
Politics (Aristotle), 51, 95, 171
Poll tax, 20, 139, 189, 206
Poor, the, disfranchisement of, 20, 130, 139, 189, 205, 206, 222. *See also* Have-nots; Rich vs. poor
"Popular government," 112
Popular sovereignty, 137, 143, 149–51
Populistic democracy, 149, 161–62

Populistic despotism, 149
Positive law, *see* Law, positive
Poverty, 31, 101, 278, 319–20, 324. *See also* Have-nots; Poor, the
Powell, Enoch, 170
Preliminary Draft of a World Constitution, The, see World constitution
Price, Richard, 162
Prince, The (Machiavelli), 270
Principles of Morals and Legislation (Bentham), 196
Privacy, right to, 203–4, 206, 209–10, 216
Private appropriation, 10–12, 40
Private-property capitalism, 6, 21, 28, 46–47, 59, 66, 76; criticism of, 45; defined, 79; socialization of, 6, 21, 26–34, 36, 46, 47, 63–64, 68, 81, 131, 226, 262
Privatization, 74; in Eastern Europe, 76, 90–94
Production: in bourgeois capitalist model, 22–23; instruments of, 11–16, 27–28, 29, 37–40, 64, 76, 79, 86–87, 226; "social ownership" of means of, 92
Profit, 13, 37–38, 47; dividends from, 42, 50
Profit motive, 21, 26, 32, 34
Progressive Party (1912), 25, 226
Proletariat, 22–23, 27–28, 49; dictatorship of, 43, 47, 52–53, 64, 87. *See also* Labor; Working class
Property: acquired vs. natural, 12–13; classless distribution of, 50; common, 9–11, 38, 40, 92; definitions, 12–13, 50; income-producing, 86 (*see also* Capital); labor theory of (Locke), 9–13, 76; Marxist view of, 14, 28, 36–37, 38–39, 40–41; as qualification for voting and office, 111, 118, 130, 139, 175
Property rights, private, 28–29, 40–42, 63, 76; abolition of, 28–29, 36–37, 39, 40–42, 47, 51, 65; erosion of, 28–29, 41–42, 47, 63; extension to the many, 41–42, 63; vs. human rights, 25–26, 226
Proportional representation, 121, 122, 175
Province of Jurisprudence Determined (Austin), 196
Public officials, 120, 174–75; incompetence in, 120; powers of, 20, 49, 108, 225; property requirement, 111, 175

Pursuit of happiness, 19, 83–85, 86, 104, 201, 224, 228

Qaddafi, Muammar, 149
Quinton, Anthony, 105, 106, 155, 156–74, 175–76, 178, 179, 181, 184–86

Racism, 98, 100, 101, 102, 241, 263, 320, 324; discrimination, 207–8; disfranchisement, 20, 118, 175, 189, 205, 206
Rainborow, Thomas, 111
Reagan, Ronald, 8, 91, 153
Real World of Democracy, The (Macpherson), 144
Reason, human, 69–70, 239. *See also* Intellect
Rebellion, revolution, 227, 259, 268, 316, 322
Reflections on the French Revolution (Burke), 162
Religion, 245, 246–47, 248, 266
Report on Manufactures (Hamilton), 14
Representation, political, 144–46, 174, 177
Representative Government (Mill), 110–11, 120, 177
Representative government, 80, 97, 110–11, 144–46, 177
Republic (Plato), 48, 195, 214–15
Republic, 19–20, 107–8, 109, 111, 117; democratic socialist, 102, 149; popular, 149–51; Roman, 109, 137–38; US, 143, 260; as world government, 260–61, 318, 321–22
Reves, Emery, 271–72
Ricardo, David, 21
Rich vs. poor: class conflict, 94, 95–96, 98; gap, 75; international gap, 251, 262, 265, 319–20. *See also* Have-nots; Haves
Right to a Living Wage (Ryan), 26
Roe v. Wade, 210, 217
Rome, ancient, 109, 137–38, 139, 149, 152, 185, 277–78
Roosevelt, Franklin D., 8, 25, 26, 183, 226, 266
Roosevelt, Theodore, 8, 25–26, 226
Ross, John, 111
Rousseau, Jean-Jacques, 51, 110, 140, 142, 144, 161, 177, 250, 267, 270, 271
Ruling class, 52–54, 94, 95, 100, 102, 111–12, 114–15, 118
Russian Revolution, 21, 43, 52
Ryan, Mgr. John A., 26, 34

Saint-Pierre, Charles, 250, 267, 271
Salaries and wages, 13, 34, 42, 50
Sanford, Nathan, 111
Schumpeter, Joseph A., 42, 45
Science, natural, 244, 246–48, 266
Second Treatise Concerning Civil Government (Locke), 9–10, 51, 268, 271
Second World, 75–76, 261–62, 264
Sex prejudice, 241
Shaw, George Bernard, 170
Sixteenth Amendment, 208
Slavery, 13, 49, 96, 101, 109, 111, 120, 130, 178, 194, 277–78; Lincoln and, 219, 220; natural, of Aristotle, 115, 177–78
Smith, Adam, 92
Social animals, 238–39
Social Contract (Rousseau), 51
Social democracy, 116, 125, 131, 157, 168
Social equality, *see* Equality
Socialism, 50, 98, 99, 102, 184, 226, 277; communist, 3, 36, 65, 68; creeping, 28–30; criticisms of, 17–18; democracy and, 3–5, 19–21, 30, 63–64; democratic, 3–5, 8, 227 (*see also* Socialist democracy); goal of, 20–21, 63, 80; Marxist, 43; misidentified with communism, 8, 21, 226; nonegalitarian, 49, 65–66, 74–75, 76; privately capitalized, 6, 21, 26–34, 36, 46, 57, 68; terminology, 6, 36, 76, 80; totalitarian, 149
Socialist democracy, 57, 102, 225, 226–27; in Eastern Europe, 3, 61
Socialist Movement, The (Vail), 39
Socialization, economic, 81, 88; of private-property capitalism, 26–34, 36, 46, 47, 63–64, 68, 81, 131, 226, 262
Social justice, 95, 98–100, 102, 183–84, 189
Social Security, 25, 35
Socrates, 195–96
Sovereignty (de Jouvenel), 150
Sovereignty, 161, 281; absolute vs. limited, 150–51; individual, 71; national, and global affairs, 101, 132–33, 256, 258–59, 263, 264, 276, 280, 281–82, 311–13, 315–16, 318; people's, 137, 143, 149–51
Soviet Union, 21, 43, 52–53, 75; in cold war, 255, 258; doctrinal extremism in, 61–63; ethnic nationalism in, 61; expansionism, 276–77; future economic system,

Soviet Union (cont.)
  6–8; reforms in, 1–3, 4, 8, 42, 46–
  47, 60–63, 227; satellites of, *see*
  Eastern Europe; standard of living
  in, 32, 47, 61; totalitarianism, 53–
  54, 56, 57, 61
Spengler, Oswald, 186
Spinoza, Benedict, 110, 191–92
Stalin, Joseph, 56
Standard of living: in capitalist
  societies, 32–33, 47, 278, 279; in
  Soviet Union, 32, 47, 61
State: abolition of, 71–72, 305; etatist
  view of, 150–52, 167; goodness of,
  304–5; origin of, 51; as protector of
  freedom, 149–51, 162; as protector
  of person and property, 57, 167,
  181, 306; purpose of, 51; withering
  away, 53–56, 64–65, 305
State and Revolution, The (Lenin), 4,
  50–51, 52, 55, 57
State capitalism, 6, 28, 36, 37, 43, 46–
  47, 50–51, 59, 64, 65–66, 80, 81,
  87, 88, 131, 226; removal of, 45,
  57, 68, 74
"State of nature," 254
State of war, 254, 268, 270, 271, 308,
  310–11, 315
State ownership, 27–28, 29, 37, 64,
  79; in Eastern Europe, 90, 92–93
Strachey, John, 31–32, 48, 50, 57–58,
  67–68, 87, 250, 275–84
Streit, Clarence, 250
Strict constructionism, 200, 208
Study of History, A (Toynbee), 48
Subject class, 52–54, 94, 95, 102,
  111–12, 114–15, 118, 120
Suffrage, 86, 114, 119, 185, 217, 223;
  exclusions from, 20, 49, 109, 111,
  118, 130, 139, 172, 173, 175, 176,
  189, 205–6, 222; extensions of, 27,
  112, 118, 121, 142, 146, 148–49;
  in totalitarian states, 159–60;
  universal, 20, 27, 49, 80, 83, 108,
  111, 112–13, 121–22, 124, 159–
  60, 161, 163–65, 169–70, 171–74,
  176–77, 180–81, 186, 205
Summa Theologica (Aquinas), 269
Sumner, William Graham, 16–18, 20
Surplus value (Marx), 14, 16, 37
Swiss democracy, 140–42, 145, 161

Tacitus, 140
Taney, Roger B., 194, 221
Taste, sphere of, 244–45, 266
Taxation: redistributive, 27, 29, 32,
  226; federal vs. state, 168
Tempting of America, The (Bork),
  187, 212, 216, 217

Thatcherism, 91
Third World, 75–76, 144, 152, 153,
  262
Thirteenth Amendment, 189, 194,
  205, 212, 222
Thrasymachus, 195–96
Thucydides, 268
Tocqueville, Alexis de, 17, 23–24, 43–
  44, 72, 96, 97, 142; on democracy,
  43, 116, 190, 212–13
Totalitarianism, 43, 44, 45, 46, 47,
  116, 261; communist, 3, 5, 6, 8, 21,
  43, 47, 65, 87, 226, 227; demise in
  Eastern Europe, 74
Totalitarian socialism, 149
Totalitarian state, 64, 80, 87, 88, 226;
  characteristics of, 46; as first phase
  of Communist revolution, 53–54;
  Soviet, 53–54, 56, 57, 61; voting in,
  159–60
Toynbee, Arnold J., 48, 101, 263
Trotsky, Leon, 52
Truman, Harry S, 8
Truth, unity of, 244, 245–48
Truth in Religion (Adler), 248
Twenty-fourth Amendment, 20, 189,
  205, 212, 222, 225
Tyler, Gus, 31
Tyranny, 43, 117–18, 120, 280, 306,
  321; international, 133. *See also*
  Majority, tyranny of

Ulpian, 196
Unearned income, 13, 35
Unearned increment, 14, 15–16, 37
Unemployment insurance, 25, 35
United Kingdom, 52, 53, 75, 76, 146,
  167, 277; anti-immigration
  sentiment, 170; democratization of,
  141–42, 143, 162, 163; economic
  system of, 21, 26–27, 63, 91; 18th-
  century, 151, 162, 165, 173–74,
  201; House of Lords, 180; lack of
  constitution and Bill of Rights, 166,
  181; suffrage extension in, 27, 142
United Nations, 243, 254, 283, 312–
  13
United States, 75, 76, 182–83, 280–
  81; anticommunism in, 62, 170; in
  cold war, 255, 258; democracy in,
  110, 142–43, 161, 163, 222, 281;
  divisions of power, 167–68;
  economic system of, 6–8, 21, 26–
  27, 63, 91–92; federalist system,
  168, 252–53, 256, 260, 263–64,
  313; human rights stance, 199–200,
  204–5; inception of ("conceived in
  liberty"), 218–19, 221; judicial
  review specific to, 181, 188, 189,

190–91; 1980s poverty, 31; 20th-century socio-economic direction, 8, 25–26, 62, 63

US Constitution, 72–73, 97, 142–43, 166, 167–68, 175, 179, 193–94, 200, 201, 260, 263, 313; amendments, 20, 189, 194, 201–6, 212, 222, 224–25; antidemocratic provisions, 73, 183, 189, 194, 205–6, 221–22; democratization of, 73, 98, 194, 205–6, 222, 224; interpretation, 188, 189, 192–93, 207, 209–10; Lincoln and, 218, 219, 221–22; strict construction of, 200, 208; unenumerated rights, 202–4, 209–10

US Senate, Bork hearings, 187–89

US Supreme Court: civil rights cases, 207–8; flag salute cases, 213–14; review powers, *see* Judicial review; right of privacy upheld by, 203, 209, 217

Universal capitalism, 87, 88, 89, 94

Utopian fantasy of anarchy, 65, 69

Utopian socialism, 34

Vail, Charles, 39

Value, labor theory of (Marx), 9, 13–14, 15, 16, 28, 37, 39–40

Veblen, Thorstein, 250, 267

Vision of the Future, A (Adler), 69, 250; excerpt, 304–14

Vocational education, 126–27, 128–29

Voltaire, 147

Voting, 159–60; lack of alternatives in, 146, 160; systems, 121, 122, 146, 175. *See also* Suffrage

Wage labor, 13, 21–25, 34–35, 37–39, 86–87, 278; raise of living standard, 32–33, 278, 279. *See also* Labor; Working class

Wages, 13, 34, 42, 50; iron law of, 21, 33, 36, 63

Wage slavery, 23–25, 130

Walesa, Lech, 90

War(s), 101, 132–35, 154, 249, 252, 259, 276–77, 308–14, 324; of capitalism, 278, 279; civil, 252, 259, 316; of communism, 276–77, 279–80; democracies and, 280–82; economic causes of, 277–8, 279–80; inevitability debate, 278, 279, 281–82; negative meaning of word, 254 (*see also* State of war); positive meaning of word, 254–55 (*see also* Warfare); writings on meaning of word, 269–72, 308–14

War crimes trials, 200, 215

Warfare, 254, 256, 308, 310–11, 315

Washington, George, 219

Wealth: power of, 85, 86; production of, 11–16, 37–38, 76, 104; reasonable maximum of, 76–77, 85, 86, 88; redistribution of, 27, 29, 32, 47, 88, 89, 226; redistribution in Eastern Europe, 89, 92–93; worldwide redistribution, 319–20

Webb, Beatrice Potter, 147

We Hold These Truths (Adler), 72

Welfare benefits, 35, 42, 75, 80, 225

Welfare state(s), 21, 26, 29, 30, 64, 80, 81, 87, 319–20; Eastern Europe, 90; Middle Europe, 91

Western democracies: socialization of economies of, 21, 26–27, 30, 47, 59–60, 63–64; standard of living in, 32–33, 47

Western societies: class conflict in, 48–49, 52, 53; move toward classlessness, 57

West Virginia State Board of Education et al. v. Barnette, 213–14

White, E.B., 271–72

Wildman, Sir John, 111

Will, George, 216

Willkie, Wendell, 266

Wilson, Woodrow, 8, 154, 226

Women's issues, 241; Bork and, 188–89, 210–11; suffrage, 20, 111, 112, 118, 139, 148–49, 175, 176, 185, 189, 205, 206, 222

Working class, 22–25, 26, 27, 30; Marx's theory of increasing misery of, 22–23, 30, 32, 33, 279; misery elimination, 33, 41–42, 47, 50, 63, 130; prejudice against, 241; suffrage, 27, 112, 121, 130. *See also* Labor; Wage labor

World communism, 153, 277

World community, cultural, 242, 243, 245–48, 257, 265–66

World constitution, 313, 318, 321; framers, 267–68; text, 284–304

World democracy, Strachey on, 275–77, 282–84

World government, 101, 133, 157, 243, 250, 256–59, 266, 314–22; desirability of, 251, 258, 316, 320–22; necessity of, 251, 256–58, 282–84, 313–14, 316, 319; obstacles to, 251, 259–65, 313, 317–20; possibility of, 251, 257–58, 314, 316–18; probability of, 251, 258, 313–14; writings on, 272–84, 314–22

World War, 312, 314, 317, 319, 320

Xenophobia, 263, 320

Grateful acknowledgment is made to the following:

Encyclopaedia Britannica, Inc., for "The End of the Conflict Between Capitalism and Communism" by Mortimer J. Adler, taken in its entirety from *The Great Ideas Today*, © 1990, used by permission; and for "A Disputation on the Future of Democracy" by Mortimer J. Adler, taken in its entirety from *The Great Ideas Today*, © 1978, used by permission.

Henry Holt and Company, Inc. (Holt, Rinehart and Winston) for excerpts from *The Common Sense of Politics*, by Mortimer J. Adler, © 1971, used by permission.

The Aspen Institute, for "Remaking Eastern Europe's Economies à la Kelso's and Adler's 'Universal Capitalism' " by James O'Toole, excerpted from *Capitalism, Communism and the Future: The Adler Seminar on Gorbachev's Reforms*, © 1990, used by permission.

The Aspen Institute Quarterly, for "Robert Bork: The Lessons to Be Learned" by Mortimer J. Adler, © 1990, used by permission; and for "Human Nature, Nurture, and Culture" by Mortimer J. Adler, © 1989, used by permission.

Encounter, for excerpts from *The Challenge of Democracy* by John Strachey, © 1963, taken from *Encounter* Pamphlet No. 10, used by permission.

"Preliminary Draft of a World Constitution" was originally published in March 1948 by *Common Cause: A Monthly Report of the Committee to Frame a World Constitution*.